The Political Economy of Saudi Arabia

D0223598

This book is a broad-ranging survey of the development of the political economy of Saudi Arabia from the 1960s right up to the present day. The first of its kind, the book analyses the social and political dynamics which have shaped economic development, the outcomes which have ensued, and the challenges which currently face the country's further development. The focus throughout is on the way in which social, political and economic factors interact and set the limits and character of development.

The context is set by the massive increase in revenues accruing to the Saudi state following the sharp rise in oil prices since 2004. The Saudi government's current economic strategy envisages Saudi Arabia emerging as a major industrial power, with a substantial stake in the global petro-chemicals market. Do the dynamics of Saudi Arabia's political economy, as it has developed since the discovery of oil, suggest that such a strategy could succeed? Is the social basis of the Saudi state, especially the state–private sector relationship, geared to that kind of outcome? Does Saudi Arabia share the characteristics which have enabled some Far Eastern and South-East Asian countries to undergo rapid industrialisation? If the strategy is successful, what will it mean for the Saudi population, and will the social impact be positive or negative? These are the issues and concerns addressed in the book.

Written by a highly respected scholar, with input from a hands-on economic analyst, *The Political Economy of Saudi Arabia* is ideal reading for those with practical involvement in Saudi Arabia and both students and academics in the area of Middle Eastern studies.

Tim Niblock is Professor in the Institute of Arab and Islamic Studies at the University of Exeter, UK.

Monica Malik has worked for a number of international financial institutions as senior economist for the Middle East, and is currently based in Dubai.

The Political Economy of Saudi Arabia

Tim Niblock

With Monica Malik

Routledge
Taylor & Francis Group

LONDON AND NEW YORK

First published 2007 by Routledge
2 Park Square, Milton Park, Abingdon, Oxon OX14 4RN

Simultaneously published in the USA and Canada
by Routledge
270 Madison Avenue, New York, NY 10016

*Routledge is an imprint of the Taylor & Francis Group,
an informa business*

© 2007 Tim Niblock with Monica Malik

Typeset in Times New Roman by Keyword Group Ltd
Printed and bound in Great Britain by Antony Rowe Ltd,
Chippenham, Wiltshire

British Library Cataloguing in Publication Data
A catalogue record for this book is available from the British
Library

Library of Congress Cataloging in Publication Data
Niblock, Tim.
    The political economy of Saudi Arabia / Tim Niblock with
    Monica Malik.
    p. cm.
    Includes bibliographical references and index.
    1. Saudi Arabia – Economic conditions.   2. Saudi Arabia –
    Social conditions.   I. Malik, Monica.   II. Title.
    HC415.33 N53   2007
    330.9538 – dc22
                                    2007018410

ISBN10: 0-415-42842-4 (hbk)
ISBN10: 0-415-42843-2 (pbk)
ISBN10: 0-203-94619-7 (ebk)

ISBN13: 978-0-415-42842-2 (hbk)
ISBN13: 978-0-415-42843-9 (pbk)
ISBN13: 978-0-203-94619-0 (ebk)

Contents

Tables and charts

Charts

Preface

This book has benefited from the advice, help and inspiration of many different people. Foremost among them I would like to thank Dr Monica Malik. The idea of the book originally came from work which she had been doing for her PhD thesis at the University of Durham. Over time, the conception of the book changed, away from a study of the private sector in Saudi Arabia to a wider study of the country's political economy. One chapter of the book, Chapter 5, is directly dependent on the excellent survey of business opinion which formed part of her thesis. I am grateful for the motivation which she initially implanted for the book, and the ideas and material which she contributed towards it. It is in recognition of this contribution that the book carries the 'with Monica Malik' label.

The contribution which one of my daughters, Kate Niblock-Siddle, has made was also substantial. She took charge of much of the fine-tuning and editing of the text and the tables, bringing to my attention a wide range of inconsistencies in layout and content which would otherwise have escaped my attention. I am deeply grateful for her assistance, offered to me from far-distant parts of the world. I must also pay tribute to the support, encouragement and understanding given to me by my two other daughters, Becky Niblock and Sally Jarmain, and by Stuart, William and Dom. They may not realise how much their presence has helped, at critical times.

Two of my PhD students, Luisa Gandolfo and Telmo Vieira, drew together some of the material which I have used in the tables. I am truly grateful that they saved me the painstaking work which this involved, and I thank them for their contribution. From a wider array of PhD students who are working, or have worked, on Saudi Arabia I have learnt much. There are many whom I could mention, but I will refer by name only to three. Their theses were being completed at a time when I was writing this book, and I found their perceptions always valuable: Dr Iqbal al-Medayan, Dr Maha Yamani and Dr Dina Khayat.

I am grateful to Henry Azzam for permission to use his chart on 'Leading wholesale trading houses in Saudi Arabia' (Chart 4.1 in this book), and to Dina Khayat for permission to draw on data on employment from her PhD thesis for Tables 3.17, 3.18, 4.17, 4.18, 6.15 and 6.16 of this book.

Those who helped and assisted me within the Kingdom of Saudi Arabia during my visits there are too numerous for me to be able to name. They gave their time, their knowledge and their enthusiasm to help me in my work. I am most deeply grateful for their generosity in providing me with so many of the insights needed to understand their complex and fascinating country. It was through them that I came to know the reserves of strength and ability which are present in the Saudi population, and gained hope and assurance for the country's future.

Tim Niblock
Exeter, April 2007

Abbreviations

ARAMCO	Saudi Arabian Oil Company
b/d	barrels per day
BOO	Build, own and operate
BOT	Build, operate and transfer
CPO	Central Planning Organisation
CRS	Congressional Research Service
EIU	Economist Intelligence Unit
EWR	Saudi Consolidated Electricity Company for the Western Region
FT	*Financial Times*
GATT	General Agreement on Tariffs and Trade
GCC	Gulf Cooperation Council
GDP	Gross Domestic Product
GOSI	General Organisation for Social Insurance
IFC	International Finance Corporation
IMF	International Monetary Fund
IPOs	Initial Public Offering of Shares
KSA-CDS	Kingdom of Saudi Arabia, Central Department of Statistics
KSA-CM	Kingdom of Saudi Arabia, Council of Ministers
KSA-CPO	Kingdom of Saudi Arabia, Central Planning Organisation
KSA-MOP	Kingdom of Saudi Arabia, Ministry of Planning
KSA-SCPM	Kingdom of Saudi Arabia, Supreme Council for Petroleum and Minerals
KSA-SCT	Kingdom of Saudi Arabia, Supreme Council of Tourism
KSA-SEC	Kingdom of Saudi Arabia, Supreme Economic Council
KSA-SSD	Kingdom of Saudi Arabia, Social Security Department
MAADEN	Saudi Arabian Mining Company
MEED	*Middle East Economic Digest*
MEES	*Middle East Economic Survey*

MNC	Multinational corporations
NADEC	National Development Company
NCB	National Commercial Bank
NCCI	National Company for Co-operative Insurance
NYT	*New York Times*
OECD	Organisation for Economic Cooperation and Development
OPEC	Organisation of the Petroleum Exporting Countries
PIF	Public Investment Fund
PLO	Palestine Liberation Organisation
RPD	Retirement Pension Directorate
SABIC	Saudi Arabian Basic Industries Corporation
SACMA	Saudi Arabian Capital Markets Authority
SADAFCO	Saudi Dairy and Foodstuffs Company
SAFCO	Saudi Arabian Fertiliser Company
SAGIA	Saudi Arabian General Investment Authority
SA-IR	Saudi Arabia Information Resource
SAMA	Saudi Arabian Monetary Agency
SAMBA	Saudi-American Bank
SAPATCO	Saudi Arabian Public Transport Company
SASE	Saudi Arabian Stock Exchange
SAUDIA	Saudi Arabian Airlines
SCPM	Supreme Council for Petroleum and Minerals
SCT	Supreme Council of Tourism
SEC	Saudi Electricity Company
SGI	Saudi Integrated Gas Initiative
SIDF	Saudi Industrial Development Fund
SOCAL	Standard Oil Company of California
SOE	State-owned Enterprise
SR	Saudi riyal. For most of the 1970s and early 1980s, trading at between $1 = SR3 and $1 = SR4. Fixed at $1 = SR3.75 since 1986.
STC	Saudi Telecommunications Company
TI	Transparency International
TRIPS	WTO Agreement on Trade Related Aspects of Intellectual Property Rights
UAE	United Arab Emirates
UNCTAD	United Nations Conference on Trade and Development
UPAP	Union of Peoples of the Arabian Peninsula
UPI	United Press International
USB	United Saudi Bank
US-CB	US Census Bureau

US-CIA	US Central Intelligence Agency
US-DOS	US Department of State
US-EIA	US Energy Information Administration
US-TRO	United States Trade Representative Office
WHO	World Health Organisation
WMO	World Migration Organisation
WTO	World Trade Organisation

Maps

Map 1 Provinces, regions and main cities of Saudi Arabia.

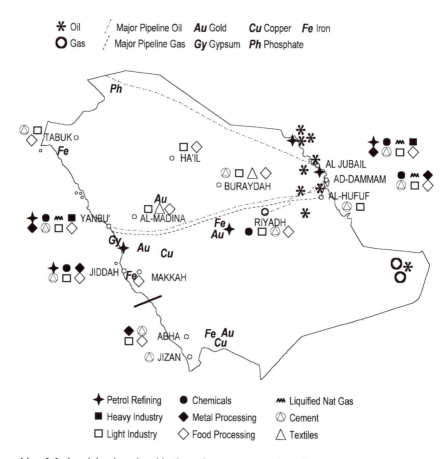

Map 2 Industrial, mineral and hydrocarbon resources of Saudi Arabia.

1   Introduction

1.1   Perspective

The objective of this book is to provide an understanding of the problems facing Saudi Arabia's economic development today, and to assess the success of the government in creating an economy which will satisfy the long-term needs of the Saudi population. The stress on 'long-term needs' is important. For states which benefit from substantial oil revenues, and a relatively small population, it may be easy to meet the immediate needs of the population. Revenues can be used to provide the services, subsidised provisions and employment which the population requires. Ultimately, however, the economy will need to survive without oil revenues, and must be geared to operate on a non-oil basis. At current rates of production, Saudi oil would last some 75 years. With the depletion of oil reserves in other parts of the world, however, the pressure on Saudi Arabia to increase its rate of production will increase–and thereby shorten the life-span of the oil resources. Conversely, there is the possibility that technological developments in the energy field may reduce global dependence on oil, lessening global demand for oil. In this case the oil revenues would last longer but perhaps not be so substantial. Whichever scenario is borne out in reality, the long-term needs of the population should not be dependent on the continued inflow of oil revenues. Saudi Arabia, moreover, has one of the highest rates of population increase in the world, so meeting the needs of the population will become steadily more expensive.

There may also be less tangible reasons for seeking to establish a sound non-hydrocarbon base to the economy. A population which lives on the proceeds of the extraction of its natural resources, with only a very small part of the population employed in the production process, will not be at ease in the international community. Living in a cocoon created by apparently unearned income, divorced from the problems facing other peoples, sets a population apart from the global community–creating attitudes and mentalities out of touch with international realities. A national society living off rent is no less uncomfortable a proposition than a class living off rent in the domestic setting. The Saudi population both deserves and needs to be dynamically engaged with developments in the wider world.

Assessing the economy's ability to survive without oil, at a time when oil revenues continue to underpin and shape almost every facet of economic activity, is not easy. By the time oil revenues have run out, the structure and attributes of the global economy will be substantially different from what they are today. How can one, then, assess whether current economic policies in Saudi Arabia will be suited to coping with a distant future, whose needs and requirements are difficult to predict? The approach taken here relies on two different strategies. The first is to identify the criteria of success: the dimensions of economic growth and development which provide a basis for economic vitality whether oil is present or not. The second is to identify the structural characteristics which underlie economic policy-making: the socio-economic and political factors which have shaped, and will continue to shape, economic policy and development. An understanding of the dynamics affecting policy and development should provide a basis on which to project likely future developments.

Four criteria of success are used in this work. The first is whether the state has been able to create the social and physical infrastructure which economies need if they are to operate effectively and competitively in the global market. The need for social and physical infrastructure is, of course, not static: the requirements change with the growth of population and the development of the economy. The criterion, therefore, must relate to whether the infrastructure which is being laid down is appropriate to the country's stage of development, and whether its quality (especially in educational provision) is suited to future expansion and refinement.

The second criterion is whether the sectors in which Saudi Arabia has the most significant comparative advantage are being developed effectively. Clearly this refers in part to the production and export of oil, gas and refined petroleum products, despite the need to reduce dependence on this resource. Advantage needs to be taken of the existing rich reserves so as to fund investments in the wider economy. The development of the petrochemicals industry and of associated downstream industries, and industries dependent on easily accessible and cheaply priced energy, however, also constitutes a crucial component of Saudi Arabia's potential comparative advantage. These industries, moreover, are mostly dependent on natural gas rather than oil. Saudi Arabia's gas supplies are currently expected to last for more than a hundred years at existing rates of production (with only 15 per cent of the country currently having been explored for natural gas) (US–Saudi Business Council 2005: 5).

The third criterion is whether the economy is providing employment opportunities to the population–of a kind which are both competitive with international labour rates, and appropriate to the levels of qualifications and training available in the Saudi population. The ability of an economy to provide adequate employment for its citizens is always crucial, but the dynamics of the global economy today give an added dimension to this issue. The process of economic globalisation, and the requirements of the World Trade Organisation (of which Saudi Arabia became a member in December 2005), mean that labour must be internationally competitive. In an open economy, of the kind envisaged and required by the WTO, investment will be attracted to those countries where goods and services can be produced cheaply and efficiently. The reduction of protective tariffs, and the removal of other measures which inhibit trade, will open the Saudi economy up to international competition in the same way as all other economies. While investment may be naturally attracted to those fields in which Saudi Arabia enjoys a comparative advantage, investment and production in other fields will move away from Saudi Arabia unless labour is internationally competitive (in costs and productivity).

Labour competitivity poses a particular problem in Saudi Arabia. Saudi governments in the past two decades have sought, no doubt justifiably, to reduce reliance on foreign labour (skilled, unskilled and professional). The impact of these measures has been to raise overall labour costs and reduce labour productivity. At most levels, Saudis benefit from better wages and working conditions than foreign labour. It is the latter, however, whose rewards and productivity reflect most accurately the rates available on the global labour market. The intention to reduce foreign labour while promoting economic production geared to the global market, then, requires one of two possible strategies. Either the remuneration and conditions of Saudi labour have to be reduced to the same level as that of foreign labour; or else the skills of Saudis (and therefore their productivity) have to be raised to exceed that which foreign labour could provide. Neither option is easy to achieve, politically, socially or humanly.

The fourth criterion is whether the private sector is sufficiently strong and effective to compete in the global market, without significant dependence on tariff protection, special favours or subsidies. This criterion is clearly linked in part to the third criterion, given that labour constitutes an important–if not the most important–cost for most private-sector businesses. Other factors, however, are also relevant, such as whether the relationship with the government bureaucracy enables the private sector to operate efficiently and flexibly. The level of managerial skill is a further important consideration. The strength and vitality of the private sector provides some indication of how well the economy could survive without oil. An enterprising private sector will have no difficulty in adapting to the changes wrought by declining oil revenues.

There is an argument for including a fifth criterion: whether a reasonable portion of oil revenues is being put aside as a 'fund for future generations'. The latter would be composed of a mixture of different foreign assets, and would provide income to the country when oil revenues are declining. Such assets would be ring-fenced against expenditure in the short term. Reference will indeed be made to the levels of foreign asset holdings, but it is difficult to use this as a measure of economic success. Some would say that current resources are better employed in building up infrastructure and existing economic capacity, and that the hoarding of money from oil revenues should be left to a later stage.

The second strategy used in this book to assess the ability of the Saudi economy to survive without oil is to examine the dynamics which underlie the pattern of development. The intention here is to identify the parameters which will shape economic growth in the future. Three theoretical approaches are used to uncover these parameters. The first focuses on the depth to which states intervene in economies. It is clearly important to identify whether the state sees itself simply as an arbitrator between different social interests, or as a major participant in economic production. The second looks at the relationship between the state and society. Of central concern here is the degree to which the state is autonomous of social groupings. Are state policies shaped by the economic interests of social groupings which are allied to the state, and on which the state is dependent? Is the state bureaucracy able to take decisions which are rationally geared towards the effective development of the economy, as opposed to simply benefiting those who are in power? The third examines the extent to which a state's dependence on externally generated 'rent' (oil revenues in the case of Saudi Arabia) determines the character of its social, economic and political structures, shaping and constraining the policies which can be pursued.

These different approaches are covered in turn in the section which follows.

1.2   Theory and Saudi political economy: useful approaches

The three different theoretical approaches which will be used here, as mentioned previously, cover the depth of state involvement, the quality and character of that involvement, and the impact of oil revenues. This section will elaborate on these approaches. The comparative and theoretical perspective is important. Patterns of development in other countries can throw light on why Saudi economic development has taken the path it has, and how it may evolve in the future. The remainder of the book makes use of these theoretical insights, showing how the changing patterns of state involvement, and the impact of oil revenues, have shaped the country's political economy. Transitions between the various stages of Saudi Arabia's economic development are interpreted in terms of the impact of, and relationship between, these factors over the period in question.

1.2.1 The depth of state involvement

The starting point for considering differing levels of state intervention in the economy is the recognition that some state action in society and economy is a necessity. Where states have collapsed, economic development or growth is not viable.[1] For example, in Somalia the state collapse occurred over a long period between 1969 and 1991. The resulting situation was a country with destroyed physical infrastructure and economic assets, private business looted, and pastoral production reduced (World Bank 1997: 159). There is a need for the state.

The issue, therefore, is what level of state involvement is present, and how this is embodied in state policy. By classifying different levels of state involvement, it becomes possible to specify where the Saudi case fits into the spectrum, and to assess whether that place in the spectrum has changed over time. Three characteristically different levels of state involvement in mixed economies will be identified here: the minimal state, state-aided capitalism and state-sponsored capitalism. The first two are in line with development led by the private sector, while state-sponsored capitalism is where the state is the main agent of growth. All three are ideal types, as in practice states do not fit neatly into such categories.

The minimal state

The role of the state in this model is purveyed as providing maximum possible freedom for citizens. It would be difficult to point today to any state which approximates to the minimal state. The notion of minimal state implies that the functions of the state should be restricted to those it alone can perform, or can carry out more efficiently than the private sector. For the state to be 'minimal' it should not:

- be concerned with, or interfere in, individuals' private lives;
- intervene in the economy, which is based on free market principles;
- involve itself in the provision of opportunities or promote equality;

- plan in detail; or
- take action intended to redistribute resources (Evans 1991: 2–3).

The philosophical underpinning to this approach lies in the view, put forward for example by Nozick, that the poor are better off in a private property/free market society than under any other system. The contention is that in such a society the economy will grow quickly and wealth will trickle down from the rich to the poor. It is also maintained, however, that the fabric of society is damaged by state interference, which violates the rights of individuals (Plant 1991: 132).

The areas the state should be involved in include:

- defence, military provision and foreign relations;
- internal law and order against illegitimate force, threats to property, theft, fraud and the violation of contracts.

The model, therefore, simultaneously emphasises some aspects of state power (e.g. the need for law and order), whilst restricting the scope of the state's action and the extent of its resource base. In practice, the proponents of the minimal state confront a dilemma. The operation of an effective market, to which they attach such vital importance, often requires a relatively strong state to provide the necessary security, ensure free competition and give investors confidence. Far from the state inevitably threatening the coherence of the market, therefore, the latter requires a strong and effective state.

State-aided capitalism

This can be defined as an economic order where the state plays a significant yet carefully circumscribed role in the economy. The appropriate role of the state is to 'to support and facilitate, rather than to manage or directly participate in, the productive sectors of the economy' (Koch-Weser 1996: 49). The state, then, retains an ideological commitment to economic development through free market capitalism, but the role of government is considered of critical importance to the proper functioning of the private-sector economy. The government provides the framework to ensure free markets, to offset distortions and to provide functions that the market would not provide on its own. In some cases, it may need to create regulatory systems to address systemic and monopoly risk. Under state-aided capitalism the government only invests in activities which have the characteristics of 'public goods', and even in this sphere some of the activities may be contracted to the private sector so as to increase efficiency (World Bank 1995: 11). In the words of Meier:

> ... the private sector ... is the engine of growth. The role of the public sector is seen as the creation of a favourable enabling environment for economic activity. The enabling environment consists of legal, institutional, and policy frameworks within which economic agents operate.
>
> (Meier 1995: 525)

The economy-related functions of the state under state-aided capitalism would normally include the following:[2]

- an appropriate legal system covering the elements needed for a capitalist framework, e.g. property law,[3] company law, and contract and patent law;[4]
- the maintenance of macro-economic stability, i.e. intervention in, or action through direction ownership of, the banking system, with a view to guaranteeing the value of money and a measure of price stability;
- action to offset or eliminate price distortions, e.g. through antitrust regulation to break up or to check monopolies;
- provision of physical infrastructure, so as to ensure that businesses can utilise an appropriate network for trade and communications; and
- provision of social infrastructure, such as education, health and environmental protection (Wade 1990: 11–12).

To varying degrees, governments operating under this model may also take action to ensure an adequate quality of labour in the economy through the provision of specialist training (World Bank 1997: 52; Meier 1995: 529); redistribute income to the poorest (if only to ensure that discontent does not threaten the capitalist system); provide some protection for the environment for long-term well-being; and offer some general services for business such as basic research, credit access for small companies and market information.

Most economies in the Western world fit into the model of state-aided capitalism. How governments interpret and apply the different elements outlined above, however, can vary considerably.

State-sponsored capitalism

Under this model, the state acts as the primary engine of growth, acting positively to promote rapid industrialisation. The latter requires a high level of productive investment, directed towards carefully selected sectors of the global economy–those which the state deems to provide opportunities for substantial export-oriented industrial growth. The primary commitment of the state, then, is to development and not to the maintenance of a free market per se. A good and supportive relationship with the private sector and the capitalist class in general is needed as a means to the ends sought by the government. As Wade has noted, the government's intervention in the market may even include distorting prices so as to change the way in which the private sector behaves, or using non-price methods to alter the behaviour of market agents. The state thus promotes investment in key industries, while at the same time ensuring that these industries are technologically advanced and internationally competitive (Wade 1990: 334; 1990a: 328).

States which follow this developmental strategy tend, at least in the initial stages of industrialisation, to be 'hard' or 'soft' authoritarian states. Corporatist relations with the private sector are maintained, with key business interests closely integrated into governmental policies and policy-making. It is deemed necessary to suppress pressures from below while the developmental impetus is built up. A frequently cited case of state-sponsored capitalism is that of Taiwan. In the post-war era, Taiwan saw rapid economic growth: real GDP grew by 10.6 per cent a year from 1965 to 1979 (Wade 1987: 30). Wade has noted that a major feature of Taiwan's development was its 'industrial deepening' (Wade 1990a: 236). The role of the state was central to industrial development: often the industries that developed were not the product of international comparative advantage, but stemmed from government policies aimed at creating 'winners' and leading industries. Among the policies which the government used to promote this strategy were the following:

- Land reform, providing a labour force for industry and enabling the extraction of a surplus from the countryside for investment in industry. This also allowed the agricultural sector to produce enough for domestic consumption and export, such that foreign exchange was available for securing inputs for manufacturing.
- Management of prices so as to enhance industrialists' profits and encourage more investment. Industrial wages were kept low, in part through curtailing union power. Concessional credits were provided so as to lower costs of production and drive investment first to heavy industry and then to electronics and machinery production.
- Creation of major state enterprises (the largest in the non-communist world). In the 1950s the state established new industries in the refining, processing and manufacture of fuel, chemicals, metals, textiles, fertilisers, glass, plastic and cement. In 1952, 56 per cent of industrial

production was in public corporations (Amsden 1979: 367). By the 1980s the share of public enterprises had fallen to under 25 per cent, and many foreign firms had entered the market, but the role of the state enterprises remained significant.

- State ownership of the banking system. Investment was controlled and channelled through the state-owned banks.
- Control of foreign competition. Rather than having a blanket policy, the protectionism was very selective and geared towards particular sectors. Between 1957 and 1976 the percentage of products with import control remained almost the same, at 36 per cent and 41 per cent respectively. Export orientation, therefore, was not achieved by free markets. There was also an emphasis on large-scale plants to obtain economies of scale as a basis for international competitivity.
- Promotion of exports. Subsidies were provided for certain types of exports, and companies exporting such products were allowed to import inputs without restrictions.
- Promotion of technology acquisition from transnational corporations. Such technology was then used to develop a national technology system. Foreign investment was directed into fields which fostered technology linkages (Schive and Maumdar 1986, cited in Wade 1990: 304).

This pattern of state-sponsored capitalism has been followed by a number of other East Asian and South-East Asian states, such as South Korea and Singapore. Most recently, the strategy of industrial development pursued by the People's Republic of China has shared some of the same characteristics.

The Asian financial crisis of the late 1990s threw doubts on the effectiveness of state-sponsored capitalism. The path to development taken in East and South-East Asia no longer seemed so impressive. Yet such a view was premature. Even at the time, Joseph Stiglitz (then senior vice president and chief economist of the World Bank) was arguing that many of the problems faced by Asian countries arose not because governments did too much, but because they did too little–and because they themselves had deviated from the policies that had proved so successful over preceding decades (Stiglitz 1998: 11). In several countries, for instance, poorly managed financial liberalisation had led to the lifting of some restrictions, including the limitations on bank lending for real estate, before a sound regulatory framework had been put in place. Kwong-Hun Lee contends that, in the case of Korea, the crisis was not caused by government involvement but by the late 1980s' trend towards liberalisation and globalisation. The latter trend undermined the industrial policy of the state, with the *chaebols* (business groups) now trying to dominate the domestic market without government involvement. Thus the problems developed as a result of the abandoning of the model, rather than being an outcome of the model (Lee 1998: 24).

1.2.2   The social dynamics of state policies

Examining the depth and character of state involvement in the economy, covered in Section 1.2.1, makes it possible to locate any economy on the continuum between minimal and maximal state involvement. To understand why a state adopts a particular economic strategy, however, requires some consideration of the social dynamics which underlie the state and of the resource base available to the government. This section covers the first of these two dimensions.

An important dimension to the social dynamics surrounding economic policy-making, in any economy which has a substantial free market, is the relationship between political decision-makers and the leading elements in the private sector. The relationship is that between political power and economic strength. To what extent are the decisions taken by the political and administrative elite influenced/determined by the leading elements in the private sector? Is the relationship between the state and these private-sector circles one which is productive for the development of the economy? And to what extent do the decisions taken by the political and administrative elite determine which individuals and groupings within the private sector are benefiting most?

The work of Peter Evans has been of particular significance in the analysis of the social dynamics underlying the state. Evans contends that effective state involvement in the economy, under free market conditions, depends on the state having a measure of 'embedded autonomy' in relation to leading business circles. The state must maintain a level of separation from and independence of such circles, so that state policy is not deflected or distorted by entrenched and self-serving business interests. Yet the administration of policy also needs to be embedded in the private sector–especially those parts of the sector which can provide the mainspring for industrial growth. Either part of this equation without the other can be damaging. A state where the personal interests of senior state personnel are interlocked with those of leading business circles will be unable to act in the best interests of the economy in general. Conversely, a state whose officials are not able to interact closely with the private sector, and learn directly what the needs and requirements of business are, will not be able to chart an effective path of economic growth.

Evans, and others who write from a similar perspective, contrast the dynamics of predatory states, where the relationship between the state and the private sector is prejudicial to coherent economic growth, to those of developmental states, where the relationship buttresses and promotes industrial development. The characteristics of these two models of state are outlined below.

The predatory state

Cypher and Dietz define the term as follows:

> The predatory state is one wherein the appropriation of unearned income via rent-seeking has become endemic and structural. Everything is for sale: the courts, the legislature, the military, the taxing authority, etc. Government employees use their authority to maximise, in the shortest possible time, their accumulation of wealth. Political offices are held not for the reason for providing services to a nation, but for the purpose of individual gain in a society that may offer few alternative avenues to wealth accumulation.
>
> (Cypher and Dietz 1997: 226)

The basic characteristic of a predatory state, then, is where the state extracts at the expense of society, undercutting development through frustrating even the most basic process of capital accumulation (Evans 1995: 12). Such a state lacks the ability to prevent incumbents from pursuing their own goals. Individual maximisation takes precedence over the pursuit of collective goals. Leading capitalists draw their benefit from the system through lobbying to capture rent, revenues and quotas, and pursuing strategies which ensure that the government allocates resources in a way that would benefit them.

Evans used Zaïre under Mobutu (1965–97) as an example of a predatory state (1992: 149, 151; 1995: 43–5). The state was controlled by Mobutu and a small number of his closest kinsmen who held the most lucrative positions (e.g. key positions in the Judiciary Council, the secret police, the Ministry of Interior, etc.). During his period in power, Mobutu and those closest to him amassed vast personal fortunes from revenues generated from mineral exports. Over the last 25 years of his rule, Zaïre's GDP per capita declined at an annual rate of 2 per cent a year and Zaïre fell towards the bottom of the world hierarchy of nations. The absence of a coherent bureaucratic apparatus was a result of personalism and a highly marketised administrative apparatus. Young (cited in Evans 1995: 46) quoted Mobutu himself characterising the system: 'Everything is for sale, everything is bought in our country. And in this traffic, holding any slice of public power constitutes a veritable exchange instrument, convertible into illicit acquisition of money or other goods'.

Defining this situation as one where the state lacks autonomy is slightly problematic, in so far as the 'relative autonomy of the state' has generally been taken to refer to the degree of independence which state actors have of class groupings in society. In this case, the state was not constrained or limited in any way by class pressures. The lack of autonomy stems from the personal interests of the decision-makers, not from class pressures. Evans explains this as follows:

> On one hand, since the state as a corporate entity is incapable of formulating coherent goals and implementing them, and since policy decisions are up for sale to private elites, the state must be seen as completely lacking in autonomy. This lack of autonomy is what permits pervasive rent seeking to prevail. At the same time, however, the Zairian State is strikingly unconstrained by society. It is autonomous in the sense of not deriving its goals from the aggregation of societal interests. This autonomy does not enhance the state's capacity to pursue goals of its own, but rather removes critical social checks on arbitrary rule.
>
> (Evans 1992: 151)

Embedded autonomy and the developmental state

As noted previously, Evans's work suggests that the key to rapid industrial development lies in the state striking the right balance in its relationship with the private sector. To create the most productive relationship, where the state cooperates closely with the private sector but retains the ability to impose its own developmental priorities on business, the state must possess an administrative machinery capable of undertaking the task. He describes this as an effective and meritocratic bureaucracy, with a strong morale and discipline. It needs to enjoy strong backing from the country's political leadership, but the latter must not interfere in the bureaucracy's day-to-day operations. The bureaucracy will have the means and the ability to identify the necessary components of national economic development, and to resist the narrow interests of particular individuals or interest groups. In the words of Rueschemeyer and Evans:

> ... a certain degree of autonomy from dominant interests in a capitalist society is necessary not only to make coherent state action in pursuit of any consistent policy conception possible, but also because some

of the competing interests in the economy and the society, even structurally dominant ones, will have to be sacrificed in order to achieve
systematically required 'collective goods' that cannot be provided by
partial interest.

(Rueschemeyer and Evans 1985: 68)

The state, therefore, stands beyond the controlling reach of vested interests, planning and guiding the rapid industrialisation of the economy.
Its decision-making process, however, needs to be embedded in the sectors of the private sector critical to rapid economic development. This is
achieved through a web of consultative committees and contacts, which
provide the state with the information it needs for effective planning.
Such contacts also enable the state to rely on the private sector for the
implementation of the goals. Policies and goals are in practice negotiated
through the relationship between the bureaucracy and the critical investors
in private-sector industry (Evans 1992: 164; 1995: 59).

Evans claims that it was this balance, characterised as embedded autonomy, which made possible the rapid industrialisation of some East and
South-East Asian economies. Their state-sponsored capitalist structures
succeeded due to the social and political dynamics which underpinned
them. The 'developmental states' of Taiwan and South Korea, in particular,
had competent bureaucratic organisations. These were grounded in a highly
meritocratic recruitment process and long-term career rewards, creating an
inner morale and commitment. In addition, along with high administrative
capacity, the state restricted its intervention to 'strategic necessities of
a transformative project, using the power to selectively impose market
forces' (Evans 1992: 164). There was a sense of 'corporate coherence'
which gave state organisations a level of autonomy.[5]

In practice, most states in the developing world are intermediate, combining some elements of predatory behaviour and some developmental
characteristics. Inadequacies in the autonomy of the state and in the
relationship between the bureaucracy and the private sector may hinder
industrial development rather than blocking it entirely. In effect, a non-
transformative dynamic is present. In many developing economies, for
example, the personal interests of state officials and individual businessmen have favoured some expansion of the private sector but no substantial
reduction in the role of the state. Both gain from continued state controls:
state officials retain the power to channel favours to those who serve their
personal or family interests, and private businessmen with government
contacts are able to limit the competition from others (Ayubi 1992: 51–2).

Evans takes the examples of Brazil and India in the 1980s to illustrate
this (Evans 1992: 166; 1995: 60). Both countries had seen a transformation

of the economy as a result of state intervention, yet the experience of transformation in both was limited by deficiencies in the state's relationship with society. In the case of Brazil the state apparatus lacked 'overall coherence and cohesiveness'. Embeddedness in the critical parts of the private sector was difficult to achieve due to the close relationship between the state and the traditional oligarchy. This relationship 'turned modernising projects into sustenance for traditional powers'. The negative dynamic, however, did not always hold. As noted by Evans, 'Brazil's industrial success involved dense ties, not insulation. Pockets of efficiency within the state apparatus sometimes had sufficient cohesion and coherence to draw industrialists into joint projects with impressive results' (Evans 1995: 73).

In the case of India the bureaucracy was designed not to be too close to the social structure to avoid the pitfall of being too closely linked to them. As a result, 'inventing' the private sector as a partner in the industrialisation process was difficult. The state's apparent successes in the 1950s came in activities 'where autonomous action could produce results, like constructing dams or building basic infrastructural capacity'. New industrial entrepreneurship in the private sector did not develop, and the success seen in Brazil in the 1970s did not take place in India. Evan concludes by noting that in the 1980s there was a 'negative sort of convergence' between the two cases and that 'in both cases, declines in the state's ability to perform as a coherent corporate actor and the erosion of the effective state–society ties went hand in hand, demonstrating once again that capacity depends on putting autonomy and embeddedness together' (Evans 1995: 73).

1.2.3   *Dynamics of the rentier state*

The third theoretical approach which is relevant to the study of Saudi Arabia's political economy is that of the rentier state.

The concept of rent itself has featured in the writing of economists ever since Adam Smith. It may be defined as 'the difference between the return made by a factor of production and the return necessary to keep the factor in its current occupation' (Bannock et al. 1992: 129). Rentier state theory was first developed by Hossein Mahdavy, in reference to Iran. He noted that the phenomenon of a state earning income through rent was itself not new, and was not always linked to oil. Payment for the passage of ships through the Suez Canal, for example, contained a substantial element of rent (Mahdavy 1970: 429).

The publication of Beblawi and Luciani's edited collection, *The Rentier State* (1987), however, marked the most significant step forward in the elaboration of the theory, and has formed the basis of much subsequent rentier state analysis of Arab oil-producing states. Beblawi, in his contribution to the book, defines 'rentier economy' as 'an economy substantially supported by the expenditure of the state whilst the state itself is supported by the rent accruing from abroad' (Beblawi 1987: 11). Two elements have to be present, therefore: rent needs to play a predominant role within the economy concerned, and the origin of that rent must be external to the state. It is not the simple inflow of oil revenues which creates a rentier economy, but the extent to which these revenues determine the form and structure of the economy, and the external source of the revenues. An oil rentier economy can survive without a productive domestic sector. Indeed, the availability of resources to finance substantial consumer imports will tend to undercut domestic production (Abdel-Fadil 1987: 84–5).

Building on his definition of a rentier economy, Beblawi defines 'rentier state' as 'any state which derives a substantial part of its income from foreign sources and under the form of rent'. While Beblawi himself does not specify what proportion of governmental income should come from oil revenues, a figure of at least 40 per cent is suggested by Luciani (1987: 70).

The contributors to Beblawi and Luciani's edited collection, and those who have written subsequently within the same framework, have contended that a number of key dynamics follow from these characteristics. The dynamics are most evident in the oil-producing states of the Gulf, which come closest to the 'ideal-type' rentier state. Their relatively small native populations, substantial oil reserves and paucity of non-hydrocarbon natural resources account for this.

The first, and perhaps most fundamental, dynamic is that of the centrality of the state. In the words of Abdel-Fadil:

> … the state becomes the main intermediary between the oil sector and the rest of the economy. It receives revenues which are channelled to the economy through public expenditure, and since public expenditure generally represents a large proportion of national income, the allocation of these public funds between alternative uses has great significance for the future development pattern of the economy.
>
> (Abdel-Fadil 1987: 83)

As oil revenues accrue directly to the state, the state becomes the origin of all significant economic and social developments, and the determinant of how resources are spread around the population.

Second, the rentier state enjoys a substantial degree of autonomy. Skocpol defines state autonomy as a situation where 'the state formulates and pursues goals which are not simply reflective of the demands or interests of social groups, classes or society' (Skocpol 1985: 9). The rentier state does not need to extract revenue from the population to finance its activities, and therefore does not need to shape economic policies or construct social alliances geared to safeguarding its financial base. Its independent resource base frees it of that necessity. Rather, all parts of society are tightly dependent on the state, with the latter operating as the major employer of labour, the source of the most lucrative business contracts, and the provider of subsidies and handouts. Not beholden to any grouping in society, the state enjoys a level of autonomy of society and freedom of action to which governments in market-driven production economies could only aspire (Skocpol 1982: 269). The state determines, exclusively in its own interest, which social groupings to favour and to what degree. It has the resources to finance effective security and infor-mation services, thereby ensuring that the less advantaged have neither the means to oppose state policy, nor even the channels through which to express opposition (Al-Dekhayel 1990: 47–62). No part of society, indeed, is left with the ability to promote or defend its own interests against the state.

Third, society in general becomes infused with rentier practice. It is not only the state whose actions and practices can be characterised in this way. A small proportion of the population (usually no more than 2–3 per cent) earns its income from the production and process-ing of hydrocarbons, leaving the remainder of the population to compete for a share in the oil rent (Beblawi 1987: 53). Social and economic interests are:

> organised in such a manner as to capture a good slice of government rent. Citizenship becomes a source of economic benefit. Different layers of beneficiaries of government rent are thus created, giving rise in their turn to new layers of beneficiaries. The whole of soci-ety is arranged as a hierarchy of layers of rentiers, with the state or the government at the top of the pyramid.

Beblawi sees this as creating a rentier mentality, which then dominates social consciousness. Living off 'unearned income', the population orients itself towards easy gain rather than productive labour. Legal processes, requiring foreign business to find local partners, buttress such attitudes. Substantial gains accrue to the citizens through serving as the necessary *kafils* (sponsors) of foreign companies, performing no serious work but earning a share of the income (Beblawi 1987: 52–3, 56). This analy-sis is often accompanied by the perception that the system is marked by corruption and a profligate and structurally driven waste of resources (Karl 1999: 32–48).

Fourth, industrial and agricultural production is a marginal component of rentier economies. Such industry and agriculture as does exist, it is contended, is supported by subsidies and its products are not competitive on the world market. The commercial and service sectors, on the other hand, are buoyant. Given that the state has the resources to permit substantial imports, and that it has an interest in satisfying popular demands for adequate and reasonably priced food and consumer goods, there is a strong dynamic against production. It is easier and more profitable to import than to produce (Niblock 1980: 1–40; Abdel-Fadil 1987: 84). Ruth First contrasts this wider developmental experience: 'The usual development is reversed. Instead of the progression from agriculture to industry to services, oil provokes the growth of only the third sector (services)…. The tertiary sector, always disproportionate in underdeveloped countries, thus grows to elephantine proportions' (First 1980: 120). The economic realities have significant effects on social and class groupings in rentier states, reinforcing the autonomy of the state as discussed above. Those parts of the population gaining their incomes from artisanal, nomadic, agricultural and petty-industrial pursuits decline in number and significance. They become increasingly dependent on the state for their livelihood. They lack the basis to press their collective interests on or against the state. The commercially based classes grow, but their interests are closely allied to the state's economic strategies. They have little reason to inhibit or challenge state policy (Niblock 1980: 15).

Fifth, trends towards political representation are weakened. Without taxation, it is contended, government is no longer perceived as being there to serve the interests of the people. The slogan of democracy, 'no taxation without representation', is reversed: 'no representation without taxation'. In practice, undemocratic states do tax their citizens, and some writers find little evidence to support the supposed linkage (Waterbury 1994: 29). Nonetheless, it does seem likely that taxation at least provides the grounds for a discourse. In the words of Luciani, 'it is a fact that whenever the state essentially relies on taxation the question of democracy becomes an unavoidable issue, and a strong current in favour of democracy inevitably arises' (Luciani 1987: 73). The state is put in a position where it 'must give credibility that it represents the common good'. The most significant respect in which rentier state structures discourage representation, however, may be one which has already been covered: social groupings are not strong enough to pursue their interests or even to claim the right of representation. Economic well-being becomes a substitute for political rights, with citizens subsuming their desire for the latter with 'the financial manna' (Beblawi 1987: 59). Even the existence of massive disparities within the country provides no basis for opposition, as Luciani explains:

> That benefits are unequally distributed is not relevant for political life, because it is not a sufficient incentive to coalesce and attempt to change the political institutions. To the individual who feels his benefits are not enough, the solution of manoeuvring for personal advantage within the existing setup is always superior to seeking an alliance with others in similar conditions. In the end, there is always little or no objective ground to claim that one should get more of the benefits, since his contribution is generally dispensable anyhow.
>
> (Luciani 1987: 74)

Sixth, expatriate labour plays a prominent part in the economy. Given the size of the revenues at the disposal of the government, and the scale of the infrastructural development which this makes possible, the need for labour and expertise is not surprising. The small population of the oil-producing states on the Arab side of the Gulf greatly magnifies the quantity of labour required, and makes its acquisition an imperative. The labour force becomes, in the process, fragmented both by national/cultural background and by rates of reward. Native labour, mostly shifting to non-manual work, is paid at a level which ensures its acceptance of the political bargain which underpins the rentier state (financial gain in return for political quiescence). Expatriate labour, on the other hand, is paid at whatever price is available on the global market (generally lower than native labour wages). Even the expatriate labour, moreover, may be subject to differential rates of pay, reflecting the wage conditions available in the country of origin. The emergence of a politically conscious labour movement is aborted by this process: there is very little basis for solidarity, whether economically or culturally. They are, moreover, in too weak a position to become politically active or to form trade union organisations: they can easily be sent home. The political interests of expatriate labour are usually focused more on their countries of origin than those of their current labour (Niblock 1980a:12).

A critique

As there has been debate over the value of rentier state theory, and some aspects of the application of the theory to the Saudi case are discussed in the section which follows, criticisms of the approach need now to be noted. These are not intended to suggest that the approach should be discarded, but rather to indicate its limitations. There is no doubt that oil revenues have a crucial and critical impact both on the economic and the social structures of

Saudi Arabia, as also of other countries whose governments are similarly dependent on hydrocarbon exports for the major part of their revenue.

First, it can be said that rentier theory carries with it an air of determinism, and that this may be unrealistic. Rentier states are seen as caught within a dynamic from which there is no escape and where the precise social and economic outcomes are predictable and inevitable. In reality, however, the rentier dimension is not the only factor shaping policy and determining outcomes. The domestic political scene, for example, may not be as subservient to short-term personal gain as rentier theory suggests, and the ability of the state to provide such gain to a rapidly growing population moved by rising expectations may be limited. The satisfaction of immediate needs, moreover, may itself create bigger problems for the future. Expanding educational provision, for example, may satisfy the immediate demands of young people, but will be destabilising in the longer term if graduates of secondary and higher education are unable to secure gainful and meaningful employment. The assumption that the technical and professional elite can be bought off by incorporation within the system, moreover, can be questioned. The reverse process can be suggested: holding key positions in the state, and determined to create a basis for post-oil economic survival, they may form an alliance within the state structure which redirects economic policies. There is, moreover, the international dimension: external influences may impose their own dynamics on the rentier state, whether through international organisations (e.g. membership of the World Trade Organisation) or the requirements of a superpower. Rentier states are not necessarily left free to chart whatever economic path they choose.

Second, the concept of the rentier state's autonomy is questionable. The definition of state autonomy which is used by Skocpol (quated above Skocpol 1985:19), and which is found in many of the classic theoretical texts on this subject (e.g. Poulanzas 1974), does indeed lead to the conclusion that oil rentier states enjoy a substantial degree of autonomy. Regimes do not rely on the support of any identifiable class groupings to remain in power, and their policies are therefore not directly influenced by such groupings. However, other theorists focus more on the state's ability to plan and pursue an economic strategy unfettered by special interests. Evans's definition of state autonomy (outlined in Section 1.2.2), for example, follows the latter line. Under this definition of the term, state autonomy can be limited or constrained by interests that are internal to the state itself. State officials, politicians or ruling family members may, through personal interests of one kind or another, frustrate the pursuit of policies which are in the country's wider developmental interest. It will be suggested in this book that, at least over some periods of Saudi Arabia's development, that dimension of state autonomy has not been present. The overall experience of Saudi Arabia's economic development, moreover, indicates the limitations on the autonomy of the state, which has often had difficulty in imposing its own economic agendas on society. Where radical reforms have been introduced, for example, it has been after a prolonged period of negotiation and postponement, frequently followed by inadequate implementation.

Third, rentier state theory, as originally formulated, does not differentiate clearly between state centrality and state capacity. While the state may be central in oil-producing states, its capacity to effect social change may be limited. A strong state, it could be argued, needs to be able to extract resources from the population as well as endow the population with goods and services. The extraction of resources from the population, through taxation, enables the state to radically transform the balance of society. The ability to extract resources may also be important when economic conditions change, perhaps following a fall in the price of oil. Most rentier states do not have this capacity, as they do not have a taxation infrastructure. The absence of such an infrastructure, moreover, deprives the state of a crucial instrument for gathering data on the economic activities of the population, further weakening its ability to change economic outcomes. This is a point which has been made by Kiren Chaudhry with regard to Saudi Arabia. Whereas the state had a developed system of taxation, and considerable data on the economic activities of the population up to the 1960s, it abandoned this with the sharp rise in oil prices and oil revenues in the 1970s. In the process it lost a powerful instrument of financial control and change (Chaudhry 1997: 141–2).

Fourth, the industrial sector is not necessarily destined for a marginal and limited role, as suggested in the theory. Although industry may be uncompetitive in some fields, there remain significant areas where it enjoys a comparative advantage in the global market. This covers, in particular, petrochemicals and all of the downstream activities (e.g. plastics production) which come from petrochemicals, and those industrial activities which rely heavily on energy use (e.g. minerals processing). The question arises, which is a central theme of this book, whether an oil-producing state such as Saudi Arabia could gain international dominance in these sectors (or parts of them), creating an industrial hub which can support a wide-ranging developmental structure–just as Taiwan did on the basis of IT production.

Whether a coherent industrialisation strategy can be pursued, links back to the debate on the autonomy and capacity of the state. While there are in Saudi Arabia many of the negative bureaucratic, social and political characteristics outlined in rentier state theory, there are also islands of efficiency and effective action. The key issue is whether those islands can be joined together, with the leading officials constituting a meritocratic bureaucracy able to plan and guide the rapid industrialisation of the economy, beyond the controlling reach of vested interests. The strong and active private sector in Saudi Arabia could, within this framework, play an important role in carrying the strategy forward.

1.3 The Saudi private sector: dependent or independent?

Of key importance in the analysis of Saudi Arabia's political economy is the assessment of the role and character of the private sector. Academic writings on this subject in recent years have provided radically different assessments. The central issue concerns the relationship between the private sector and the state, which links directly into the theoretical discussion introduced in Section 1.2.2. As this is of key importance to the themes pursued in this book, an outline of the ongoing debate will be given here.

Two different positions emerge with regard to the relationship between the private sector and the state. The two positions share a common basis, both contending that the Saudi government has at times been influenced by elements in the private sector. The difference between them is whether the influence of the private sector comes from its collective significance in the economy or from personal links between individual businessmen and individual state officials. Setting this within the theoretical framework discussed earlier, the individual-to-individual influence is one which can involve predatory behaviour (individuals taking benefit at the expense of a coherent strategy of economic development), whereas the collective influence of a strong private sector can create an interaction with state bodies which can buttress effective economic development. The latter could, in appropriate circumstances, lead to the country emerging as a 'developmental state' as outlined earlier–with a high rate of growth and a broadly based and intensive involvement in the international economy.

The starting point for both sides is an acceptance that the rentier basis of the economy had the initial effect of creating a state with a high degree of autonomy of any social grouping within the country. There can be little doubt that the influx of oil revenues into the country after 1948, and particularly after the price rises of the early 1970s, freed the Saudi state from economic dependence on any social grouping in the country. Whereas in the pre-oil era, the state needed to raise money for its administration and activities from taxation, customs duties, loans from merchants, etc., and all of these required political actions which maintained a form of economy that enabled the economy to produce the taxes and duties that needed to be raised, this was no longer the case by the 1970s. On the contrary, the state was now the provider, with no reason to raise money from the population.

The one critical need was to ensure the security of the oil sector, and the funds which financed governmental activities would continue. The substantial revenues in the hands of the government could be used to buy off discontent, favour those who could help promote the government's objectives, and create the infrastructure and many of the key producing installations which were needed for economic development. Even at this time, it would be wrong to suggest that this high level of state autonomy enabled the state to cut itself free from any connection with society. On the contrary, the state still needed to work with key religious and social figures to ensure popular quiescence, if only to counter radical influences coming from outside the country. The state, however, had the means available to determine how its relationship with key figures would be shaped, and what role they would play in carrying forward governmental objectives.

The divergence between the two approaches lies in their analyses of the impact which the boom period following the early 1970s' rise in oil prices had on the country's political economy. The boom years (or the 'first boom') covered the years between 1973 and 1983. Prices fell in the early 1980s and with them the income accruing to the state. This was followed by a gradual recovery in revenues in the later part of the 1980s. The latter recovery, however, was not sustained: the government's finances were stretched by the state bearing the major financial burden of the 1991 Gulf War, and despite a spike in prices and production during 1991 and 1992, the oil revenues reaching the government were low relative to the early 1980s and subject to sudden and abrupt decline. It was not until the turn of the millennium that a gradual and sustained improvement in oil prices and production, and therefore in the revenue base of the Saudi state, took place.

The writings of Kiren Chaudhry will be taken here as representing one pole in the debate (Chaudhry 1997). Her view, based largely on the rentier state hypothesis, is that the boom period in Saudi Arabia led to the establishment of personalistic links between individual investors and state officials. The state officials were mainly from Najd and they tended to support individuals who came from the same background. The investors who won out at this stage, therefore, were mainly from the Najd region, and many were coming into the business sector without an established background in business. The schemes in which they invested brought benefit to them and also to the state officials who had helped them. Some analysts who adopt a similar line to this identify the royal family as constituting the key element in forging personalistic links between the state and the private sector. Royal princes, it is claimed, used their family connections to secure contracts for businesses in which they had a stake. While it is certainly true that in the 1970s and 1980s members of the Al Su'ud were more active in business than before, and making considerable gains as a result, Chaudhry claims that this was not the key dimension. Of greater importance, she says, were the lower-level contacts which stemmed from individual state officials' personal and family connections.

Whichever element was of most importance, however, the critical point remains the same: new elements were coming into the business sector, where some key state officials or government personnel facilitated this entry and stood to gain from it. The emergence and strengthening of this element of the private sector, Chaudhry maintains, resulted in the weakening of the country's established merchant families, most of whom were based in Jiddah. The overall impact on the business sector, therefore, was to weaken and divide the private sector, and to defeat any attempts by the state to reform the economy. Those within the state apparatus with interests at stake in the existing framework were able to block moves made by the state towards the significant liberalisation of the economic system. The existing, relatively controlled and subsidised, economic system suited their personal interests. The private sector as a whole stood to gain from a more liberalised system, but those businessmen who had made gain through preferential personal contacts with individual state officials did not.

The opposing pole in the debate is found in the writings of Giacomo Luciani. To him, the private sector has been steadily advancing over the years towards constituting a counterpoise to governmental power (Luciani 2005). The boom period provided a basis on which the private sector could establish itself as an important force within the economy, and the years of recession revealed the importance of the private sector to the future development of the economy. While it was not strong enough through the 1980s and most of the 1990s to influence the government away from its determination to drive forward a development programme led by the state, due to the continued strong autonomy enjoyed by the Saudi state, it was increasingly showing signs of its independence from governmental control and guidance. The work of Mary Okruhlik also emphasises the positive impact which the recession after 1983 had on the private sector, making it more reliant on its own resources and more inclined to be critical of governmental policy. Luciani sees the developments which occurred after 2000, when the government did come to promote a wide-ranging programme of economic reforms, as stemming from the role which the private sector was now playing, and from a governmental recognition that the cooperation and involvement of the private sector was now a necessity.

The fact that Luciani's work was published in 2005, whereas Chaudhry's was published in 1997, may be significant. Luciani had the advantage of taking account of developments through an important stage of economic reform. His conclusion is that Saudi Arabia now has a business leadership which is autonomous of the state, pressing for an economic system characterised by transparency and lack of corruption, and with an independent judicial system giving effect to clearly defined regulations. Whereas Chaudhry sees a system which has some of the characteristics of a predatory state, therefore, Luciani sees one which has the potential to operate as a developmental state (although he does not specifically use this concept). In the latter case, the state would be operating on the basis of embedded autonomy.

A variant of Luciani's approach, which is rather more negative in terms of its evaluation of likely developments, is that of Stephen Hertog (2006). In Hertog's analysis, policy-making (at least from the late 1990s) was not 'unduly encumbered by organised social interests which could thwart reforms', and the 'higher echelons of the technocracy contained a whole host of qualified figures with a liberal outlook' (Hertog 2006: 289). Within the structures of the state, moreover, there were 'a number of rather efficient state agencies–the Saudi Arabian Monetary Agency (SAMA), the Saudi Arabian Basic Industries Corporation (SABIC), the Saudi Ports Authority etc. (ibid.: 39). Economic reform and development, therefore, were not constrained by personalistic relations between state and business personnel. Yet there was a critical constraint: the system was imbued with 'segmental clientalism'. State institutions had developed as 'fiefdoms', dominated by individuals who held their positions by virtue of deals made and compromises reached within the royal family. This pattern of administrative organisation became 'locked in' through the dynamics of elite politics and bureaucratic growth. While each fiefdom might be internally efficient, integrated decision-making (involving more than one ministry or institution) was and is weak. This, therefore, is not a form of state which could reform itself quickly or operate flexibly and effectively in devising new policies.

The character of the private sector, and the nature of its relationship with the state, will be a theme pursued through the different chronological phases covered in this book. The line taken here is closer to that of Luciani than of Chaudhry. Indeed, the contention is that developments since 2003, which was the date Luciani's material goes up to, provides further evidence of the growing strength and resilience of the private sector. The relationship between the private sector and the state, moreover, has increasingly taken on characteristics akin to those found in a developmental state. Over the years since 2004, Saudi Arabia has benefited from a massive rise in oil revenues. These are conditions in which, if rentier influences were still predominant in setting Saudi economic agendas, the state could be expected to resist economic reform (deemed as unnecessary and risky). Yet it is precisely over these years that the process of economic reform has moved ahead. The conclusion must be that there are factors more powerful than those of the rentier economy which are driving the process forward.

It should be noted, however, that the analysis given here does not necessarily regard the strengthening of the private sector's influence on the state as providing the solution to Saudi Arabia's developmental problems. The importance of the developmental state experience in the Far East has been to show that a particular relationship between the state and the private sector (embedded autonomy) may constitute the most critical dynamic towards export-oriented industrialisation. Whether it solves the wider problems of society, however, is a different matter. The impact of industrialisation on social relations in Taiwan will not be the same as that in Saudi Arabia.

The most crucial difference is labour. Saudi Arabia's resource and population base, the expectations to which Saudi citizens have become accustomed, and the forces of globalisation currently shaping global economic development, all affect critically the balance of benefit/loss to different parts of the Saudi population as a result of industrial success. Unless state policy can ensure that Saudi citizens gain employment within the burgeoning private sector, on a basis where it is economically beneficial for employers to provide them with this employment, successful industrialisation could well be socially disruptive. The forces of economic globalisation currently work against a positive outcome–towards the employment of migrants rather than Saudis. Attempts now being made to boost Saudi employment, and to reduce migrant labour, are an indication of governmental concern on the issue. The problem, however, will not be solved simply by restrictions on migrant employment. What is needed is a relationship between the state and the Saudi labour force which is conducive to creating a productive and creative workforce, paid at rates which are internationally competitive. There are political as well as administrative and economic dimensions to the development of such a workforce.

The embedding of the Saudi state perhaps needs to be wider than that which has been appropriate in East Asia. It needs to encompass a broad range of social interests, covering labour as well as capital.

1.4 Defining the Saudi private sector: a complication

Analysing the role of the state in the economy, with particular regard to how it relates to the private sector, raises one immediate problem. The definition of what is comprised by the private sector is not always clear.

In offering a definition of the private sector, the World Bank points to the indistinct character of the dividing line between public and private sectors:

> The private sector is usually defined as the collection of enterprises that are owned by individuals or groups not representing the state, where the public sector comprises government agencies and state owned enterprises. In practice, however, the dividing line between the public and the private sector is always blurred, especially since ownership and control of the state may vary in degree and over time. Furthermore, countries differ in their legal or customary definitions of what is private and what is public.
>
> (World Bank 1989: 1)

The blurred nature of the dividing line is particularly apparent in the case of Saudi Arabia (Presley 1984: 27–8; Montagu 1994: 61). The main problem lies in the extent to which the state controls or partly owns many of the enterprises which operate in the commercial/industrial sector. The most notable example of this is SABIC, the second-largest company in the country (after Prince Alwaleed's Kingdom Holdings). Almost 25 per cent of the total net income accruing to companies listed on the Saudi stock market (the *Tadawal*) in 2006 was contributed by SABIC. Yet the company is 70 per cent owned by the state, most of its activities are closely linked into governmental strategies and plans, and its board is chaired by the Minister of Industry. The second-largest contributor to total net income of listed companies was the Saudi Telecommunications Company, which is also 70 per cent owned by the state. The largest bank in the country is the National Commercial Bank. Up to the late 1990s it was owned by the bin Mahfouz and Kaki families, but in 1997 it was converted into a joint-stock company and in 1999 the government took a 70 per cent stake in its share capital. Nonetheless its activities are still included in governmental statistics covering the private sector. Among other companies which combine private and public shareholding are a number of smaller banks (e.g. the Riyadh Bank and the Saudi Investment Bank), cement companies (e.g. the Saudi Cement Company), transport companies (e.g. the Saudi Public Transport Company [SAPTCO]) and agricultural companies (e.g. the National Development Company [NADEC]). The extent of state involvement in companies whose contribution to the economy is classified in national accounts as part of the private sector is clearly substantial. In fact, approximately one-third of the capitalisation of the companies listed on the *Tadawal* in recent years has been governmental.

A further complication arises from the extent to which foreign companies participate in joint enterprises with state organisations. National accounts attribute this production to the private sector, yet in practice the foreign companies may be simply building and operating industrial undertakings owned and controlled by the state. While this economic activity can be useful, it does not necessarily contribute to the vitality and strength of the Saudi business sector.

While these problems make it difficult to define clearly the weight and importance of the private sector, the direction and extent of change can nonetheless be apparent. The growing proportion of GDP coming from the private sector, for example, is significant however the private sector is defined–as long as the same definition is consistently applied over the period in question. The application of the term 'private sector' to something which might be more accurately termed the 'corporate sector' or perhaps the 'business sector', moreover, is not wholly inappropriate. Corporations which retain a majority public-sector ownership, but whose business practices cohere with those of private companies, may help to reduce needless bureaucracy and create a more flexible environment for economic growth.

1.5   The structure of the book

Chapters 2–4 and 6 trace the development of the Saudi economy through four main stages or time-periods. Each of the four chapters is structured in a similar way. This is intended to enable the reader to follow through, from one stage to another, progress made on each of the 'criteria of success' outlined previously. Achievements in laying down an appropriate infrastructure and in developing the hydrocarbons sector are treated integrally in the account of economic development in each stage. Employment and the development of the private sector, however, are given separate sections in each chapter. Their importance in the analysis warrants this separate treatment: they contain the central dilemmas which need to be resolved if the Saudi economy is to satisfy the long-term needs of the population. The following elements are brought into the analysis of all of the time-periods:

1 The resource base, in terms of revenue and foreign assets. This is to provide an overview of the sums accruing to the government in revenues, comparing oil with non-oil revenue sources, and the holdings of foreign assets.
2 The development plans. An account of the development strategies of each plan, and the planned allocation of spending between the various sectors.
3 The articulation of development strategy and economic policy. Changes in the resource base, and perhaps in political or social priorities,

will lead to economic policy and expenditure diverging from that which was planned. The policies actually pursued, and the money actually spent in each sector, are the key issues here.

4   The record of achievement in economic and social development. The growth and composition of Gross Domestic Product, the strengthening of the country's physical infrastructure and social provision, and movements in the balance of payments are taken as the key measures of economic achievement.

5   The policy and regulatory framework affecting the private sector. The focus here is on the range of governmental regulations and measures which impinge on private-sector activity.

6   The strength and composition of the private-sector economy. This is measured by factors such as the contribution of the private sector to Gross Domestic Product, and the distribution of private-sector activity across agriculture, industry and services.

7   The social dynamics of the private sector, and the relationship with the state. The concern here is to identify the character of the social groupings promoting private-sector growth, and their relationship with the Saudi state.

8   Employment. How the labour force developed, paying attention to the breakdown between Saudi and non-Saudi labour, and between male and female. Also of concern are the rates of remuneration of the different elements.

Chapter 2 covers the years between 1962 and 1970. This was the critical period when the basis for economic development was being laid down: planning organisations were created, investment was directed towards a significant expansion of the social and economic infrastructure, and the economy was put back onto a solid basis after the crises of the late 1950s. The level of oil revenues at this stage, however, remained limited–at least relative to the situation after 1972.

Chapter 3 covers the 1970–85 period. Over these years, Saudi Arabia passed through its first three development plans: the First Development Plan (1970–5), the Second Development Plan (1975–80) and the Third Development Plan (1980–5). The definition of this period as a stage, co-terminous with the first three plans, requires some explanation. The dynamics of the Saudi economy in fact undergo several major changes over this period, caused more by rising and falling oil prices than by the intrinsic content of the development plans. The sharp rise in prices in 1973–4 put into the hands of the government a vastly greater revenue than it had ever had before; this was further complemented by the price rises of 1979–81. After 1982 the government had to adapt to a significant fall in oil revenues.

Yet there remains good reason to focus on the whole period covered by the plans. This is partly due to practical considerations: the economic statistics and information which Saudi institutions provide–especially in tracing the achievements of the economy–are mostly presented within the framework of the periods covered by the plans. This, of course, applies to all of the chronologically based chapters, each of which takes a period defined by plan-periods.

There is, however, also a more substantive reason for taking the 1970–85 years together. This is because the whole period was characterised by policies which envisaged social and economic transformation through massive investment in infrastructure and production. Even the First Development Plan, framed before the 1973–4 price rises, held that vision–based on the knowledge that investment in the oil industry in the 1960s was about to yield higher oil production and therefore higher exports. The cautious approach of the 1960s, then, was replaced in the 1970s by an ambitious attempt to transform the economy, with a modern agricultural sector, health and social provision similar to that in the developed world, a well-skilled professional and technical labour force, and (especially from the Second Plan onwards) a developed industrial base. During the mid-1970s international attention was caught by the Shah of Iran's boasts of Iran's rapid emergence as a significant developed country. The Saudi plans attracted less attention, as they were promoted with less extravagant fanfare, but in practice the vision was similar. As for the years after 1982, when oil revenues were declining, the vision remained in place through necessity: the plans were already being implemented, and could be financed through accumulated assets. There was also the expectation and the belief that the global demand for oil would sooner or later resume its growth, and that oil revenues would return to levels more comparable to the past.

Chapter 4, covering 1985 to 2000, again encompasses three development plans: the Fourth Development Plan (1985–90), the Fifth Development Plan (1990–5) and the Sixth Development Plan (1995–2000). Over these years, the vision of a transformed economy was still in place, but the government now had to take more account of constraints. Most of the major infrastructural projects envisaged in the 1970–85 plans, moreover, had now either been completed or (in the late 1980s) were being completed. The oil price falls of the 1980s, and the fluctuating prices through the 1990s, drove the government to borrow on the international market–indicating that limited capital availability now had to be figured into development plans. The rapid rise in migrant labour, moreover, was raising concern, requiring the government to think through the labour requirements of planned developments–and to introduce more programmes aimed at replacing non-Saudi labour with Saudi labour, as well as to intensify the educational and training programmes which would enable more Saudi labour to be used. Much of the focus of economic policy over this period, therefore, was on coping with changing conditions–some of them brought on by the ambitious plans of the previous period–rather than enthusiastically embracing a new strategy.

Chapter 6, from 2000 to the present, begins with the introduction of the Seventh Development Plan (2000–4) and continues into the first years of the Eighth Development Plan (2005–9). This period has been marked by a new vision–that of an economy shaped around a dynamic private sector able to compete in global markets. The vision has developed in stages. Initially, the emphasis was on economic reform aimed at creating the market conditions required for membership of the World Trade Organisation. There were strong fiscal reasons for the government to pursue such a policy at the turn of the millennium, given the low level of oil revenues in 1997 and 1998. Government expenditure needed to be cut and hopes for economic growth therefore depended on the expansion of the private sector. By 2003, however, oil prices and production were considerably stronger and more stable, and in 2005–6 oil revenues reached a level which had not been seen since 1981. Rather than this leading to a retrenchment in the pace of reform, the opposite occurred. Economic reform now came to be linked to a strategy for using private capital to create a new industrial infrastructure for Saudi Arabia. Global predominance could even be attained in those fields where the Kingdom held significant competitive advantage. The period since 2003 can be seen as constituting the second Saudi oil boom.

The chronological chapters in this book, it will be noted, have an overlapping year with the previous period and also with the subsequent one (1962–70, 1970–85, 1985–2000, 2000–6). This follows the format of the first six development plans which carry an ambiguity as to the precise start- and end-points of the planning periods. The procedure is, however, useful in its own right. It enables the reader to keep track of how developments in one period relate to those in the previous one. The ambiguity in the chronological divisions, moreover, reflects the reality that the processes of change do not take place in neatly separated stages.

The two non-chronologically based chapters (Chapters 5 and 7) pursue themes of relevance to the accounts of economic developments given in the other chapters, but with a specific focus. Chapter 5, based on a survey of business opinion in the late 1990s, examines the problems facing the growth of the private sector at that time. The intention here is to provide a picture of these problems on the eve of the major reforms which the government was to initiate after 2000.

The final chapter in the book (Chapter 7) provides an assessment of the record and achievement of economic reform since 2000, indicating also what additional reforms may be desirable if the objectives of the government are to be attained. While the planning of reform is covered in Chapter 6, therefore, the record of achievement/limitations in actual reform is the subject of Chapter 7. The chapter covers, among other aspects, the appropriateness of existing legal and institutional structures; the extent to which the social and physical infrastructure can sustain a developing globally-oriented private sector; the impact of membership of the World Trade Organisation; the record on privatisation; the operation of the stock market; the competitiveness of Saudi labour and the changing pattern of employment; the shaping of the relationship between the private sector and the state in the light of the reforms; and the social impact of the current pattern of economic development. Some of the material in this chapter is drawn from interviews with businessmen in Saudi Arabia conducted in 2006 and early 2007.

2 Laying the basis for development, 1962–70

2.1 Introduction

Before the beginning of oil exports, Saudi Arabia clearly came close to the minimal state model. This did not stem from a philosophy of economic liberalism, but from the practical reality of resource poverty. There was simply no money for the state to play a more active role, or even to create the administrative organisations necessary to support such a role. Governmental structures were very light and basic. Up to 1952 the only ministries in existence were those of Finance (founded in 1932), Foreign Affairs (1933) and the Interior (1944).

The state operated, in practice, with a large element of predatory behaviour. The King was able to, and did, use state resources for his own purposes. Yet it is difficult to compare this element of predatory behaviour with that of the predatory states mentioned in Evans's work (see Chapter 1). Even the concept of a distinction between the King's resources and those of the state was not present for much of King Abd al-Aziz's reign: the main use to which state/royal resources were put was in ensuring the security of the state and the stability of the regime, whether this was done through the purchase of weaponry, the granting of provisions and funds to tribal leaders whose loyalty was needed, the financing of royal marriages to the daughters of crucial tribal leaders, the provision of hospitality to those who came to express their loyalty to the King, the salaries of the officials who served the King and the ministries, payments to the small number of foreign advisers who gathered around the King, or whatever. The characteristics of predatory behaviour in a state like Mobutu's Zaïre, where state resources were siphoned off into the Swiss bank accounts of leading members of the regime, were very different from this.

Once oil exports began in 1948, and significant resources became available to the regime, the potential of the state to move beyond the activities of a minimal state grew. The development of the economy now became financially feasible. But in practice this did not change the state's mode of operation: it continued to function through the 1950s as a minimal state. There was no coherent plan for economic development. Indeed, most aspects of the state's economic management lacked coherence. A new range of government ministries was established from 1952 onwards, but they neither controlled economic policy nor determined the distribution of resources. The edifice of a modern state was developed, but not its reality. Rather than the Saudi state undertaking a programme of economic and social development, much of the new wealth was used to finance lavish expenditure by the King (especially after Saud became King in 1953), pay more generous subsidies to the tribal and religious elements whose loyalty underpinned the state, and expand the armed forces. The lavish expenditure by the King was now more clearly of a predatory nature. Resources were being used for the personal benefit of the ruler and those around him, rather than for the state and the population.

Socially, however, there were important developments taking place in Saudi Arabia during the 1950s, stemming from the initiation and development of oil production. The first was that a small but politically conscious industrial working class was developing. At its core were the largely Shiite workers employed in the oil industry in the Eastern Province. Strikes, combining pay demands with political concerns, occurred in 1953 and 1956 (Niblock 2006: 40). Second, merchant families whose influence and contacts with the King enabled them to obtain agencies for the import of particular goods, or contracts for the construction of buildings and infrastructure, benefited greatly. The oil income made possible the import of substantial quantities of consumer goods of all kinds. Those who were in a position to conduct this trade, and to build the palaces and ministries which were now needed, came to occupy strong positions in Saudi Arabia's economy and society. The gains, it should be stressed, stemmed from the patrimonial favours of the monarch, not from a governmental strategy to facilitate the accumulation of private capital. Third, the rural and artisanal population tended to suffer from the new developments. The goods they produced could not compete effectively with imports. Many of them abandoned their traditional pursuits and moved into the urban and modern economy.

Change away from this minimal/predatory model of state organisation came with the rising influence and authority of Crown Prince (later King) Faisal, who was appointed Prime Minister in March 1958. The appointment was effectively imposed on King Saud by the wider royal family, concerned that the King's political and economic mismanagement would lead to the undoing of the Saudi monarchy. Over his first two years as Prime Minister, however, Faisal could not pursue an active development policy.

His central concern had to be on the restoration of financial stability. His efforts were focused on reducing and controlling the predatory and wasteful expenditure which had forced the Kingdom to seek help from the IMF early in 1958. These penny-pinching policies proved unpopular among many members of the Al Saud, and others who had benefited from Saud's profligacy. King Saud managed, aided in part by the reaction to Faisal's policies, to regain enough support within the family to reassert his authority in June 1960, taking the prime ministership back into his own hands and leaving Faisal on the sidelines.

In October 1962 the struggle for political control between King Saud and Crown Prince Faisal came to an end. Faisal was reinstated as Prime Minister. His control of government policy was never again effectively challenged. When Saud did seek to resume his powers in 1964, he lost the throne and Faisal was appointed King. Faisal's transition from Crown Prince to monarch, however, made little difference: the power to make governmental decisions remained where it had been before. The period between 1962 and the introduction of the First Development Plan in 1970 therefore constitutes a definable stage in Saudi Arabia's development. Policy was now directed towards articulated developmental objectives, albeit without a document which laid out the strategy for attaining these objectives.

Economic developments in Saudi Arabia between 1962 and 1970 hold more in common with those in other state-centric developing countries than they do with any of the models of state involvement in mixed economies outlined in Chapter 1. The state, as in the socialist-oriented regimes in the major Arab republics at this time (Egypt, Syria, Iraq, etc.), was seeking to develop the country's economy and infrastructure through its own direct efforts and resources. This was not akin to state-sponsored capitalism, in so far as the role of the private sector was more as an appendage than a partner in the economic expansion. The main targets of development at this stage, moreover, were not industrial. Expenditure was directed mainly to social and physical infrastructure. Such funding as was devoted to the productive sectors went to agriculture.

The major difference between the economic strategies of Saudi Arabia and those of the more radical Arab regimes lay in the scope of the activity which the private sector could undertake. In the Kingdom, the private sector continued to dominate the commercial sector, whereas under radical Arab regimes the state appropriated the larger commercial and manufacturing enterprises. The difference was, to some extent, attributable to the different forms of rent on which each depended. Nasser's Egypt, for example, saw the need to acquire resources from the private sector, through nationalisation and controls. In practice, the extraction of resources from the private sector in this manner operated as a form of rent. Foreign aid, which Nasser was able to acquire from both the East and the West during the Cold War, also constituted rent. The Saudi regime had no need to extract resources from the private sector. Oil rent provided the funding for state-centric development. Saudi Arabia in the 1960s, moreover, was not as administratively and educationally developed as Egypt. It did not as yet have the administrative and planning structures, nor the physical infrastructure, necessary for an ambitious industrial strategy. A key element of Faisal's policies during the 1960s, indeed, was to develop the institutions and procedures appropriate to such a strategy. The establishment of the Central Planning Organisation in 1965 was the most important move in that direction.

2.2   The economy before 1962

2.2.1   *Before oil exports*

In 1932, when Saudi Arabia was created, the state of the economy was not significantly different from what it had been, in techniques and composition of production, for centuries. Knauerhase (1975: 57) noted that the wheel was not in general use in most areas of the country. This observation is misleading, carrying with it a hint of civilisational backwardness. The reality was that the terrain of most of Saudi Arabia made nomadic production and the transport of trade by camel more appropriate than any wheel-based economic activities. The seaports, and sea trade with India and elsewhere, moreover, provided the setting for some of the larger merchant enterprises in existence at that time, on the eastern and western shores of the Kingdom. Nonetheless, the absence of wheeled transport or implements does indicate the character of the economic activity and exchange which were practised in substantial parts of the country.

Before the development of the oil industry, the main sources of the Saudi population's livelihood were pastoral agriculture and trade (Lipsky 1959: 204; Knauerhase 1975: 57–9; Bashir 1977: 40; Azzam 1993: 11). Inhabitants of the interior of the country were mainly pastoralists, raising goats, sheep and camels. Settled agriculture was present in Asir and in the oasis areas of al-Hasa. The inhabitants of the small towns were mainly engaged in commercial and artisanal activities. There was virtually no industry. The traditional economy was generally based on a complex of small, self-sufficient units, the largest boundaries of which were those of oasis, village or tribe. The social characteristics which accompanied this form of economic life were those of relative poverty, a high level of illiteracy, and substantial isolation from developments outside of the local area.

Nonetheless, there were areas where economic activity was sufficient for wealth to accumulate. On the Gulf coast, some merchant families – often with interests which spread across Saudi and non-Saudi territories in the Gulf (including Persia/Iran) – benefited from the pearl fisheries, the shipment of Arabian horses to India, trade in agricultural produce, etc. The Hijaz had the most significant commercial infrastructure, based on services provided to the pilgrimage traffic. Earnings from this source provided a significant source of income for the holy cities of Makkak and Madinah and the nearby port of Jiddah. For four months of the year, a large number of people were engaged in supplying goods, accommodation and other support for pilgrims. The main fields of trade were furnishing, food and clothing. Most of the domestic goods, apart from food and artisanal products, were imported.

Levies on pilgrimage traffic also constituted a major source of income for the state before the development of the oil industry (Niblock 1982: 93). Following the signature in 1933 of the agreement with the Standard Oil Company of California granting concessions for oil exploration, income from the latter source exceeded that from pilgrimage levies.

2.2.2   From the export of oil

The turning point in the economy came with the beginning of oil exports in 1948. Oil had been discovered in 1938, but the initiation of oil production and export was held back by the Second World War. Oil exports greatly increased the revenues available to the government. Governmental revenues, which had averaged $13–16 million annually between 1938 and 1946, rose to $53.6 million in 1948. By 1953 they had surpassed US$100 million and by 1960 stood at US$333.7 million (Niblock 1982: 95–6). The economic basis for an oil rentier state was now present. The economy was dominated by the oil sector, which accounted for 85 per cent of the government's revenue and 90 per cent of foreign exchange earnings. Oil revenue provided the major impetus to commercial activity and infrastructural development (Lipsky 1959: 154).

In comparison with many states in receipt of new revenues from oil, however, the economic development which ensued was limited. Despite the new ministries which had now come into existence, a significant part of governmental revenues remained directly under the personal control of the King. Table 2.3 shows that in 1959 the opaque category 'private treasury' accounted for about 20 per cent of total budget appropriations, more than twice that expended on economic projects (approximately 9 per cent). Some 24 per cent of appropriations went to defence, and 14 per cent to the upkeep of ministries. In practice, large amounts were spent on the construction of palaces, misguided foreign adventures, and hand-outs to individuals close to the King. Much simply disappeared through corruption. It is likely that the figures for 1959, moreover, represent a considerable improvement on earlier years. Accurate figures on the latter are not available. In 1958 Prince Faisal had become Prime Minister and was following a plan produced by a mission of the International Monetary Fund to restore financial stability to the country, and this had some impact on the 1959 figures.

Some worthwhile development expenditure was taking place, especially in education (to which some 10 per cent of budget appropriations were devoted in 1959), and in health services (5 per cent), but this was limited relative to the potential offered by rising oil revenues. Projects could often not be carried forward effectively, moreover, due to inadequacies in the administrative and financial frameworks. Although the Saudi Arabian Monetary Agency (SAMA) had been established in 1952, and had a reputation from the outset for probity and professional conduct, it did not at this stage have the practical instruments to manage the financial system. Until 1958 its activities were effectively limited to the execution of the government's policies, and up to 1966 it had no defined responsibility over the country's commercial banks (Knauerhase 1975: 239).

The majority of the population benefited little from the oil wealth. The standard of living of significant parts of the population, indeed, was deteriorating, as the basis of the livelihood of those in the traditional sectors was being undermined. The situation was particularly bad outside of the main cities. New forms of transport, and the rapid growth of food and consumer imports, led to a decreased demand for rural products and services. The market for camels, horses and agricultural produce was badly affected, as also were the markets for maritime, craft and artisanal goods (Lipsky 1959: 152–3, 156). There was, as a result, considerable hardship in the countryside, which was only partially alleviated by the increased subsidies that the King made available to the tribal leaders.

The declining prosperity (or increased poverty) of much of the population stood in sharp contrast to the substantial profits accumulated by those benefiting from the patrimonial favours of the King. As a result of these increased inequalities, and the wasteful use of resources, there was growing social tension and discontent.

2.3 Governmental revenue and foreign assets, 1962–70

The economic development which Saudi Arabia witnessed over this period was built on the increasing resources which could be spent on development. These increased resources, however, were not simply a fortunate windfall from which Faisal's government was able to benefit. It was largely the outcome of the government's own efforts. There were two aspects to this. The first was that, Faisal's rigorous control over wasteful state expenditure released resources which could now be devoted to development. The scale and impact of this diversion of resources will be covered in Section 2.5.

The second aspect was the growth in revenue from oil sales. Unlike the gains which Saudi Arabia made from this source during the mid- and late 1970s, this did not come from a rise in the price of oil. Indeed, for most of the 1960s the posted price of oil (the price agreed with ARAMCO for calculating the share of oil sale revenue allocated to the Saudi government) remained constant. The increased revenue, rather, stemmed in part from increased production and in part from a series of renegotiations with ARAMCO of the terms on which revenue was shared. The gains, in both cases, can be attributed to the greater effectiveness and strength of the government, buttressed by a gradual change in the balance of the relationship between governments and oil companies which followed the establishment of the Organisation of Petroleum Exporting Countries (OPEC) in 1960. The establishment of the General Organisation of Petroleum and Minerals (Petromin) in November 1962 signalled to the oil companies that the Saudi government was intent on gaining more influence over oil industry operations in the Kingdom. This was followed by the granting of prospecting and exploration licences and oil concessions to Petromin in 1967, and also to some relatively small foreign oil companies which had no previous involvement in Saudi Arabia (Knauerhase 1975: 184–9).

Table 2.1 shows the rise in oil production and exports which occurred over the 1962–70 period. Table 2.2 covers the growth in revenues accruing to the government over the same years, and the sources from which they were coming. The key point is that over this period oil production approximately doubled, while revenues accruing to the government approximately tripled.

In comparison to the major increases in revenue which were to occur in the 1970s, the rise during the 1960s was relatively limited. Up to 1965, moreover, Faisal's main concern was to restore financial stability and to avoid international indebtedness. The resource base over the period covered in this chapter, therefore, dictated a considerably more restrained approach to development than that which was to characterise strategies pursued in the 1970s. Nonetheless, governmental expenditure did increase, and between 1966 and 1970 this exceeded the growth of revenue. Government finances were in deficit over that period.

Table 2.1 Saudi crude oil prices, production and exports, 1962–70 (million barrels)

Year	Posted price per barrel (Arabian Light 34 API) (US $)	Total	% Change	Daily average	Total exports
1962	1.8	599.76	10.96	1.64	501.30
1963	1.8	651.71	8.66	1.79	544.83
1964	1.8	694.13	6.51	1.90	587.21
1965	1.8	804.94	15.96	2.21	678.83
1966	1.8	948.57	17.84	2.60	829.31
1967	1.8	1,023.84	7.94	2.81	888.57
1968	1.8	1,113.71	8.78	3.04	968.30[a]
1969	1.8	1,173.89	5.40	3.22	1,020.05
1970	1.8	1,386.67	18.13	3.80	1,174.17

[a] Including Petromin exports.
Sources: Prices from World Bank (1962–70) *Commodity Trade Price Trends.* Washington: World Bank. Other data from Saudi Arabian Monetary Agency (various years) *Annual Surveys*. Riyadh: SAMA.

Foreign assets rose gradually during the 1960s, but did not exceed the level which was needed to maintain the value of the Saudi riyal (Knauerhase 1975: 245–51).

2.4   Planning without a development plan: the Ten-Point Programme and development strategies, 1962–70

Faisal's control saw the introduction of a more coherent vision of economic and social development in the Kingdom. The key document which introduced that vision was the Ten-Point Programme of 1962, which was announced within a month of Faisal's reinstatement as Prime Minister.

The Programme contained provisions with regard to political, administrative and judicial organisation as well as economic and social development. Many of the political and administrative proposals, such as the introduction of a Basic Law and a system of provincial administration, were not put into effect at that time (in fact not until the 1990s). The points which related to economic and social development took the form of broadly phrased aspirations, yet they conveyed governmental determination to pursue a developmental agenda and identified areas for expenditure which were indeed those given attention over the remainder of the decade. Point Seven promised to improve the position of Saudi citizens through the enactment of a variety of social measures. Point Eight stressed the need to intensify and coordinate economic development, envisaging

Table 2.2 Governmental revenues, 1961/2 to 1970/1 (SR million)

	1961/2	1962/3	1963/4	1964/5	1965/6	1966/7	1967/8	1968/9	1969/70	1970/1
Oil sector revenues	1,648.8	1,917.8	2,267.9	2,571.8	3,144.2	3,944.1	3,515.4	4,198.3	5,197.8	5,440.0
1 Royalties	564.3	674.5	721.4	813.4	954.4	1,160.7	1,126.6	1,177.0	1,738.5	1,573.0
2 Income tax	1,084.5	1,243.3	1,528.0	1,756.6	2,186.5	2,783.4	2,388.8	3,018.8	3,459.3	3,863.5
3 Tapline	–	–	18.5	1.8	3.3	–	–	2.5	–	3.5
Tax revenues	229.6	214.8	219.3	234.7	272.9	308.5	331.2	392.7	441.3	654.0
1 Direct taxes	66.8	65.5	58.0	59.5	62.0	76.7	81.0	88.1	110.4	202.5
2 Indirect taxes	153.5	140.2	152.2	163.0	198.5	215.0	233.3	286.0	303.7	421.7
3 Fees and licenses	9.3	9.1	9.1	12.2	12.6	16.8	16.9	18.6	27.2	29.8
Non-tax revenue (charges and miscellaneous)	61.0	77.8	121.5	140.1	176.0	188.3	211.0	299.1	316.2	275.9
Other revenues, n.e.c.	–	–	–	–	4.9	7.4	6.4	8.5	8.0	6.2
Total current general revenues	1,939.4	2,210.4	2,608.7	2,946.6	3,598.0	4,448.3	4,064.0	4,898.6	5,963.3	6,376.1

Source: Saudi Arabian Monetary Agency (2005) *Forty-First Annual Report*. Riyadh: SAMA.

a new structure of laws and regulations which would make this coordinated strategy possible. It was clear that the strategy would cover the private as well as the public sector, as there was reference to measures which would attract capital. Point Nine laid out the priorities which would guide development plans, with the immediate emphasis being on physical infrastructure (especially roads and water supply) and industry (both heavy and light). Agricultural and industrial banks were to be created to promote private-sector growth in those fields, and there was to be an Economic Development Fund to provide the funding which public corporations would need for developing their operations (De Gaury 1966: 147–51).

The vision put forward in the Ten-Point Programme was similar to that advanced in many other developing countries at that time, with an emphasis on the state introducing the social legislation needed for development, creating the infrastructural basis for a modern state, and promoting industrialisation. The main difference from the transformationist programmes of Arab socialist regimes lay in the absence of a dialectic emphasising social equality (with accompanying policies redistributing wealth and productive resources). At this stage, moreover, the Saudi government had not placed its vision within the text of a development plan, as had been done in most of the other major states of the region. The administrative infrastructure for planning, and in particular for introducing development plans, was nonetheless being put in place. The Central Planning Office, established in 1965, was given responsibility for preparing periodic reports on the economy and five-year plans, and for ensuring that development programmes were compatible with the amount of finance available (Al-Farsy 1989: 142). From 1966 the role which SAMA could play in regulating the economy was strengthened through the issuing of the Banking Control Law. This gave the agency the power to set limits to the total value of loans which commercial banks could extend, fix some of the critical terms and conditions for loans, and set the level of assets which each bank should maintain (Knauerhase 1975: 238). Some of the legal frameworks which were introduced during the 1960s were also crucial for a coherent development programme. The 1968 Land Apportionment Act clarified the rights of ownership of land: all land which was undeveloped belonged to the state (Hajrah 1982: 21). The 1969 Labour Law introduced the first systematic regulation of the conditions under which Saudis and non-Saudis could be employed (Mutawakil n.d.: 123–72).

Despite the absence of a formal development plan, the manner in which expenditure was allocated in the national budgets between 1962 and 1970 indicates a reasonably coherent development strategy. Table 2.3 gives details of these allocations. Figures for 1959 are also included, so as to indicate the longer-term changes which were occurring. Among the

Table 2.3 Distribution of financial allocations in budgets, 1959 and 1961/2 to 1969/70 (SR million)

	1959	1961/2	1962/3	1963/4	1964/5	1965/6	1966/7	1967/8	1968/9	1969/70
Administration										
Private Treasury	236.0	248.0	199.0	183.0	173.0	173.0	173.0	173.0	173.0	173.0
Royal Cabinet	0.5	10.0	10.0	10.0	6.0	8.0	8.0	15.0	13.0	14.0
Council of Ministers	7.0	9.0	11.0	11.0	14.0	19.0	19.0	17.0	19.0	18.0
Foreign Affairs	19.0	43.0	50.0	39.0	49.0	51.0	56.0	52.0	65.0	56.0
Interior	90.0	129.0	162.0	228.0	276.0	345.0	370.0	406.0	528.0	546.0
Finance and National Economy	39.0	41.0	46.0	61.0	63.0	57.0	62.0	58.0	71.0	68.0
Justice	19.0	21.0	21.0	24.0	25.0	31.0	33.0	32.0	36.0	36.0
Total	409.5	501.0	499.0	556.0	606.0	684.0	721.0	753.0	905.0	911.0
Defence										
Defence	262.0	340.0	392.0	502.0	548.0	572.0	1,163.0	723.0	841.0	831.0
Civil Defence	–	–	40.0	28.0	39.0	31.0	31.0	20.0	30.0	20.0
Total expenditures	262.0	340.0	432.0	530.0	587.0	603.0	1,194.0	743.0	871.0	851.0
Budgetary reserve	–	–	–	–	–	–	–	–	–	–
Social										
Labour and Social Affairs	–	47.0	77.0	55.0	62.0	78.0	87.0	84.0	92.0	92.0
Education	118.0	171.0	223.0	271.0	305.0	360.0	399.0	383.0	483.0	558.0
Health	60.0	69.0	87.0	103.0	117.0	128.0	154.0	122.0	156.0	155.0
Information	–	–	31.0	32.0	34.0	39.0	42.0	43.0	44.0	43.0
Religious Affairs	23.0	29.0	61.0	66.0	73.0	81.0	90.0	91.0	68.0	67.0
Subsidies	–	25.0	30.0	30.0	30.0	20.0	20.0	20.0	20.0	15.0
Total	201.0	341.0	509.0	557.0	621.0	706.0	792.0	743.0	863.0	930.0

Economic										
Agriculture	20.0	34.0	43.0	58.0	67.0	84.0	88.0	80.0	89.0	82.0
Communications	24.0	18.0	21.0	79.0	87.0	103.0	119.0	98.0	111.0	106.0
Petroleum and Minerals	–	11.0	11.0	11.0	12.0	14.0	17.0	16.0	19.0	19.0
Commerce and Industry	3.0	5.0	6.0	10.0	11.0	12.0	15.0	13.0	16.0	14.0
Projects	55.0	400.0	550.0	550.0	762.0	1,402.0	1,717.0	2,146.00	2,570.0	2,682.0
Total	102.0	468.0	631.0	708.0	969.0	1,615.0	1,956.0	2,353.0	2,805.0	2,903.0
All other										
Emergency expenses	–	–	60.0	60.0	60.0	44.0	46.0	31.0	40.0	41.0
Other Expenditures	138.0	115.0	174.0	251.0	311.0	313.0	339.0	322.0	396.0	328.0
Budgetary reserve	–	–	–	–	–	–	–	–	–	–
Total	138.0	115.0	234.0	311.0	371.0	357.0	385.0	353.0	436.0	369.0
Grand total	1,112.0	1,765.0	2,279.0	2,686.0	3,112.0	3,961.0	5,025.0	4,037.0	5,885.0	5,966.0

Source: Knauerhase, Ramon (1975) *The Saudi Arabian Economy.* New York: Praeger.

key elements worth noting here are that the growth of expenditure on the administrative institutions, and on education and health, was relatively limited in comparison to that on economic development. By the end of the period, indeed, about 50 per cent of expenditure was devoted to the latter, and most of this was for new projects.

2.5   The record of achievement in economic and social development

2.5.1   *The growth and composition of GDP*

Gross Domestic Product (GDP) rose sharply through the 1960s. In 1970/1, the overall GDP total stood at 266 per cent above what it had been in 1962/3, at current prices. The fastest rate of growth was in the final year. Table 2.4 covers this period, with GDP subdivided according to the contribution made by different sectors. Saudi statistics do not provide information on GDP growth at constant prices over these years. It should be noted, however, that the difference between measurement in constant and current prices would not be so great as in later years, given that the price of oil remained stable and that the oil industry made the biggest contribution to GDP.

For most of the period, the oil sector accounted for between 44 per cent and 47 per cent of GDP, rising to 55 per cent in the final year. As a result of the substantial increase in the latter year the oil sector registered the highest percentage increase in the value of production, among the different economic sectors. The agricultural sector witnessed the least growth, with the percentage contribution of this sector to GDP falling from 10 per cent in 1962/3 to 4 per cent in 1970/1. Growth in other sectors was well balanced, with substantial growth being recorded. The steady expansion of the electricity, construction and transport sectors was significant, given that these provided the infrastructure necessary for further economic growth.

The governmental emphasis on industrialisation began to bear some fruit, although at this stage the developments were mainly restricted to oil refining. The newly established Petromin built a refinery in Jiddah, which began production in August 1968, complementing the production from ARAMCO's refinery at Ras Tanura. Another company operating in the oil-related industry was Petromin Lubricating Oil Company (Petrolube), founded in 1968 with 71 per cent ownership by Petromin and 29 per cent by Mobil and other private interests. It produced basic lubricants in a Jiddah factory which began production in 1970. Petromin was also involved in the establishment of the Saudi Arabian Fertiliser

Table 2.4 Composition of the Gross Domestic Product by type of economic activity, 1962/3 to 1970/1 (current prices, SR million)

Industry group	1962/3	1963/4	1964/5	1965/6	Old Series 1966/7	New Series[a] 1966/7	1967/8	1968/9	1969/70	1970/1
Industries and other producers, except for producers of government services										
Agriculture, forestry, fishing	866.2	908.8	874.4	839.4	862.4	846.3	881.0	957.4	984.1	1,015.5
Mining, quarrying										
Petroleum, natural gas	4,049.2	4,068.8	4,508.8	5,441.5	6,052.2	6,130.7	6,892.8	7,269.8	8,106.3	12,581.3
Other	15.5	18.4	25.1	31.7	35.4	36.4	43.5	48.9	46.7	50.3
Manufacturing										
Petroleum refining	528.6	586.4	658.3	698.2	736.2	759.8	901.6	984.7	1,240.9	1,474.2
Other	157.0	172.9	191.3	212.4	237.0	308.9	344.1	385.3	431.2	483.6
Electricity, gas, water	100.9	112.8	128.2	150.3	166.9	198.7	219.6	247.2	273.1	297.9
Construction	310.8	368.3	501.7	633.4	707.1	727.4	869.1	977.4	933.9	1,007.0
Wholesale and retail trade, restaurants, hotels	516.0	599.7	718.0	823.2	876.3	721.8	806.5	937.8	1,007.5	1,067.5
Transport, storage, communication	537.3	636.6	739.4	855.5	976.4	937.9	1,009.7	1,173.2	1,242.5	1,479.3
Finance, insurance, real estate, business services										
Ownership of dwellings	382.0	405.9	430.0	462.0	494.0	494.0	545.0	601.0	661.0	727.0
Other	n.a.	n.a.	n.a.	n.a.	n.a.	266.7	314.7	334.9	354.9	376.6

continued

Table 2.4 Continued

Industry group	1962/3	1963/4	1964/5	1965/6	Old Series 1966/7	New Series[a] 1966/7	1967/8	1968/9	1969/70	1970/1
Community, social and personal service	212.7	222.1	246.2	284.8	310.8	171.0	191.4	214.7	238.3	265.4
Less imputed bank service charge	n.a.	n.a.	n.a.	n.a.	n.a.	−34.5	−39.1	−43.2	−46.0	−49.6
Nongovernmment production	7,676.2	8,100.7	8,591.4	10,432.4	11,454.7	11,565.1	12,979.9	14,089.1	15,474.2	20,776.0
Producers of government services										
Public administration and defence	659.7	771.7	853.3	900.2	1,079.5	752.2	801.0	891.5	942.1	992.7
Other services	226.0	285.5	323.7	374.7	462.5	613.8	648.3	723.7	736.3	812.4
Government production	885.7	1,057.2	1,177.0	1,274.9	1,542.0	1,366.0	1,449.3	1,615.2	1,678.4	1,805.1
Total public and private output	8,561.9	9,157.9	9,768.4	11,707.3	12,996.7	12,931.1	14,429.2	15,704.3	17,152.6	22,581.1
Import duties	n.a.	n.a.	n.a.	n.a.	n.a.	211.4	227.4	271.0	246.0	340.1
GDP	8,603.7	9,205.2	10,257.5	11,775.6	13,078.6	13,142.5	14,656.6	15,975.3	17,398.6	22,921.2

[a] Small changes were made in the way the different activities were classified before and after 1966, hence the listing of 'New Series' and 'Old Series' figures for 1966/7.

Source: Knauerhase, Ramon (1975) The Saudi Arabian Economy. New York: Praeger, pp. 58–9.

Company (SAFCO) in 1965, which began the production of urea and sulphuric acid at its Dammam factory in 1969. Petrolube and SAFCO constituted the first moves into downstream industrialisation in petrochemicals in Saudi Arabia – an area which was to witness major developments over the 1970–85 period.

2.5.2 The strengthening of infrastructure and social provision

There was a steady, although not spectacular, strengthening of social and physical infrastructure between 1962 and 1970. Many of the key indicators witnessed a doubling or tripling: the capacity for electricity generation, the length of the road network, the numbers of school and university students, and the numbers of medical personnel and hospital beds. As a result of the improvement of port facilities, the goods offloaded at Saudi ports increased by about ten-fold over the period. Expanded port facility was deemed particularly important in ensuring that development was not impeded by bottlenecks (KSA-CDS 1971).

Yet the increases were in reality not exceptional. In all of these areas the expansion was starting from a low base. To achieve several-fold increases, with the injection of a reasonable level of expenditure, was not difficult. Much of the growth, moreover, occurred after 1966, once the institutions to support expansion were in place and the country's finances had been brought back into balance.

There was also, over this period, a steady increase in the funds being devoted to social welfare. Again, the growth was steady but not exceptional. Whereas 25,197 individuals were gaining support from the Social Security Department in 1962/3, the number had risen to 72,681 in 1970/1 (KSA-SSD n.d.: 59–61). The major increase in such support was to occur in the decade which followed.

2.5.3 The balance of payments and trade

The steadily increasing revenues from oil through the 1960s led to a similar increase in current account receipts, with a surplus on the balance of payments through to 1967. The surplus, however, gradually declined as a result of development expenditure bringing in increased levels of imports. In the final two years of the decade, moreover, there was a new strain on the balance of payments: the grants and loans which were extended to Egypt and Jordan following the 1967 war. In 1968 and 1969, consequently, the balance on the current account moved into deficit, and the Saudi government drew on its foreign assets to fill the gap.

The deficit position was one of the factors which impelled the Saudi government to seek a further renegotiation of its agreements with the oil companies. Despite the improvements in the apportionment of oil sales proceeds which had taken place during the 1960s, the conviction grew that the Kingdom was not obtaining a fair share. It was at this time, moreover, that the Central Planning Office was putting together the First Development Plan. The government was, therefore, aware of the heavy expenditure on, and substantial imports of, capital goods and materials which would be needed to fulfil the plan's objectives. The problem, it was believed, lay in the control which the oil companies had not only on oil production but also on pricing and production. This pattern was to shift significantly after 1970.

2.6 Growth and structure of the private sector

Outside of the commercial field, most of the private sector at this time was characterised by small-scale units of production. Settled agriculture consisted of small farms, where most of the labour came from within the family. In pastoral agriculture, some of the tribal leaders owned large herds of camels, which had been important for the conduct of trade. By the 1960s, however, this was no longer a significant element in the national economy. Pastoral agriculture, moreover, was shrinking rapidly. The manufacturing sector was also composed mainly of small operations. Of the 9,174 'manufacturing establishments' in existence in 1966/7, according to Central Department of Statistics records, 4,394 of them employed no more than one person (presumably the owner), and 3,769 between two and four people. Most were, therefore, little more than artisanal undertakings (KSA-CDS 1968: 190–1). There was almost no private-sector industrial activity. The main obstacles to the private sector developing industrial projects were the absence of financial facilities necessary for the establishment of industrial projects, the lack of local raw materials, the paucity of skilled labour available locally, and the weakness of the country's physical infrastructure. It was easier and more profitable to import than to produce locally.

The commercial sector accounted for some 62 per cent of the business establishments in existence in 1966/7, with a total of 26,870 units. While 20,838 of these were run by the owner with no one else involved, a small number were substantial. Twenty-five employed more than 50 people, and ten of these employed more than 100. Some of the business establishments in the commercial field, moreover, were closely linked to construction companies (KSA-CDS 1968: 190–1). In construction there were 34 establishments employing at least 50, and 24 employing more than 100. The size of the workforce does not do justice to the strength of the commercial establishments. The major merchant houses and family businesses employed relatively few people but maintained trading networks which stretched across the Red Sea and the Gulf, and had outposts on the shores of the Indian subcontinent. They had also, since the beginning of the oil era, become the agents for the major Western companies which were selling consumer and capital goods to the Saudi population and government. The significance of their activities to the well-being of the population and the economy was considerable. Unlike the role played by the state in the economies of the Arab republics at that time, the Saudi state had no direct role in importing or construction. The private sector was expected to fulfil these needs. About 50 per cent of all commercial establishments were retailers of food and other consumer goods, and 17 per cent retailed textiles, clothing and home furnishings (Knauerhase 1975: 133).

Approximately 50 per cent of the 42,886 commercial establishments in 1967/8 were based in the Western Province, which was regarded at this time as the Kingdom's main commercial centre. Some 25 per cent were in the Central Province and 16 per cent in the Eastern Province (KSA-CDS 1968: 190–1). Most of the larger family businesses were situated in the Western Province, especially the port city of Jiddah.

The commercial elements which played a leading role during the 1960s had mostly established their positions of strength prior to the beginning of the decade. They were not a new commercial elite, therefore, but a strengthened old one drawing benefit from the increased need for their services arising from economic development. The elite based in Jiddah constituted a reasonably cohesive grouping, with links of marriage, social interaction and commercial partnership bringing them together, despite the families often coming from different geographical and ethnic origins. Many came from families which had settled in the holy cities of the Hijaz in former times, coming from Iran, Hadhramaut, central Arabia, the Indian subcontinent and elsewhere.

Four different categories can be identified, according to how and when their wealth was established. First, there were those whose family wealth had pre-dated the establishment of the contemporary Saudi state (1902), and whose social and economic position had in fact helped King Abd al-Aziz establish his authority over the territories of what is now Saudi Arabia. At times Abd al-Aziz was heavily dependent on these merchant families as they provided him with resources at critical points in his reign. Some of the families carried social prestige by virtue of descent from the Prophet or his companions, or else for performing functions associated with the annual pilgrimages. With the advent of the oil era, the well-established merchant families naturally benefited from the good relations which they enjoyed with the King, gaining concessions for the supply of specific goods. Important among these families were the Alirezas and Zahids, who had maintained strong trading establishments in the Hijaz since the 1840s. Others who also fell into the same category were the al-Attas's, Attars, Ba'eshans, Bin Himds, Binzagrs, Buqshans, Hafiz's, Jamils, Jamjooms, Najis, Nashars, Nassifs, Sanies, Sharbatlis, Shobokshis and Shinkars (Carter 1984: 12). All of the families mentioned above were based in Jiddah, but there were also some similarly well-established merchant families elsewhere, such as the al-Rajhis, al-Rashids and Umrans in the Central Province, and the Algosaibis, al-Turkis, Babtains, Seihaitis and Tamimis in the Eastern Province.

Second, there were the merchants who, from a limited resource base, succeeded in establishing good links with King Abd al-Aziz or King Su'ud during the 1940s and 1950s, and were able to obtain key agencies and construction contracts through these contacts and their inherent skills. Many were important in the fields of banking and construction. Among them were the Abu Nayyans, al-Esayis, Bin Ladens, Bin Mahfouz's, El Khereijis, Juffalis, Kakis, Rajabs and Silsilahs.

Third, there were those individuals in the Eastern Province who established close relations with ARAMCO, and built their initial wealth on the supply of goods to ARAMCO. Among these were the Olayans.

Fourth, there were those who had served the King as physicians or advisers, or else held senior administrative positions, and had been able to enter business on this basis. Among these were the al-Sulaimans, Khashoggis and Pharaons.

Despite the strength of these family businesses, they were also heavily dependent on the state. There had been a time, in the 1920s and 1930s, when the merchant families could exert powerful influence over the economic policies pursued by the King. Merchant pressure had, for example, ensured in 1933 that the King cancelled a contract which he had signed with the Soviet Vostogorg organisation, which would have threatened their control over the import market (Niblock 1982: 93). With this economic influence there was also a significant element of political influence, not only through their access to the King but also through positions which they were given in some of the institutions that were established (such as the Consultative Assembly of the Hijaz, established in 1926). By the 1960s, the position had changed. Merchants still often benefited from good personal relations with the royal family, but there is no evidence of this affecting overall economic policy. There was no longer a balance of dependency: the merchant families were now dependent on the government for the contracts and concessions on which their businesses depended.

2.7 The changing pattern of employment

Saudis still made up the great majority of the labour force throughout the 1960s. In 1962/3, according to figures produced by the Central Planning Organisation in 1970, there were some 60,000 foreign workers in the Kingdom, with the overall workforce standing at some 722,050 (KSA-CPO 1970). Some 92 per cent of the workforce, therefore, was Saudi. Most of the non-nationals were employed in the private sector, with a total of only 5,000 working for the government.

In the course of the decade, however, numbers of foreign workers grew. In 1966/7 the number was estimated at 240,400, out of a total workforce of 1,006,600 (Birks and Sinclair 1980b: 94–5). By 1970 it had probably reached about 500,000, out of a total of some 1.3 million. The fields of activity of the workforce were also changing. Whereas about 72 per cent of the workforce were recorded as being 'agricultural workers and bedouin' in 1962/3 (Birks and Sinclair 1981: 162), the proportion fell through the decade. It probably stood at less than 60 per cent in 1970. The next reliable figures which are known are that the agricultural sector accounted for only just more than half (51.4 per cent) of total employment in 1974.

2.8 Conclusion

The centralisation of power in the hands of Prince/King Faisal made it possible for the Saudi state, over the 1962–70 period, to pursue a state-led development policy: creating the administrative, planning and legal structures necessary for development, raising the revenues coming to the state from oil sales, and using resources more effectively than before, for the development of physical (and to a lesser extent social) infrastructure. Some progress was also made in promoting oil-related industrialisation. The 1962–70 period should, however, be thought of as a transitional stage, where the economy was being taken in a new direction with a vision of substantive change, but where the resources, availability of trained Saudi personnel and infrastructure were insufficient to bring about a major social or economic transformation. The oil rentier base of the state ensured that the private sector was dependent on the state rather than vice versa. While the oil rentier dimension weakened the position and influence of the private sector, however, it also underpinned its prosperity and survival. The state had no need to dispossess it of its assets or its role, as was occurring in many Arab states.

3 Planning for transformation, 1970–85

3.1 Introduction

The 1970–85 period covers a stage of Saudi economic policy when the development strategy becomes framed around a vision of social and economic transformation. The previous period had laid the basis, although in practice inadequately, for such a strategy to be pursued. There was now at least a modicum of administrative and planning structures, physical and social infrastructure and actual developmental plans to sustain a bold attempt at social and economic change.

Most of those who have written on the evolution of the Saudi economy have chosen to take the years between 1973 and 1982 as a key time-period for analysis. They describe these years as Saudi Arabia's 'first boom', initiated by the sharp rise in oil prices in 1973–4, further boosted by the price rises of 1979–81, and finishing with the fall in prices and production after 1982. These years do indeed represent the height of the expansion generated by rising oil prices. Revenues reached levels which had been barely imaginable during the 1960s. In 1982 they stood at $328.6 billion, whereas in 1969 they had totalled only $5.1 billion. Each of the three development plans covering the period, however ambitious when announced, was outpaced by actual development. Expenditure was able to, and did, greatly exceed the allocations specified in the plans.

Yet there is a rationale for taking the whole period covered by the first three development plans as an appropriate unit of analysis. Developments after 1973 were to dwarf those of 1970–2, but the first two years of the First Plan do nonetheless form an integral part of the strategy which guided and dominated economic policy between 1970 and 1985. Oil revenues almost doubled between 1969 and 1972, mainly through the increase in production. The increased production stemmed from the substantial investment devoted to the oil sector in the late 1960s. Saudi Arabia had, therefore, boosted its long-term ability to generate oil revenues. Moreover, the Tehran agreement of 1970, between OPEC and the major oil companies, gave oil-producing countries more leverage on the international pricing of oil. By 1970, therefore, the Saudi government had acquired a sound basis on which to frame a more ambitious development programme than before. The 1970–5 plan (made public for the first time in September 1969) embodied this approach. The scale of the planned projects and expenditure after 1973 was to be greatly expanded, but the First Plan contained the main conceptions inspiring the transformative vision of the 1970–85 period.

A further reason for keeping to the periods of plans is that development strategies do not change immediately with changes in the available revenue. The plan can continue to provide the framework within which long-term economic decisions are made. More revenue than expected can lead to more profligacy, and less revenue to penny-pinching measures and perhaps a slowing down of development. But the direction of development may remain unchanged. The immediate response to a fall in revenue, moreover, may be to draw down foreign assets or else borrow money on the international market, thereby ensuring that the critical areas of development expenditure are protected. In practice this latter development is what happened in Saudi Arabia when oil revenues fell after 1982. At least through to the end of the Third Plan (1985), expenditure on the major development projects envisaged in the plan was maintained.

Saudi Arabia's first three development plans (1970–5, 1975–80 and 1980–5), then, contain within them programmes for massive economic and social transformation. Little trace was left of the minimal state of the past. The state was now the initiator, mainspring and sustainer of a transformative project which envisaged the reconstitution and reconstruction of social and economic life in the Kingdom. Yet the final eclipse of the minimal state still did not bring with it a major move towards either the state-aided capitalist or the state-sponsored capitalist models of economic organisation. The domestic private sector remained what it had been during the 1960s: an adjunct and beneficiary of the development process, but not a critical instrument in creating the basis for an industrialised economy.

The adjunct role of the private sector at this time nonetheless enabled the private sector to expand substantially. This expansion was largely a spin-off from state expenditure on infrastructural, administrative and industrial development, although state support through cheap loans and protected markets also played a role. The private sector was needed, as before, to maintain the commercial networks which supplied goods to the population, and to take on construction contracts. Through involvement in irrigated agriculture it also now had a role in reducing the country's dependence on imported food. An element of state-aided capitalism was present in this strategy for the private sector, but not as an element in developing the industrial basis of the new economy. The responsibility for significant industrial development lay with the state.

This model of development, in fact, remained characteristic of developing countries (normally with a socialist ideology) using the state as the instrument of development—not as an aid or sponsor of the private sector, but as a substitute for it. Effectively it was a state socialist model of development, without the socialism. The ability to pursue this hybrid development strategy stemmed, of course, from oil revenues. This was the period when the rentier state aspects of the economy reached their zenith. The oil revenues made it possible for the state to undertake economic transformation on a scale which, elsewhere, would normally be associated with the expropriation of private capital.

Much of the emphasis in the plans remained focused on building up the infrastructural base. This was natural, given the underdevelopment of the country's infrastructure, both social and physical. There was also now, however, a significant new emphasis on state investment in productive sectors of the economy. The focus was centred on downstream petrochemicals—using oil and gas to develop a wide range of petrochemical products. This was a major development, and given the expectations that Saudi petrochemicals would become a significant component of Saudi exports in the future, it pointed towards the export-oriented industrial development of developmental states. Yet the Saudi state did not resemble the model of a developmental state at this stage. The petrochemicals ventures were too narrowly based, too isolated from other dimensions of industrial development in the country, and too deficient in local private-sector involvement, to fit that model. The heavy subsidisation, moreover, raised questions as to whether Saudi petrochemicals would be accepted easily into global markets.

3.2   Governmental revenues and foreign assets, 1970–85

While the rapid rise in oil prices after the 1973 war was the main factor which boosted Saudi oil revenues dramatically in the mid-1970s, revenues were already growing quickly prior to the war. Table 3.2 shows that revenues for 1972 were almost twice the level of 1970. The major cause of the rapid increase at this time was the growth of production. Table 3.1 shows that average daily production rose from 3.80 b/d in 1970 to 6.02 b/d in 1972.

Nonetheless, the main increases in revenue through the 1970s and early 1980s clearly came more from rises in prices than increased production. The price for Arabian Light oil stood at $1.90 per barrel in 1972, rising

Table 3.1 Saudi crude oil prices, production and exports, 1970–85 (million barrels)

Year	Nominal price (Arabian Light 34 API)	Total	% Change	Daily average	Total exports
1970	1.30	1,386.67	18.13	3.80	1,174.17
1971	1.65	1,740.68	25.53	4.77	1,528.19
1972	1.90	2,201.96	26.50	6.02	1,992.53
1973	2.70	2,772.61	25.92	7.60	2,560.34
1974	9.76	3,095.09	11.63	8.48	2,891.68
1975	10.72	2,582.53	−16.56	7.08	2,409.39
1976	11.51	3,139.28	21.56	8.58	2,939.64
1977	12.40	3,357.96	6.97	9.20	3,142.05
1978	12.70	3,029.90	−9.77	8.30	2,812.70
1979	17.26	3,479.15	14.83	9.53	3,218.47
1980	28.67	3,623.80	4.16	9.90	3,375.69
1981	34.23	3,579.89	−1.21	9.81	3,291.54
1982	31.74	2,366.41	−33.90	6.48	2,058.40
1983	28.77	1,656.88	−29.98	4.54	1,431.08
1984	28.06	1,492.90	−9.90	4.08	1,167.89
1985	27.52	1,158.80	−22.38	3.17	780.72

Sources: Prices from World Bank (1970–85) *Commodity Trade Price Trends.* Washington: World Bank. Other data from Saudi Arabian Monetary Agency (various years) *Annual Surveys.* Riyadh: SAMA.

to $9.76 per barrel in 1974. In the four years which followed it increased slowly, and then rose again sharply. The latter rise was prompted by the Iranian revolution (with the overthrow of the Shah in February 1979), and a further twist was added by the outbreak of the Iran – Iraq war in September 1980. The oil price stood at $12.70 in 1978, rising to a peak of $34.23 in 1981. Production had also risen between 1972 and 1981, but had not doubled. The overall impact on oil revenues was very substantial, as can be seen from Table 3.1. They stood at SR328.6 billion in 1981, as against SR13.5 billion in 1972. Over these years, therefore, oil revenues had risen to a figure which was about 25 times what it had been in 1972. From these figures, it is easy to see that the oil rentier dimension of the Saudi economy had reached a level at this time which was quite unlike what had gone before – and in practice unlike that which was to follow.

After 1982, through to the end of this period, there was a gradual fall in the price of oil, which had moved back down to $27.52 by 1985. An even more substantial impact on revenues, however, came from the fall in production over those years. This stemmed from Saudi Arabia's role as a swing producer of oil: boosting production when the price was high so as to keep it from becoming excessive, and cutting it when the price was low

Table 3.2 Governmental revenues, 1969–85 (SR million)

Year	Oil revenues	Other	Total revenues
1969	5,119	549	5,668
1970	7,122	818	7,940
1971	9,685	1,435	11,120
1972	13,480	1,888	15,368
1973	39,285	2,420	41,705
1974	94,190	5,913	1,00,103
1975	93,481	9,903	1,03,284
1976	1,21,191	14,766	1,35,957
1977	1,14,042	16,617	1,30,659
1978	1,15,078	16,427	1,31,505
1979	1,89,295	21,901	2,11,196
1980	3,19,305	28,795	3,48,100
1981	3,28,594	39,412	3,68,006
1982	1,86,006	60,176	2,46,182
1983	1,45,123	61,296	2,06,419
1984	1,21,348	50,161	1,71,509
1985	88,425	45,140	1,33,565

Source: Saudi Arabian Monetary Agency (2005) *Forty-First Annual Report*. Riyadh: SAMA.

so as to prevent a total collapse in price. As the world market for energy had been greatly affected by the price rises of the 1970s, with demand falling both through some consumers succeeding to cut energy or moving to other energy sources, and through a slowing in the growth of the global economy, the price came under strong downward pressure in the first half of the 1980s and Saudi Arabia responded by cutting production. It was therefore losing both through the lower price of oil and a lower level of its own oil production. Daily average oil production had fallen from 9.81 barrels per day in 1981 to 3.17 in 1985. Oil revenues in 1985 came to some 28 per cent of what they had been in 1981. Clearly there was a very substantial impact on the resources which were available to the government.

A stabilising influence on governmental income at this time was provided by the government's non-oil revenue. Although this did rise and fall, the changes were not so abrupt as with oil income, and the rises and falls did not coincide exactly with changes in oil revenue. This is apparent from Table 3.2, which shows that 'other revenue' continued to increase through to 1983, and that the decline thereafter was relatively gradual. Other revenue receipts in 1985 remained higher than they had been in 1981. In 1985, in fact, other income made up more than a third of all governmental income. A major reason for this was that the scale of the revenues from oil at their height was considerably greater than what the

Table 3.3 Foreign assets, 1970–85 (US$ billion)

1970	1.0
1971	1.6
1972	2.9
1973	4.6
1974	22.0
1975	38.7
1976	51.2
1977	59.4
1978	60.0
1979	61.7
1980	86.8
1981	126.5
1982	137.7
1983	125.3
1984	109.7
1985	87.7

Sources: Calculated from data in Saudi Arabian Monetary Agency (various years) *Annual Surveys.* Riyadh: SAMA; and International Monetary Fund (various years) *International Financial Statistics.* Washington: IMF.

government could spend. The level of foreign assets, therefore, had risen and this gave the government a substantial flow of investment income in the years which followed. Most of the 'other income' coming to the government at this time, indeed, came from this source. The level of the income did, nonetheless, decline as the government was having to sell off some of its foreign assets to finance its development strategy. This in turn reduced the investment income.

Table 3.3 shows the movements of foreign assets. Rising from $1 billion in 1970, they grew sharply between 1974 and 1976, and again between 1980 and 1982, reaching a peak at $137.7 billion in the latter year. Thereafter the government was selling off assets, and they fell back to $87.7 billion in 1985. Not all of the fall can be attributed to emergency measures to fill the deficit in governmental finances caused by the fall in oil revenues. The high level of assets at the beginning of the decade came from the inability to spend money, rather than a strategy geared to maintaining such a high level of assets.

3.3 Development strategy: overall targets and objectives

All of the development plans in Saudi Arabia refer to a set of principles which underpin the development effort in general. Their formulation varies slightly from one development plan to another, and in the case of the First Plan they are given a very brief mention, but the underlying ideas remain the same. The central elements are that development will occur within a framework which:

- safeguards the ethical principles of Islam and the cultural values of Saudi society;
- assures the defence of the country and maintains the internal security and social stability of the Kingdom;
- ensures balanced economic growth throughout all regions of the Kingdom, making use of the oil resource yet also conserving depletable reserves;
- diversifies the economic base, reducing dependence on the production of crude oil as the primary source of national income;
- develops human resources through education, training and the raising of health standards;
- completes the basic infrastructure which is required for the attainment of all other goals; and
- supports free enterprise, subject to the interests of the community at large.

These generalised commonalities, all of which are given some emphasis in the strategic conceptions and detailed targets in the plans, give the plans an appearance of continuity and long-term coherence. In reality, however, there are significant differences of emphasis and rhetoric.

All three of the plans covered in this chapter are characterised by their emphasis on the role of the state in shaping and leading the developmental process. None of them gives significant attention to the role of the private sector, and in fact none devotes a chapter to the sector. Such mentions as there are of the sector mainly occur tangentially when there is reference to support services which government agencies will make available to those working in the private sector. The First Plan makes a surprising reference to the private sector already accounting for '85 per cent of GDP, 54 per cent coming from the oil companies and 31 per cent from other private sector activities' (KSA-CPO 1970: 45). The figures cohere neither with statistical realities nor with the development strategy which the plan proposes. All of the country's oil production appears to be attributed to the private sector's GDP, presumably on the grounds that ARAMCO had at that time not been brought under state ownership. Most of the rest of the plan, in any case, rests on the assumption that economic development can be brought about with little reference to the private sector.

Unlike the First Plan, the Second and Third Plans have short sub-sections on the private sector in their chapters on Plan Management and Implementation. These, however, are no more than two-page commentaries on how the private sector might relate to the plan.

The limited space given to the private sector in the plans is not simply an oversight. The perception of the government at this time was that the public sector would carry, almost to the exclusion of the private sector, the burden of developing the economy. The Third Development Plan states very explicitly the all-encompassing role of governmental expenditure. After pointing out that the oil revenues dispense with the need for the government to levy taxes on other sectors in order to finance current and capital expenditure, and provide the necessary means to finance investment, the plan says:

> Since the development process begins with the conversion of oil revenues into domestic assets, and given the Government administers each stage of this process, economic development is largely a government activity. This applies not only to financing and administration of the development projects, but also to the conceptual and organisational phase of planning. Development is a public sector responsibility also in the sense that the ownership and the operation of most of the newly created assets continue to be controlled by the central or local government.
>
> (KSA-MOP 1980)

All of the three plans, in fact, embody a project approach to development planning, rather than a sectoral approach. That is to say, they focus on the specific projects which the government will support in each field of economic activity, rather than on how the sectors are expected to develop over the planning period. The latter approach would need to include more specific indications as to the part which the private sector would play in the developmental process. The First Plan, in particular, reads very much as a listing of projects which will benefit from government finance.

Comparisons between the overall developmental expenditure allocations in the first three plans (and others) cannot be made simply on the basis of the overall expenditure figures found in the plans. The overall figures provided there do not cover the same elements. The First Plan and the Second Plan, for example, include administration and defence as expenditure items. Later plans limit themselves to expenditure which is strictly developmental. Some plans include expenditure by the state-controlled development banks (the Saudi Industrial Development Fund and the Saudi Agricultural Bank), while others do not.

The figures on developmental expenditure provided in Tables 3.4, 3.5 and 3.6, therefore, have been adapted so as to ensure that the same elements are covered in each. They are restricted to the genuinely developmental fields of expenditure, and do not include loans made by state-owned banks. The developmental fields are divided into four main sectors: Economic Resource Development, Human Resource Development, Social Development and Physical Infrastructure.

The scale of the growth in planned development expenditure over the three plans comes out clearly and starkly from Tables 3.4, 3.5 and 3.6. Starting from SR24 billion in the First Plan, it reached SR318 billion in the Second Plan and SR698 billion in the Third Plan. Between the First and Second Plans, therefore, the increase was more than 13-fold, and between the Second and Third Plans more than two-fold. While this increase was substantial, this does not in itself represent a disjunction in the path of development. The expansion of planned expenditure in the Second Plan was dependent on the infrastructure which the First Plan had put in place. The longer-term perspectives of economic development which became concrete in the Second Plan had already been given expression in the First Plan – although as distant goals rather than immediate objectives. At the time when the plan was being drawn up, Petromin was actively developing projects for petrochemical development. The plan states that 'the foreign exchange earnings of oil provide relatively unconstrained access to the foreign management skills, trained manpower, technology, raw materials, equipment and machinery required for development' (KSA-CPO 1970), and that:

> ...there are opportunities for large-scale petrochemical industries; for utilising more capacity of the steel mill and expanding its capacity; and for other industries ... because manufacturing's contribution to GDP is still relatively small ... implementation of large-scale enterprises on the order contemplated by Petromin would have dramatic effect.
>
> (KSA-CPO 1970: 34)

It is nonetheless true that the three plans do embody different emphases. This is evident from the phraseology used in describing the strategic objectives of each. The First Plan is more cautious, as one would expect of a plan drafted at a time when governmental finances had been in deficit for two years. The plan refers to the impact which the Middle East crisis had had on the Saudi economy, and the need to rebuild the foreign assets which had been depleted by Saudi loans to front-line states. Most of the 'policies, programmes and projects' covered in the overview of development presented at the beginning of the plan are in the fields of social

Table 3.4 First Development Plan, 1970–5: projected financial allocations (SR million)

Development sector	Recurrent costs	% of recurrent costs	Project costs	% of project	Total	% of overall total
Economic Resource Development	**1,397.1**	**11.5**	**1,396.4**	**11.8**	**2,792.5**	**11.6**
Agriculture and water	973.8	8.0	493.9	4.2	1,467.7	6.1
Energy and minerals	339.8	2.8	858.7	7.2	1,197.5	5.0
Manufacturing and commerce	83.5	0.7	43.8	0.4	127.3	0.5
Human Resource Development	**6,150.2**	**50.6**	**1,227.5**	**10.3**	**7,377.7**	**30.7**
General education	4,386.0	36.1	558.0	4.7	4,944.0	20.6
Higher education	1,179.0	9.7	439.0	3.7	1,618.0	6.7
Training	585.2	4.8	230.5	1.9	815.0	3.4
Social Development	**1,612.9**	**13.3**	**308.2**	**2.6**	**1,921.1**	**8.0**
Health	1,097.2	9.1	242.8	2.0	1,340.0	5.6
Labour and social affairs	515.7	4.2	65.4	0.6	581.1	2.4
Physical Infrastructure	**2,996.2**	**24.6**	**8,953.6**	**75.3**	**11,949.8**	**49.7**
Transport and communica-tions	1,767.3	14.5	5,709.2	48.0	7,476.5	31.1
Municipal residential development	1,228.9	10.1	3,244.4	27.3	4,473.3	18.6
Overall total	**12,156.4**	**100.0**	**11,885.7**	**100.0**	**24,041.1**	**100.0**

Overall totals composed from the figures for the highlighted development sectors.

Note: The overall totals of development expenditure under the First Plan given here are different from those given in the plan itself. The reason for this is that the plan includes defence and administration. Later plans do not include these elements, but restrict themselves to development expenditure as it is normally conceived. To enable realistic comparisons between development expenditure under different plans, therefore, expenditure on defence and administration has been excluded here.

Source: Figures taken from, or calculated from data in, Kingdom of Saudi Arabia, Central Planning Organisation (1970) *First Development Plan, 1970–75*. Riyadh: CPO.

Table 3.5 Second Development Plan, 1975–80: projected financial allocations (SR million)

Development sector	Recurrent costs	% of recurrent	Project costs	% of project	Total	% of overall total
Economic Resource Development	**4,518.5**	**5.7**	**87,616.5**	**36.6**	**92,135.0**	**28.9**
Agriculture and water	2,307.5	2.9	36,442.0	15.2	38,749.7	12.2
Energy and minerals	1,620.4	2.1	6,944.0	2.9	8,565.0	2.7
Manufacturing and commerce	590.6	0.7	44,230.5	18.5	44,820.3	14.0
Human Resource Development	**43,907.3**	**55.5**	**36,216.6**	**15.1**	**80,123.9**	**25.2**
General education	35,044.5	44.3	26,291.0	11.0	61,335.5	19.3
Higher education	5,993.7	7.6	6,831.8	2.8	12,825.5	4.0
Training	2,879.1	3.6	3,093.8	1.3	5,962.9	1.9
Social Development	**18,148.8**	**23.0**	**15,064.0**	**6.3**	**33,212.8**	**10.4**
Health	5,098.6	6.5	12,396.0	5.2	17,494.6	5.5
Labour	13,050.2	16.5	2,668.0	1.1	15,708.2	4.9
Physical Infrastructure	**12,530.8**	**15.8**	**100,413.8**	**42.0**	**112,944.6**	**35.5**
Transport and communications	5,340.8	6.8	40,013.0	16.7	45,353.8	14.2
Municipal residential development	7,190.0	9.0	60,400.8	25.3	67,590.8	21.3
Overall total	**79,105.4**	**100.0**	**239,310.9**	**100.0**	**318,416.3**	**100.0**

Overall totals composed from the figures for the highlighted development sectors.

Note: The detailed expenditure allocations given in the plan for the sub-categories of Economic Resource Development are not easily compatible with the overall total for the sector. It has been necessary to make assumptions as to which activities are counted under each specific sub-category. The plan contains data on expenditure on construction, for example, which has been divided according to the sub-category where the expenditure occurred.

Source: Figures taken from, or calculated from data in, Kingdom of Saudi Arabia, Ministry of Planning (1975) *Second Development Plan, 1975–80*. Riyadh: Ministry of Planning.

Table 3.6 Third Development Plan, 1980–5: projected financial allocations (SR million)

Development sector	Recurrent costs	% of recurrent	Project costs	% of project	Total	% of overall total
Economic Resource Development	**30,424.3**	**16.7**	**230,785.5**	**44.7**	**261,208.8**	**37.5**
Agriculture and water	12,767.2	7.0	59,318.2	11.5	72,084.4	10.4
Energy and minerals	14,013.7	7.7	79,509.9	15.4	93,522.6	13.4
Manufacturing and commerce	3,643.4	2.0	91,958.4	17.8	95,601.8	13.7
Human Resource Development	**78,873.6**	**43.4**	**49,463.1**	**9.6**	**128,337.0**	**18.3**
General education	56,652.9	31.1	20,200.0	3.9	76,852.2	11.0
Higher education	20,467.7	11.3	25,164.5	4.9	45,632.2	6.5
Training	1,753.0	1.0	4,098.9	0.8	5,851.9	0.8
Social Development	**26,033.7**	**14.3**	**35,166.3**	**6.8**	**61,200.0**	**8.7**
Health	24,422.8	13.4	35,100.7	6.7	59,523.5	8.5
Labour	1,610.9	0.9	65.6	0.1	1,676.5	0.2
Physical Infrastructure	**46,562.7**	**25.6**	**200,781.6**	**38.9**	**247,344.3**	**35.5**
Transport and communications	27,725.8	15.2	115,292.3	22.3	143,018.1	20.5
Municipal residential development	18,836.9	10.4	85,489.0	16.6	104,326.2	15.0
Overall total	**181,894.3**	**100.0**	**516,196.5**	**100.0**	**698,090.1**	**100.0**

Overall totals composed from the figures for the highlighted development sectors.

Note: In the Third Plan's statistics on allocations, there is a small inconsistency between the totals which are given for each of the major development sectors (e.g. Human Resources) and the total of the allocations for the sub-categories (e.g. general and higher education, etc.) within that sector. The figures provided here are drawn from the detailed expenditure allocations for each field.

Source: Figures taken from, or calculated from data in, Kingdom of Saudi Arabia, Ministry of Planning (1980) *Third Development Plan, 1980–85.* Riyadh: Ministry of Planning.

and physical infrastructure. The Second Plan talks ambitiously of laying 'the foundations of economic self-sufficiency in the future as a precautionary measure against the gradual depletion of oil, when revenues and foreign exchange from oil may decline' (KSA-MOP 1975: 58), while at the same time undertaking substantial infrastructural change. To achieve the production objectives:

> ... large investments are to be made in industrial ventures based on natural gas and mineral resources; individual and joint investments in other industries will be encouraged with special incentives; and agricultural production will be stimulated through government research extension activities, credit and input subsidies, and expansion of productive land.
>
> (KSA-MOP 1975: 58)

The Third Plan implicitly criticises the Second Plan, saying that the strategy must now be to focus the development effort more sharply. For the first time in a Saudi development plan, there is a concern with the economy's reliance on foreign labour and a strategy to limit that dependence. This was to be a feature of all subsequent plans. The plan states:

> The strategies of the First and Second Plans emphasised high growth rates in all sectors, and as a corollary, the relatively free import of foreign labour. The Third Plan emphasises high growth more selectively, and aims to consolidate rather than expand the foreign labour force. This reduced emphasis on all-round growth constitutes the most important element in the series of structural changes intended for the Third Plan period.
>
> (KSA-MOP 1980: 16)

The plan lays emphasis specifically on developing the productive sectors, and among these 'a key element will be the maximisation of domestic value-added from crude oil production through hydrocarbon industries'. Infrastructural investment would be 'concentrated in areas with proven potential for growth of productive activities' (ibid.: 17). Overall, then, a significant part of the huge development expenditure envisaged in the plan would be used for the creation of a viable and effective petrochemicals industry.

The allocation of expenditure in the plans follows the pattern which the plans' rhetoric suggests, as can be seen from Tables 3.4, 3.5 and 3.6. All but 11.6 per cent of planned expenditure in the First Plan was for infrastructural and social development. In fact, the 11.6 per cent allocated to economic resources is itself an overstatement. More than half was for 'Agriculture and Water', and the plan reveals that most of this was specifically for the improvement of water supplies. The latter should really count as infrastructural expenditure, given that the water supplies were mainly for domestic and industrial purposes rather than agricultural. Only a very small part of the planned funding, then, was directly for economic resource development, with half of the overall total going to physical infrastructure, and almost one-third to human resource development. Such industrial investment as was envisaged in the plan was almost entirely restricted to the energy sector.

The Second Plan saw a major increase in planned expenditure on economic resource development (to 28.9 per cent), and a consequent reduction in the proportions going into physical infrastructure and human resource development. Nonetheless, in absolute terms, the plan envisaged the level of expenditure in both of these latter fields increasing dramatically. Human resource development expenditure was to increase more than 10-fold, and physical infrastructure some 11-fold. Social development expenditure was expected to rise, both absolutely and proportionately.

In the Third Plan there was a further substantial rise in the proportion going to economic resource development, now accounting for 37.5 per cent of all planned expenditure. Physical infrastructure retained the same proportion (35.5 per cent) as under the Second Plan. Much of the planned expenditure in the latter sector, however, was allocated to projects which would be of productive value (such as the infrastructure needed for the development of the new industrial cities in Jubail and Yanbu). The proportion going to human resource development declined substantially (from 25.2 per cent to 18.3 per cent), and even in absolute terms the increased spending did little more than keep up with inflation.

3.4 The articulation of development strategy and economic policy

3.4.1 Factors shaping the articulation of policy

The key factor which had shaped the development plans was the amount of revenue expected to come from the sale of oil. The most important factor affecting the implementation of the plans was the extent to which those expectations were fulfilled. In the course of the first two plan-periods, actual expenditure significantly exceeded that which had been projected in the plan concerned. The extent and the speed of the rise in the price of oil was much greater than the planners had envisaged, with particularly sharp rises taking place half-way through the First Plan and in the last two years of the Second Plan. Not to have spent a significant part of these revenues on development would have led to domestic criticism, given that the Kingdom remained underdeveloped in so many ways. In its annual budgets, therefore, the government allocated more funds to the development sectors than had been envisaged in the plans.

The period covered by the Third Plan opened with a further rapid rise in oil revenues, with the government again raising the allocations for development expenditure above that which had been envisaged in the plan. After 1981, however, revenues declined sharply (see Table 3.1), and by 1983 were below the level they had been at when the plan was formulated. Over the last two years of the plan, therefore, budget allocations were cut back. The overall effect of this was that development expenditure over the third plan-period did not exceed that which had been planned.

The 1970–85 period can be seen, therefore, as having passed through the following phases:

1970–2: Following the introduction of the First Development Plan, but prior to the rapid rise in the oil price, expenditure was kept within the bounds of the plan. In practice bottlenecks in the economy, and the slow start made on some projects, meant that expenditure fell short of projections.

1973–5: Rising revenues after the October 1973 war encourage the government to raise budget allocations beyond the planned levels of expenditure, and actual development expenditure exceeds the planned First Plan allocations.

1976–9: Expenditure rises quickly within the framework of the more ambitious targets set by the Second Plan. Oil revenues, meanwhile, had reached a plateau, such that expenditure exceeded revenues in 1978 and 1979. Nonetheless, budget allocations for development were not cut back significantly.

1980–2: Expenditure rises within the framework of the highly ambitious Third Plan, but is exceeded by the even more rapid rise of revenues at this time (with the impact of the Iranian revolution and the outbreak of the Iran – Iraq war on oil prices).

1983–5: Revenue declines sharply, through falls in both oil prices and oil exports. Deficits are recorded in 1984 and 1985. Budget allocations are reduced in 1984 and 1985, and actual developmental expenditure also declines. Nonetheless, there are no major cutbacks in governmental plans (Rehfuss 1996: 50).

3.4.2   *Changes in the regulatory framework*

The contribution of the government to the development of the economy cannot be seen simply in terms of the development plans and the sums invested in development sectors. Also relevant are the efficiency of the governmental machine, the framework of laws and procedures which regulate economic development (especially the private sector), and the support available from government agencies for business and commercial activities.

The administrative machinery of the Saudi state grew substantially over the 1970–85 period. The numbers employed in the civilian public sector rose from 112,000 in 1970 to 469,000 in 1985 (see Table 3.17). While this indicated an increase in administrative capacity, however, it does not necessarily reflect an increase in administrative efficiency. Some administrative developments were clearly productive, such as the creation and development of specialised credit funds: the Agricultural Bank (established in 1964, but substantially expanded after 1970), the Saudi Industrial Development Fund (1974), the Saudi Credit Bank (1971) and the Real Estate Development Fund (1974). The first two were significant for economic resource development in the private sector, and the latter two catered for the social needs of the population. The Public Investment Fund (1971) was set up to provide loans to public enterprises and organisations for projects which were commercial in nature. Also important was the creation of the Saudi Ports Authority (1976), the Saudi Arabian Basic Industries Corporation (SABIC) (1976), the Ministry of Industry and Electricity (1975) and the Royal Commission for Jubail and Yanbu (1975).

While some government departments, and some of the bodies created by governmental action, were operating effectively and efficiently, however, the overall machinery of government remained cumbrous and bureaucratic. Ministries tended to operate as fiefdoms of individual ministers (Hertog 2006: 93–103). Civil servants enjoyed little room for taking decisions on their own, with even minor issues needing ministerial endorsement. Contact between the different parts of the administrative machine was limited, such that there was frequently an overlap between the work which different ministries were doing. Sometimes this resulted in contradictory policies being pursued. The coherence of the development plans was not reflected in a coherence of actual policy. Some procedures could be swiftly completed through communication with the relevant minister, but the normal processes of administrative action were time-wasting and inefficient.

Three significant changes in the private/public division of activities took place over this period. Two involved measures to strengthen governmental control of the economy. First, the nationalisation of ARAMCO. Contrary to the impression held by many observers during the 1970s, this was not simply an outcome of the 1973 war and the rebalancing of the relationship between Saudi Arabia and the West which followed from it. The process was underway before the war, with the Saudi government taking a 25 per cent stake in ARAMCO's assets and concessions in 1972. In 1974 the Saudi government's stake moved up to 60 per cent. The move was generally described in terms of governmental participation in the company rather than nationalisation, so as not to associate it with the nationalisation of foreign assets which had occurred in many Arab countries during the 1950s and 1960s. In practice, the term 'participation' was appropriate: the former owners (Texaco, Mobil, Exxon and the Standard Oil Company of California) continued as the managers of the company's oil production, with the government determining the overall strategy pursued. The government was, through these means, able to control more effectively the pricing and levels of production of Saudi oil.

Second, the government gained control of the electricity sector through bringing the existing privately owned electricity companies into consolidated regional companies. Majority shareholding of the new companies lay with the public sector. The process of creating the new regional companies took place in 1976 and 1977. Again the process involved the government gaining majority ownership and hence control, rather than the expropriation of the previous owners. It had become clear that the private sector was neither up to meeting the economy's rapidly growing demand for electricity nor was it able to meet the government's increasing emphasis on standardisation of voltages and frequencies – a prerequisite to modernisation (Soufi and Mayer 1991: 11).

A third change in the public/private division involved a shift back to the private sector. In 1984 the government sold to the public 30 per cent of its shares in SABIC. This was expected to be the harbinger of a gradual move towards majority private ownership of the corporation. Despite many reports over the years of more share sales impending, however, none has materialised. The private sector's involvement in the corporation emphasised the commercial basis on which it was intended to run, although in practice the private shareholders have subsequently played little part in key decisions.

3.4.3   Government subsidies and loans for business and commercial enterprises by state-owned banks

The welfare of the population, and the buoyancy of some parts of the economy, were also affected by subsidies and subsidised loans to particular parts of the population and sectors of the economy. A large array of subsidies was introduced in the course of the 1970s. The main elements here were subsidies to reduce the cost of food, direct payments to farmers, subsidies for the production of wheat and barley, social security payments, subsidies to electricity companies to reduce the price of electricity, and a variety of payments related to social care. In 1970 the total cost of subsidies came to SR17 million. By 1984 this had increased to SR12.1 billion (KSA-MOP 1989: 55).

The creation and expansion of the Agricultural Bank and the Saudi Industrial Development Fund have been mentioned above. Over the period 1970–85 they played a significant role in financing developments in the productive sectors of the economy. The Agricultural Bank's activities were at a height between 1975 and 1983, when it extended SR11.8 billion worth of loans to a total of 27,000 farmers or farming enterprises (Looney 1990a: 49). Lending by the Saudi Industrial Development Fund increased from SR16 million in 1974 (its first year of operation) to SR6.8 billion in 1979, although the number and value of new loans gradually declined after that (KSA-MOP 1989: fig. 11).

3.4.4 Changing patterns of governmental expenditure

Table 3.7 shows that the government changed its budgeted expenditure radically from year to year to take account of rises and falls in revenues. In 1973, 1974 and 1975 budgeted expenditure was approximately doubling every year, with very substantial rises also taking place in 1979, 1980 and 1981. In both cases this followed the major increases in oil prices. The ability of the government to spend the money, however, was not so great: expenditure lagged behind the budgeted targets in each of those years. Nonetheless, government expenditure tended to catch up with revenue rises three or four years after these rises had taken place. In 1977 and 1978 government finances, therefore, had moved back into deficit, as also between 1983 and 1985. In the latter case this was in part the result of a fall in revenue, whereas in the former case revenue had simply reached a plateau. Between 1976 and 1978 the government put a cap on spending, but in practice this proved ineffective: expenditure continued to rise. After 1982 the attempt to limit expenditure was more strongly and effectively pursued, such that there was a steady and substantial year-by-year reduction through to 1985.

The main increases and decreases in government spending were on administrative expansion, subsidies and defence rather than on development. This is clear from the data in Tables 3.7 and 3.8. The former covers all government expenditure, while the latter is confined to

Table 3.7 Budgeted and actual revenues and expenditures, 1969–85 (SR million)

| | Revenues | | Expenditures | | Surplus/deficit |
	Budgeted	Actual	Budgeted	Actual	Actual
1969	5,966	5,668	5,966	N/A	N/A
1970	6,380	7,940	6,542	5,418	1,522
1971	10,782	11,120	10,782	8,303	2,817
1972	13,200	15,368	13,668	10,148	5,220
1973	22,810	41,705	22,810	18,595	23,110
1974	98,247	100,103	45,744	32,038	68,065
1975	95,847	103,384	110,934	81,784	21,600
1976	110,935	135,957	110,936	128,273	7,684
1977	146,493	130,659	111,400	138,048	−7,389
1978	130,000	131,505	130,000	147,971	−16,466
1979	160,000	211,196	160,000	188,363	22,833
1980	261,516	348,100	245,000	236,570	111,530
1981	340,000	368,006	298,000	284,650	83,356
1982	313,400	246,182	313,400	244,912	1,270
1983	225,000	206,419	260,000	230,185	−23,766
1984	214,100	171,509	260,000	216,363	−44,854
1985	200,000	133,565	200,000	184,004	−50,439

Source: Saudi Arabian Monetary Agency (2005) *Forty-First Annual Report.* Riyadh: SAMA.

Table 3.8 Breakdown of governmental expenditures in the First, Second and Third Plan periods

		Economic resources development	Human resources development	Social and health development	Infrastructure development	Total
First Plan	SR billion	9.5	7.0	3.5	14.1	34.1
	%	27.7	20.6	10.3	41.4	100.0
Second Plan	SR billion	97.3	51.0	27.6	171.3	347.2
	%	28.0	14.7	8.0	49.3	100.0
Third Plan	SR billion	192.2	115.0	61.2	256.8	625.2
	%	30.7	18.4	9.8	41.1	100.0

Source: Kingdom of Saudi Arabia, Ministry of Planning (2000) *Seventh Development Plan, 2000–2004.* Riyadh: Ministry of Planning.

development spending. Table 3.7 shows rapid changes in expenditure occurring, with little relationship to the needs of the development plans and the actual expenditure which was going into development. In the second plan-period, for example, total government expenditure came to SR684 billion, whereas development expenditure stood at SR347 billion.

It was a pattern which was to be expected, at least when revenues were rising: it was easier to spend money by expanding ministries, raising salaries, increasing subsidies and buying weapons than it was to instigate new development projects.

As indicated earlier, development expenditure exceeded planned allocations in the first two plan-periods, and fell slightly short of planned allocations in the third. Table 3.8 gives the figures: expenditure over the First Plan period came to a total of SR34.1 billion, as against the planned SR24.5 billion; over the Second Plan period to SR347.2 as against SR318.4 billion; and over the Third Plan period to SR625.2 billion as against SR698.1 billion. In practice the differences are not very substantial. The rapid rise in revenues in the first and second plan-periods came in the later part of each, and the bottlenecks in the economy and administrative apparatus had in both cases already held back the pace at which money could actually be spent. In the third plan-period, the fall in revenues after 1981 reinforced the problems caused by over-ambitious targets, yet actual expenditure remained substantially higher than the level reached prior to the inception of the plan.

The differences between planned expenditure (as shown in Tables 3.4, 3.5 and 3.6) and actual expenditure (as shown in Table 3.8) show up some interesting trends in the composition of development expenditure. In the period covered by the First Plan, there was an actual underspending of the planned allocation on social development, and the amount allocated to human resources was only just met. Spending on physical infrastructure was significantly in advance of planned allocations, but the major difference was in economic resource development, which attracted more than three times as much expenditure as had been planned. The latter made up 27.7 per cent of total development spending, rather than the 11.8 per cent which had been planned. Much of the additional spending was in the energy and minerals sector of the economy, with the government taking a stake in ARAMCO and then investing in oil development so as to take advantage of the changing conditions on the world oil market.

In the period covered by the Second Plan, expenditure on social development again fell substantially short of the planned targets (SR28 billion as against SR33 billion), but on this occasion human resource development fell even further short of the target (SR51 billion as against SR80 billion). Economic resource development slightly exceeded the targets (SR97 billion as against SR92 billion), but the major excess over targets was recorded by physical infrastructure (SR171 billion rather than SR113 billion). The government was clearly finding it easier to achieve its objectives in building roads, housing and communications than it was in developing the educational and health services. Some of the excess expenditure on economic resource development, moreover, is accounted for by spending on urban water supplies, which could better be classified as infrastructural spending.

In the Third Plan period, the government achieved its objective of substantially increasing expenditure on economic resource development, but not nearly to the extent which it had intended (SR192 billion as against SR261 billion). Expenditure in that sector accounted for 30.7 per cent of total expenditure rather than the 37.5 per cent which had been planned. Spending on physical infrastructure, on the other hand, slightly exceeded the target (SR257 billion as against the planned SR247 billion, making up 41.1 per cent of total spending as against the planned 35.5 per cent). Social development spending on this occasion reached the planned level (SR61 billion), but human resource development expenditure again fell significantly short of the target (SR115 billion as against SR128 billion).

Overall, there is little evidence that the decline in oil prices after 1981 significantly slowed the pace at which the government's development projects went forward. The plans were already in place, and most of the major construction projects contracted, before the fall in prices. Foreign assets remained at a high level through to 1984, and these could be and were used to ensure the completion of projects. Some of the shortfalls in government spending, moreover, seem to have come from a policy of delaying payment on bills, with the government hoping that payment could be staved off until oil prices recovered. Besides that, the bottlenecks in the infrastructure and the administration were continuing to slow the development process down.

3.5   The record of achievement in economic and social development

3.5.1   The growth and composition of GDP

Gross Domestic Product at current prices grew quickly in the first two plan-periods. As can be seen from Table 3.9, the rise between 1970 and 1975 was more than seven-fold, from SR22 billion to SR163 billion. The rapid growth continued over the 1975–80 period, reaching SR544 billion in 1980. Given that GDP at current prices (i.e. the prices prevailing in the year covered) includes the effect of rising oil prices, the many-fold increases are hardly surprising. The figures do, however, show the size of the economy's resource base.

Table 3.9 Growth in Gross Domestic Product,
          1970–85 (current prices, SR million)

Year	Total GDP[a]
1970	22,279
1971	30,124
1972	37,819
1973	53,047
1974	159,276
1975	163,156
1976	224,441
1977	259,548
1978	270,439
1979	373,309
1980	544,070
1981	619,538
1982	520,949
1983	441,533
1984	416,416
1985	372,408

[a] Total except import duties.

Source: Kingdom of Saudi Arabia, Central Department of Statistics (1970–85) *Statistical Abstracts.* Riyadh: Ministry of Planning.

A more significant measure is the growth of GDP at constant prices, in so far as this shows a real measure of economic production and is not skewed by sudden changes in prices. There is a difficulty in providing accurate figures for real GDP growth in the 1970s and early 1980s, however, because there are substantial discrepancies between the figures produced by different Saudi bodies. The most widely used figures in the past have been those produced by the Ministry of Planning. The Ministry's Third Development Plan records real GDP having risen by 13.4 per cent annually in the First Plan period and by 8.4 per cent in the Second Plan period (KSA-MOP 1980: 20). The base year for the constant prices was set at 1970 for the first period, and 1979 for the second. The First Plan had set a target for GDP growth at 9.5 per cent, while the Second Plan set a target of 10 per cent. Whereas GDP growth was estimated as having significantly exceeded the First Plan target, therefore, it fell short of the Second Plan target.

The Ministry of Planning appears, perhaps surprisingly, to have underestimated the actual rate of real GDP growth. Its figures were prepared at a time when the gathering of data on the economy was not well advanced, which may explain the anomaly. Later figures from the Saudi Arabian

Monetary Agency, prepared on the basis of data from the Ministry of Finance, show a more substantial growth in real GDP. The latter is consistent with other indications of how the economy was developing. The SAMA figures are those used in Tables 3.10 and 3.11. They are based on constant prices at 1999, making it possible to compare GDP levels over the whole period covered in this book. The difference in base year means that the amounts given for GDP in Table 3.10 could not be expected to tally with figures produced at the time (nor, of course with the current price GDP figures in Table 3.9). The variance in the figures, however, is not explained simply by the different base years used. Table 3.11, covering percentage growth in GDP (based on the SAMA figures), provides evidence of this. Percentage growth should not be greatly affected by changes in the base year, yet the pattern of development shown in those figures is substantially different from that shown in the earlier data.[1]

Tables 3.10 and 3.11 show the significant trends taking place in real GDP between 1970 and 1985. Over the First Plan period (1970–5), real GDP growth greatly exceeded the plan target, averaging 21.7 per cent per annum as against the targeted 9.5 per cent. Not all sectors, however, were performing equally well. The crude oil and natural gas sector grew substantially, more than double the 9 per cent growth which the First Plan had targeted for it, and made the largest absolute contribution to GDP growth. The tables show that much of this growth took place before the Middle East war of October 1973, and therefore was not an outcome of the rise of prices associated with the conflict. Substantial growth was also taking place at this time in the construction, trade, finance and community services sectors – the sectors which could be expected to benefit most from the rise in government expenditure now fuelling developments. Growth in the agricultural and manufacturing sectors was more limited. Overall, then, this was a period when GDP growth stemmed from the development of the oil industry, the construction projects financed by rising revenues, and the commercial and community services which enabled the population's needs to be met.

Over the period covered by the Second Plan, between 1975 and 1980, the rate of real GDP growth did not meet the target set in the plan. The latter had predicted an annual growth rate of 10 per cent, whereas the actual growth was approximately 6.8 per cent per annum. The main reason for the shortfall was that oil production did not increase at the rate which had been expected in the plan (4.8 per cent as against the planned 12 per cent). This stemmed from the reduction of world demand for oil following the price rises of 1973–4. The impact of this on the economy was especially acute in 1978, where a negative growth rate in the economy was recorded. In other sectors, growth targets were

Table 3.10 GDP by kind of economic activity, 1970–85 (producers' value, at constant prices at 1999, SR million)

	1969	1970	1971	1972	1973	1974	1975	1976	1977	1978	1979	1980	1981	1982	1983	1984	1985
Industries and other producers except producers of government services:																	
Agriculture, forestry and fishing	5,510	5,493	5,707	6,028	6,371	6,751	7,186	7,721	11,893	10,510	9,207	10,386	10,888	11,716	12,734	15,146	17,865
Mining and quarrying	74,038	87,360	109,606	138,667	174,729	195,363	160,085	198,289	212,021	191,410	219,522	229,157	225,964	150,078	105,632	95,315	74,306
(a) Crude petroleum and natural gas	73,595	86,935	109,129	138,048	173,824	194,041	158,521	196,811	210,521	189,954	218,119	227,752	224,435	148,358	103,875	93,595	72,649
(b) Other	443	425	477	619	905	1,322	1,564	1,478	1,500	1,456	1,403	1,405	1,529	1,720	1,757	1,720	1,657
Manufacturing	8,312	10,325	10,562	11,181	12,178	15,219	15,186	16,047	17,351	18,835	20,777	22,081	24,624	26,821	28,902	32,350	35,565
(a) Petroleum refining	5,345	6,982	6,792	6,897	7,288	7,350	6,534	7,978	8,273	8,787	9,443	9,374	9,436	9,630	10,344	10,828	12,868
(b) Other	2,967	3,343	3,770	4,284	4,890	7,869	8,652	8,069	9,078	10,048	11,334	12,707	15,188	17,191	18,558	21,522	22,697
Electricity, gas and water	801	890	941	1,003	1,151	1,024	1,299	761	885	1,429	2,109	2,552	2,635	-892	-2,089	-658	3,624
Construction	9,431	8,836	9,476	12,170	17,131	30,600	44,339	46,099	45,475	46,372	50,329	56,008	61,593	60,323	54,992	47,528	39,489
Wholesale and retail trade, restaurants and hotels	3,991	4,203	4,429	5,235	7,103	9,563	11,539	12,601	14,325	18,058	21,867	25,873	31,223	35,127	35,987	33,605	33,633
Transport, storage and communication	5,604	6,127	7,131	8,384	10,461	10,105	10,602	11,707	12,967	15,502	16,363	16,271	18,269	19,673	20,899	21,718	21,666
Finance, insurance, real estate and business services	16,715	17,746	18,988	21,240	25,518	43,395	56,321	58,685	58,664	67,827	75,293	81,263	88,325	94,680	96,170	89,372	81,509
(a) Ownership of dwellings	11,051	11,910	12,921	14,416	17,040	28,428	40,180	44,291	43,902	50,799	55,738	57,611	59,443	62,423	64,338	60,072	53,722
(b) Other	5,664	5,836	6,067	6,824	8,478	14,967	16,141	14,394	14,762	17,028	19,555	23,652	28,892	32,257	31,832	29,300	27,787
Community, social and personal services	4,510	4,916	5,399	6,261	6,549	11,953	12,633	9,644	9,977	11,272	12,946	12,360	14,609	15,668	15,281	15,485	17,604
Less imputed bank services charge	25,571	27,506	27,469	27,245	26,781	21,079	6,408	3,736	4,120	5,096	6,081	6,885	8,447	8,578	8,604	8,838	7,332
Sub-total	103,341	118,388	144,772	182,922	234,409	302,894	312,245	357,942	379,982	376,798	422,573	449,065	469,684	404,615	359,904	341,022	317,928
Producers of government services	25,875	26,649	29,000	32,185	36,928	44,615	53,584	54,883	61,041	60,255	58,211	63,339	67,364	72,300	77,119	82,089	86,757
Import duties	2,921	3,002	3,790	4,171	4,116	3,673	3,710	3,715	4,689	4,315	3,952	3,934	3,510	3,650	4,057	4,347	4,289
Gross Domestic Product	132,137	148,039	177,562	219,278	275,452	351,181	369,539	416,540	445,713	441,369	484,736	516,337	540,558	480,566	441,080	427,458	408,974

Note: The official data give no explanation as to how the Electricity, gas and water sector could have achieved a minus figure for their GDP contribution in 1983 and 1984. It is probably explained by adjustments to the statistics being necessary after the electricity companies were brought within the public sector.

Source: Kingdom of Saudi Arabia, Ministry of Planning (1987) Achievements of the Development Plans. Riyadh: Ministry of Planning.

Table 3.11 Percentage growth in sectors of the Gross Domestic Product, 1969–85 (constant prices at 1999)

	1969	1970	1971	1972	1973	1974	1975	1976	1977	1978	1979	1980	1981	1982	1983	1984	1985
Agriculture, forestry and fishing	5.66	-0.31	3.90	5.62	5.69	5.96	6.44	7.45	54.03	-11.63	-12.40	12.81	4.83	7.60	8.69	18.94	17.95
Mining and quarrying	5.36	17.99	25.46	26.51	26.01	11.81	-18.06	23.86	6.93	-9.72	14.69	4.39	-1.39	-33.58	-29.62	-9.77	-22.04
(a) Crude petroleum and natural gas	5.40	18.13	25.53	26.50	25.92	11.63	-18.31	24.15	6.97	-9.77	14.83	4.42	-1.46	-33.90	-29.98	-9.90	-22.38
(b) Other	-1.56	-4.06	12.24	29.77	46.20	46.08	18.31	-5.50	1.49	-2.93	-3.64	0.14	8.83	12.49	2.15	-2.11	-3.66
Manufacturing	7.91	24.22	2.30	5.86	8.92	24.97	-0.22	5.67	8.13	8.55	10.31	6.28	11.52	8.92	7.76	11.93	9.94
(a) Petroleum refining	5.74	30.63	-2.72	1.55	5.67	0.85	-11.10	22.10	3.70	6.21	7.47	-0.73	0.66	2.06	7.41	4.68	18.84
(b) Other	12.05	12.67	12.77	13.63	14.15	60.92	9.95	-6.74	12.50	10.69	12.80	12.11	19.52	13.19	7.95	15.97	5.46
Electricity, gas and water	12.98	11.11	5.73	6.59	14.76	-11.03	-25.68	16.29	61.47	47.59	11.38	8.64	3.25	-133.85	134.19	-68.50	-650.76
Construction	-0.45	-6.31	7.24	28.43	40.76	78.62	44.90	3.97	-1.35	1.97	8.53	11.28	9.97	-2.06	-8.84	-13.57	-16.91
Wholesale and retail trade, restaurants and hotels	12.68	5.31	5.38	18.20	35.68	34.63	20.66	9.20	13.68	26.06	21.09	18.32	20.68	12.50	2.45	-6.62	0.08
Transport, storage and communication	13.81	9.33	16.39	17.57	24.77	-3.40	4.92	10.42	10.76	19.55	5.55	-0.56	12.28	7.69	6.23	3.92	-0.24
Finance, insurance, real estate and business services	6.34	6.17	7.00	11.86	20.14	70.06	29.79	4.20	-0.04	15.62	11.01	7.93	8.69	7.20	1.57	-7.07	-8.80
(a) Ownership of dwellings	7.74	7.77	8.49	11.57	18.20	66.83	41.34	10.23	-0.88	15.71	9.72	3.36	3.16	5.03	3.07	-6.63	-10.57
(b) Other	3.70	3.04	3.96	12.48	24.24	76.54	7.84	-10.82	2.56	15.35	14.84	20.95	22.15	11.65	-1.32	-7.95	-5.16
Community, social and personal services	8.88	9.00	9.83	15.97	4.60	82.52	5.69	-23.66	3.45	12.98	14.85	-4.53	18.20	7.25	-2.47	1.33	13.68
Less imputed bank services charge	5.27	7.57	-0.13	-0.82	-1.70	-21.29	-69.60	-41.70	10.28	23.69	19.33	13.22	22.69	1.55	0.30	2.72	-17.04
Sub-total	6.09	14.56	22.29	26.35	28.15	29.22	3.09	14.63	6.16	-0.84	12.15	6.27	4.59	-13.85	-11.05	-5.25	-6.77
Producers of government services	5.71	2.99	8.82	10.98	14.74	20.82	20.10	2.42	11.22	-1.29	-3.39	8.81	6.35	7.33	6.67	6.44	5.69
Total except import duties	6.01	12.24	19.81	23.79	26.14	28.07	5.27	12.85	6.83	-0.90	10.01	6.58	4.81	-11.20	-8.36	-3.18	-4.35
Import duties	7.19	2.77	26.25	10.05	-1.32	-10.76	1.01	0.13	26.22	-7.98	-8.41	-0.46	-10.78	3.99	11.15	7.15	-1.33
Gross Domestic Product (GDP)	6.04	12.03	19.94	23.49	25.62	27.49	5.23	12.72	7.00	-0.97	9.83	6.52	4.69	-11.10	-8.22	-3.09	-4.32

Source: Calculated from data in Saudi Arabian Monetary Agency (1970–86) Annual Surveys. Riyadh: SAMA.

largely met, with a steady increase occurring. Growth of the non-oil sector averaged 15.3 per cent per annum over the plan period. The contribution of the manufacturing sector (excluding oil refining) to GDP exceeded that of agriculture over this period. This marked a substantial change from former times, when the agricultural contribution had been the larger.

Following from the different patterns of sectoral growth just mentioned, the share of the oil sector in GDP declined between 1975 and 1980, although the sector's contribution still far outpaced that of any other sector. Having reached a peak of 58.1 per cent of total GDP (constant prices) in 1973, it declined to 43.5 per cent in 1979 (figures compiled from Table 3.10). This did not, however, indicate that the economy was moving away from its dependence on oil. The vitality of the non-oil sectors derived from the oil-derived revenues which the government was spending in those sectors – and the multiplier effects stemming from such expenditure. Construction was the major contributor to GDP outside of the oil sector, contributing some 10 per cent of overall GDP. At its peak the construction sector accounted for 30 per cent of non-oil GDP. The heavy investment which was directed to manufacturing in the petrochemicals sector was not reflected in high growth rates at this time. The schemes were still in the process of construction, rather than production. Non-petrochemicals manufacturing recorded higher rates of growth, but still made up a relatively limited share of GDP. The share of agriculture continued to decline, with a relatively modest growth rate. Table 3.11 shows the sectoral growth percentages.

As a result of the investment in infrastructure over the first two development plans, Saudi Arabia had by the end of the 1970s developed its infrastructure considerably, placing the government in a position to pursue agricultural and industrial development more effectively in subsequent plans – an aspect which had not achieved significant success so far. Some of the other effects of the pattern of development between 1970 and 1980, however, were not so positive. One was that the economy had become critically dependent on foreign labour. While this was initially seen as necessary while the country was building its infrastructural base, foreign labour was in practice becoming a necessary part of all economic activity. This will be discussed later. Another problem was the rate of inflation. The period of the Second Plan, in particular, saw a rapid rise in prices, with money supply increasing by 62.6 per cent and 83.2 per cent in 1976 and 1977. These were the highest rates recorded since Faisal had brought the financial structure under control in the early 1960s, and had a severe effect on parts of the population which were not able to benefit from rising governmental expenditure. In the final year of the plan, strong action by the Saudi Arabian

Monetary Agency brought the expansion down to 11.5 per cent, and this lower level was maintained through the 1980s (KSA-MOP 1989: 174).

In the Third Plan period, between 1980 and 1985, GDP initially rose quickly relative to the 1979 level, but declined steadily after 1981. The scale of the rise and fall of GDP was less marked in terms of current prices than constant prices (see Tables 3.9 and 3.10). This is explained by the causal factor behind the rises and falls – the oil market. Up to the end of this period, the Saudi government was supporting the world price of oil by cutting its own production. In the figures on GDP at current prices, therefore, the impact of falling oil production is partially offset by the high price of oil.

Over the Third Plan period, real GDP was declining at an average of 3.1 per cent per annum. By 1985 it had sunk to a level it had not been at since 1975. While the decline over the 1981–5 period was substantial, it could nonetheless be contended that the main anomaly in Saudi Arabia's real GDP at this time was the high point reached in 1979–81 rather than the lower levels thereafter. GDP at constant prices did not regain the high level of 1981 until 1992, while GDP at current prices took until the year 2000 to surpass the 1981 peak. Analyses of the performance of the Saudi economy which highlight the falling per capita income of Saudis during the 1980s and 1990s, where per capita income in 1998 had fallen to one-third of the 1981 level ($22,000 as against $7,000 at current prices), are neglecting the abnormality of the 1981 economy.

The cuts in government expenditure which followed from falling oil revenues after 1981 had a substantial impact on the sectors of the economy most affected by the reduced spending. Among the sectors which were particularly hit by this were construction and finance. The decline in the construction sector over the period (see Table 3.11) also stemmed from the completion of some of the major infrastructural projects. When these projects were finished, no new projects came in to replace them. Some sectors, however, grew quickly through the first half of the 1980s, in particular non-oil manufacturing and agriculture. The substantial growth of the non-oil manufacturing sector stemmed largely from the contribution now made by the petrochemicals industry, in which the government had invested so heavily since the mid-1970s. With regard to agriculture, this was a period when the government was placing emphasis on food security, encouraging investment in irrigated agriculture. The loans made to private investors by the Saudi Agricultural Bank were boosting production significantly.

Overall, the non-oil sector grew over the period of the Third Plan, although not by the margin which the plan had envisaged (5.1 per cent per annum as against the targeted 6.2 per cent). The sectoral growth rates in the non-oil economy were, in fact, starting to reflect the structural change which the government wanted, with the increasing significance of agricultural and industrial production in GDP. The Fourth Plan referred to this, stressing the importance of the strong growth in manufacturing (14.1 per cent) and agriculture (8.7 per cent) over the Third Plan period (KSA-MOP 1985a: 14).

3.5.2 The balance of payments and trade

The trend of the overall current account of the balance of payments (surplus or deficit) moved roughly in tandem with the rise and fall of oil prices. When oil prices rose, substantial surpluses built up on the balance of payments. With the explosive growth of government expenditure following such rises, however, imports increased rapidly and within three or four years overtook the value of exports. The overall account then went into deficit. Deficits were recorded in 1978 and 1983–5 (see Table 3.12). There was, therefore, a swing backwards and forwards between massive surpluses and sometimes substantial deficits. The surplus of $17.7 billion in 1974 was followed four years later (1978) by a deficit of $0.6 billion. The rising oil prices in 1981 returned the balance of payments to substantial surplus ($40.0 billion in 1981), but deficits were recorded over the three years between 1983 and 1985 – reaching a peak of $16.1 billion in 1984. The planning of a coherent development policy was, at times, adversely affected by these huge changes.

The most important determinant of the Saudi balance of payments and trade over the 1970–85 period, then, was oil exports. Through to 1982 oil exports accounted for all but a small part of the positive side of the current account: between 86 per cent and 92 per cent of all exports and 'incoming transfers' (the latter being investment income). Even after 1982, when the price of oil and the level of oil production and exports were falling, the oil component never sank significantly below 60 per cent of all exports and incoming transfers.

There are, nonetheless, some other significant trends which can be observed over this period. Between 1974 and 1983 a steady increase was taking place in investment income. This came from the substantial foreign assets which the government was building up (see Table 3.3), itself a product of rising oil revenues in the mid-1970s and between 1979 and 1981. Investment income was able to palliate some of the effects of the falls in oil revenues after 1981. In 1985 the value of investment income came to almost 50 per cent that of oil income. This helps to explain why the government was able to keep up a large part of its development expenditure despite the drastic fall in oil revenues. The gradual fall in the

Table 3.12 Balance of payments, 1970–85 (US$ billion)

	1970	1971	1972	1973	1974	1975	1976	1977	1978	1979	1980	1981	1982	1983	1984	1985
Current account																
Exports and incoming transfers																
Oil exports	2.2	2.6	3.9	5.8	32.6	27.2	35.5	40.2	36.8	57.9	100.6	111.0	72.9	44.6	36.2	25.8
Other commodity exports	0.0	0.0	0.0	0.0	0.1	0.1	0.1	0.1	0.1	0.1	0.2	0.9	1.0	1.0	1.3	1.5
Investment income	0.1	0.1	0.1	0.2	1.2	1.9	2.9	4.0	4.3	4.9	7.4	11.0	14.1	15.9	13.4	12.4
Service exports	0.2	0.3	0.4	0.6	1.4	1.3	1.7	2.0	2.2	2.8	3.8	5.1	4.9	4.4	4.2	3.6
Total	2.5	3.0	4.4	6.7	35.3	30.5	40.2	46.4	43.5	65.7	112.9	127.9	92.8	65.9	55.0	43.5
Imports and outgoing transfers																
Commodity imports	0.8	0.8	1.0	1.8	2.6	3.8	7.4	12.3	17.4	21.1	25.6	30.7	35.4	34.2	29.8	21.9
Payments for services	1.4	2.0	1.0	2.0	9.1	11.8	7.5	20.6	25.5	28.8	40.4	50.8	44.5	43.4	38.3	29.3
Workers' remittances	0.2	0.2	0.3	0.4	0.5	0.6	1.0	1.5	2.8	3.8	4.1	5.3	5.3	5.2	5.3	5.2
Total	2.4	3.0	2.3	4.2	12.2	16.2	15.9	34.4	45.7	53.7	70.1	86.8	85.2	82.8	73.4	56.4
Current account balance	0.1	1.0	2.1	2.5	23.1	14.3	14.3	12.0	-2.2	12.0	42.8	41.1	7.6	-16.9	-18.4	-12.9
Capital movements																
Oil sector and government capital transactions (net)	0.0	0.1	0.1	-0.6	-3.7	1.9	-0.4	0.8	0.5	-1.3	-3.2	6.5	11.1	4.9	4.9	0.4
Private capital movements (net)	-0.1	0.0	-0.7	-0.4	-1.6	1.2	-1.7	-1.3	0.7	-8.9	-9.7	-1.4	-7.9	2.9	-1.5	3.9
Commercial bank movements (net)	0.0	-0.0	-0.2	0.0	-0.1	0.0	-0.5	-1.0	0.4	-1.5	-3.7	-6.2	-3.1	-0.1	-1.1	-0.8
Total	-0.1	-0.1	-0.8	-1.0	-5.4	3.1	-2.6	-2.5	1.6	-11.7	-16.6	-1.1	0.1	6.7	2.3	3.5
Balance of payments surplus/deficit	0.0	0.8	1.3	1.5	17.7	17.2	11.7	10.5	-0.6	0.3	26.2	40.0	7.7	-9.2	-16.1	-9.4

Source: Calculated from data in Saudi Arabian Monetary Agency (1970–2006) *Annual Surveys.* Riyadh: SAMA.

level of investment income, however, shows that such a strategy could not continue for long. The government was using not only the interest accrued on its assets but some of the assets themselves to finance development. There was, therefore, a decline in the level of investment income after 1983.

Non-oil exports remained relatively low over this period. Such growth as there was came mainly from petrochemicals sales. Service exports, on the other hand, rose significantly, although with a reduction after 1983 in keeping with the wider developments in the economy. These exports were composed mainly of services required by the oil industry, in particular shipping.

The steady rise of imports throughout the period, with the exception of 1984 and 1985, constitutes an important characteristic of the economy over these years. It followed from the rising level of governmental expenditure, with all the multiplier effects on capital and consumer spending which followed. The speed with which Saudi Arabia increased its imports is clear from its rise in the international table of importers. Johany et al. (1986: 71) point out that in 1974 Saudi Arabia was already ranked 34th among the world's importers, and three years later had advanced to 11th place. Johany et al. (ibid. 72–4) also note that the nature of the imports changed. Whereas in 1972 the most important imports were mass consumption products (food items, cigarettes, medicines, cars and textiles), by 1977 the relative importance of consumer goods had declined (except for cars). Investment goods had now become more important. With the change in the nature of imports the origins of the imports also changed. The share of the countries producing industrial goods increased, that is, the United States, Japan and Europe.

One element in the balance of payments figures which did not register a significant decline after 1982 was workers' remittances. These increased rapidly between 1975 and 1982, and then remained on a plateau through to the end of the period. Although the government was attempting to reduce the numbers of migrant workers in the country at this time, there was no significant reduction in the number. The amount of money being repatriated by them to their home countries, therefore, did not decline.

On the capital side of the account, the item 'private capital movements' mainly registered negative figures over this period (see Table 3.12). Saudi citizens were investing more money outside of the country than was coming into the domestic economy from outside. The account becomes positive in 1983 and 1985, probably as a result of Saudi investors having to bring money back into the country to make up for losses in their domestic businesses. The latter stemmed from the economic downturn caused by cutbacks in government expenditure.

3.5.3   *The strengthening of infrastructure and social provision*

The growth of infrastructure and social provision advanced quickly over 1970–85 period. Most of the figures on physical infrastructure show many-fold growth: generated electric power rose more than 38-fold; the length of paved road more than five-fold; and the volume of cargo handled in the ports some 30-fold (KSA-MOP 1985b: 150–87). Yet there were areas where provision did not satisfy the needs of economic development or the personal needs of the population. Housing, for example, did not keep pace with urban growth (Al-Farsy 1990: 151), the national telecommunications system did not nearly meet demand, and there remained considerable bottlenecks in the transport sector.

In human resources, the educational system was developing quickly. Over the 1970–85 period the number of boys' schools more than tripled, while the number of girls' schools (starting from a low base) increased some 15-fold. Educational enrolment rose sharply, by some five-fold at the primary level, 12-fold at the intermediate level, and 40-fold at the higher educational level (KSA-MOP 1985b: 154–61). Yet, while most of the younger generation were able by the end of this period to benefit from ample opportunities for education – up to whatever level they were capable of going – there were increasing indications that the products of the educational system were not competitive in the employ-ment market. Most young Saudis were going into the public sector, where they enjoyed privileged employment conditions, rather than the more competitive employment market of the private sector. A signif-icant part of the expansion in higher education was in the religious universities.

With regard to social provision, there was a rapid growth in health pro-vision. The number of hospital beds increased more than three-fold over the period, and medical staff by some 15-fold. The support given to indi-viduals and families in need of assistance registered the most substantial increase of all over the period. The amount paid for social security relief assistance rose some 50-fold, that for old age and disability pensions some 30-fold. The cumulative number of employees covered by social insurance rose from 145,400 to 3.3 million (KSA-MOP 1985b: 166–74), ensuring a measure of social protection to those in the private sector as well as the public sector.

The character of the relationship between the state and the population was affected by these developments of infrastructure and social provision. On the one hand, the population was afforded greater support and facilities than before. On the other hand, the dependence of the population on state institutions increased.

3.6 The contribution and composition of the private-sector economy

The growth and significance of the private sector will be assessed in terms of the size of its output (measured in constant prices), the percentage share of this output relative to the contributions made by the government and oil sectors, the size and share of the private sector's contribution to gross fixed capital formation (investment), and the number of companies operating in the private sector. There will also be a consideration of the distribution of private-sector activity across different parts of the economy. In keeping with Saudi statistics, the oil sector will be treated as distinct from both the private and government sectors. Prior to the nationalisation of ARAMCO in 1974, oil production was coming from a privately owned company yet the main part of the gains of production were accruing to the government. To combine the oil figures with either the private or government shares of the economy (at least before 1974) would distort realistic comparisons.

Table 3.13 shows that the output of the private sector was growing steadily over the 1970-85 period, with the exception of a relatively small

Table 3.13 Private-sector share in Gross Domestic Product, 1969–85 (constant prices at 1999, SR million)

	Private sector	% of total	Oil sector	% of total	Government sector	% of total	GDP
1969	18,855	14.5	80,445	62.3	29,916	23.2	129,216
1970	18,753	12.9	95,362	65.8	30,922	21.3	145,037
1971	22,511	13.0	117,446	67.6	33,795	19.4	173,772
1972	30,385	14.1	146,886	68.3	37,835	17.6	215,107
1973	43,442	16.0	183,796	67.7	44,098	16.3	271,336
1974	88,400	25.4	205,987	59.3	53,121	15.3	347,508
1975	130,689	35.7	171,508	46.9	63,632	17.4	365,829
1976	135,643	32.9	211,494	51.2	65,687	15.9	412,825
1977	142,758	32.4	225,530	51.1	72,736	16.5	441,024
1978	157,504	36.0	205,812	47.1	73,737	16.9	437,054
1979	172,677	35.9	235,341	48.9	72,766	15.2	480,784
1980	187,841	36.7	245,843	48.0	78,719	15.3	512,403
1981	209,124	38.9	243,580	45.4	84,344	15.7	537,048
1982	222,289	46.6	167,454	35.1	87,172	18.3	476,916
1983	223,020	51.1	122,932	28.1	91,070	20.8	437,023
1984	214,356	50.7	112,160	26.5	96,594	22.8	423,111
1985	208,543	51.5	92,525	22.9	103,617	25.6	404,685

Source: Kingdom of Saudi Arabia, Ministry of Planning (1987) *Achievements of the Development Plans.* Riyadh: Ministry of Planning.

reduction in the two final years. It is noteworthy that the latter reduction was not nearly as substantial as that experienced by Saudi GDP as a whole at that time. The rate of growth of the private sector was more than three times that of overall GDP between 1970 and 1985. As a result of this, the private sector's share of GDP over this period steadily rose, starting at 12.9 per cent of total GDP in 1970 and ending at 51.5 per cent. In this case, the 1983–5 period constituted a high point, rather than one of decline as characterised most other aspects of the economy at this time. Over these three years the private sector maintained a position where it accounted for more than half of GDP. The private sector was clearly growing in strength and activity, contributing positively to the economy when the governmental and oil sectors' output was in sharp decline.

Yet it would be wrong to conclude from this that the private sector was becoming the driving force behind the economy's development. The rising private-sector activity was mainly the product of governmental expenditure. As the plans themselves point out, the biggest contribution made by the private sector to GDP was in areas which were heavily dependent on government contracts: construction and the maintenance of infrastructure (KSA-MOP 1980: 32; 1995: 44). The most profitable elements of this activity, indeed, were the government-financed projects. In the late 1970s, construction accounted for about 30 per cent of all private-sector output. Table 3.14 shows that whereas construction was growing quickly

Table 3.14 Percentage growth in private-sector fields of activity, 1970–85, by plan-period (compounded, at current prices)

	Plan I average	Plan II average	Plan III average	Average of 3 plans
Agriculture, fishing and forestry	3.6	6.9	9.5	6.7
Construction	21.4	15.8	−2.4	11.6
Electricity, gas and water	3.4	21.9	21.2	15.5
Manufacturing (total)	3.9	9.8	7.3	7.0
Refining	0.9	6.1	3.0	3.3
Other	10.8	15.4	11.7	12.6
Transport, storage and communications	0.7	19.3	7.1	9.0
Wholesale and retail trade, restaurants and hotels	13.8	22.7	8.7	15.1
Finance, insurance, real estates and business services	7.9	23.7	2.5	11.4
Community social and personal service	7.1	10.6	4.4	7.4

Source: Kingdom of Saudi Arabia, Ministry of Planning (1987) *Achievements of the Development Plans*. Riyadh: Ministry of Planning.

in the First and Second Plan periods, when the construction of the key government-financed infrastructural projects was in process, this turned into a negative rate of growth in the Third Plan. Many of the projects had been completed in the latter plan-period, and cutbacks in government expenditure were slowing the progress on others. The sectors of trade, transport and finance, although not so dependent on government contracts, were also greatly affected by the multiplier effects of government expenditure, with output rising quickly in the First and Second Plan periods, and registering more modest growth after 1981.

In the Third Plan period there was a change in the balance of private-sector activity, which suggested a more significant role for this sector in the long-term development of the economy. Agriculture and manufacturing (excluding oil refining) now became the fields which were expanding most substantially. In agriculture, private investors began transforming the sector through massive schemes based on irrigation. This development had little to do with the traditional agricultural sector, and was led by businessmen rather than farmers. While this development moved the country towards self-sufficiency in some agricultural products, it came at considerable cost to the environment. The impact of drawing on the ground reserves of water was to lower the water-table, which in turn negatively affected some existing surface vegetation. Private-sector involvement in manufacturing was also growing. At this stage, however, this was not in the fields where Saudi manufacturing was at its most significant, namely the downstream hydrocarbons sector (petrochemicals and their derivatives). Private-sector manufacturing up to the mid-1980s was mainly restricted to petty manufacture for the local market. Investors were not intent on exploiting opportunities inherent in the country's rich mineral resources and obtaining a stake in export markets. In both agriculture and manufacturing, there was still a heavy dependence on governmental resources. Almost all of the projects undertaken were dependent on subsidised loans from the Saudi Agricultural Bank and the Saudi Industrial Development Fund.

The scale of the private-sector investment within the Kingdom also bears witness to the sector's increased activity. Table 3.15 shows a steady increase in gross fixed capital formation coming from the private sector, with a relatively small decline taking place in the two final years. It is significant that the latter decline still left the contribution higher than it had been in 1982/3.

Given the massive governmental investment which was going into development projects in the 1970s and early 1980s, the private sector's share of total investment remained surprisingly high over the 1970–85 period. Its share of gross fixed capital formation, as shown in Table 3.15,

Table 3.15 Gross fixed capital formation by sectors, 1969/70 to 1985/6 (current prices, SR million)

Year	Govt. (non-oil)	% of total	Private sector (non-oil)	% of total	Oil sector	% of total	Total
1969/70	1,214	46.7	1,056	40.7	327	12.7	2,597
1970/1	1,204	41.1	1,150	39.2	577	19.7	2,931
1971/2	1,443	42.4	1,290	37.9	671	19.9	3,404
1972/3	1,985	34.9	1,669	29.3	2,040	35.8	5,694
1973/4	3,416	40.7	2,351	28.0	2,632	31.3	8,399
1974/5	7,370	41.6	6,670	37.7	3,659	20.7	17,699
1975/6	17,491	52.1	10,627	31.7	5,422	16.2	33,540
1976/7	27,352	53.4	16,523	32.3	7,316	14.3	51,191
1977/8	40,484	60.5	18,354	27.7	8,053	11.8	66,891
1978/9	49,031	64.0	19,401	25.3	8,222	10.7	76,654
1979/80	61,598	63.5	23,207	23.9	12,264	12.6	97,069
1980/1	66,874	62.9	28,691	27.0	10,811	10.1	106,376
1981/2	73,881	60.4	35,830	29.3	12,604	10.3	122,315
1982/3	66,411	57.5	34,162	29.6	14,882	12.9	115,455
1983/4	50,026	48.5	41,320	40.0	11,882	11.5	103,228
1984/5	46,314	48.0	40,624	42.1	9,554	9.9	96,492
1985/6	32,775	42.9	35,236	46.2	8,303	10.9	76,313

Source: Saudi Arabian Monetary Agency (1970–86) *Annual Surveys*. Riyadh: SAMA.

began the period at 40.7 per cent, went on a downward trend through to 1979/80 when it reached 23.9 per cent, then rose again. In the two final years of the period it stood at 42.1 per cent and 46.2 per cent – in excess of the share at the start of the period. The record of private-sector investment after 1983 shows that it was helping to cushion the economy against the negative impact of declining governmental spending.

Table 3.16 provides further evidence of increasing private-sector activity. Whereas there were only 592 private sector establishments in the country in 1973 (the date from which reliable figures on this are available), the number had reached 12,020 by 1985. At the beginning of the period, the number of private-sector establishments only marginally exceeded governmental units, while in 1985 the number was almost 11-fold greater. Even though some businesses were going bankrupt as a result of the cuts in governmental expenditure after 1982, the overall number of private-sector establishments continued to grow. Although the figures on private-sector employment at this stage are unreliable, estimates suggest that the private-sector employed some 90 per cent of the Kingdom's labour force in the mid-1980s. There were, however, relatively few Saudis in this workforce.

Table 3.16 Number of establishments by sector, 1973–85

Year	Private	Government	Total
1973	592	470	1,062
1974	749	488	1,237
1975	1,417	517	1,934
1976	1,816	541	2,357
1977	2,385	561	2,946
1978	3,217	583	3,800
1979	4,460	623	5,083
1980	5,472	647	6,119
1981	6,447	729	7,176
1982	8,992	1,020	10,012
1983	10,723	1,199	11,922
1984	11,746	1,324	13,070
1985	12,020	1,367	13,387

Source: Kingdom of Saudi Arabia, General Organisation for Social Insurance (1974–86) *Annual Statistical Reports.* Riyadh: GOSI.

Significant though the rise in private-sector activity was, the conditions under which the private sector operated were in many ways not conducive to its growth. Among the structural characteristics hindering the private sector at this stage were the following:

- The financial markets were underdeveloped. Lacking the support of such markets, investors could not easily obtain the resources to invest in major industrial projects. There was, furthermore, ambiguity over the charging of interest for bank loans, which restricted the ability of banks to support private investment within the country. Potential investors were, therefore, heavily dependent on the government-subsidised credit institutions (the Saudi Agricultural Bank and the Saudi Industrial Development Fund), and on the contacts they maintained with those bodies.
- Foreign investment had to comply with regulations which were discouraging, such that foreign companies found it easier to import goods into the country than to produce them locally. The major exception here was those companies operating in partnership with the Saudi state.
- The low population base limited the size of the market for consumer goods. Local producers, moreover, had to compete against imports which carried relatively low tariffs. The possibility of export was limited due to restricted access to international markets.
- The major areas where Saudi Arabia enjoyed comparative advantage on the international market were ones where the scale of investment

required was substantially greater than what the private sector could reasonably undertake.

- Prices of some local resources were high, relative to other countries with which Saudi Arabia would need to compete on the global market. In particular, prices for land and non-industrial properties were high.
- Labour was expensive. The remuneration of Saudi labour, in particular, tended to follow the trends of inflation and oil revenues, and was only remotely connected with real productivity.

These structural hindrances are of significance to the section which follows. In practice the gains of private-sector development were linked to the ability of entrepreneurs to circumvent or overcome the obstacles to investment. Who they were, and what contacts they had, therefore helped to determine their success.

3.7   The social dynamics of the private sector

Significant changes were taking place in the composition of the private sector over the period covered by this chapter. As the trends continued to develop over the subsequent period, however, they will be examined in detail in the relevant section of Chapter 4. For the moment, the main changes will be outlined.

The growth of the private sector, as documented in the previous section, brought considerable numbers of new investors into the sector. A study conducted in 1996 showed that, of the top 100 companies in Saudi Arabia at that time, most were established after 1973. This applied to 85 per cent of the banks, 29 per cent of trading establishments, 67 per cent of contracting firms, 70 per cent of manufacturing enterprises, 86 per cent of utility companies and 50 per cent of diversified companies (Metwally and Abdel-Rahman 1996: 170–1). While the old merchant families remained important, especially in trading and petty-manufacturing activities, three new elements were now becoming important. The first was that referred to by Okruhlik as the 'nouveau riche' (Okruhlik 1992: 148) – those who made their fortunes quickly in the boom period through gaining key contracts (usually in construction or the supply of goods and services to the royal family), or as agents who negotiated arms deals with foreign suppliers of weaponry. Many of these were of non-Saudi origin, although with Saudi citizenship. Among them were Adnan Khashoggi, Muhammad al-Fassi and Rafiq Hariri (who enjoyed both Saudi and Lebanese citizenship).

The second element was composed of a Najdi 'new middle class' (Chaudhry 1997: 159–162). This came about due to the growth of the administrative structure of the state and the extent to which key civil service positions were occupied by Najdis. The latter trend became particularly marked after the death of King Faisal in 1975. Many of those who were now occupying key positions in the state had resources to invest and would enter business either as a side-activity while still in office or after leaving their governmental positions. In other cases, the personal linkages with Najdis in the private sector or from leading tribal families encouraged and facilitated the entry of the latter into new schemes of investment. The loans made available by the government-supported credit institutions were of crucial importance here. It was in the expanding agricultural sector that this new investment was particularly prominent. Chaudhry:62 explains how this process operated:

> Family, tribal and kinship connections with bureaucrats were utilised by aspiring Nejdi businessmen not only to get permits, register agencies and so on, but also to gather and peddle supposedly confidential information about upcoming government tenders and projects. Such practices are common in many countries. In Saudi Arabia, however, they were unique, not just because of the amounts of money involved and the proportion of economic activity covered but also because the distribution system was deliberately constructed to facilitate the entry of nationals into intermediary positions between government and foreign companies. Thus, although the government had no stated position of helping Nejdis enter the business world ..., the regulations governing the economy were clearly designed to generate a domestic entrepreneurial group.

The third element was composed of elements from the royal family. The coy attitude which many members of the royal family had previously had towards involvement in the private sector (an attitude which was specifically promoted by King Abd al-Aziz) was now finally abandoned. With resources coming from the major land grants from which they had benefited in the late 1960s, aided by such income which they gained directly from state sources, a significant number of royal family members now went into business. In some cases this was done on an unproductive basis, such as taking a share in business so as to use their privileged links with those responsible for the award of contracts. In other cases, however, it involved genuinely productive investment. The latter tended to be directed more towards manufacturing than to agriculture or commerce.

3.8   The changing pattern of employment

The employment figures which will be used here are those which appear in Saudi Arabia's development plans, in the sections which trace how employment grew in previous plan-periods. It will be shown later, in Chapter 7, that these Ministry of Planning figures are unreliable. One indication of their unreliability is that the figures given in different plans are inconsistent: the plan which immediately follows one plan-period will almost invariably show higher figures for that period than are found in subsequent plans for the same period. It may be suggested that the high initial estimates may be intended to show that the employment of foreign labour will be reduced under the subsequent plan. Nonetheless, for most of the years covered in this book, there are no other figures which are available. The Ministry of Planning figures, moreover, do appear to show real trends. The actual size of the labour force, and the exact breakdown between Saudi and non-Saudi labour, may not be portrayed correctly, therefore, but the figures probably do reflect accurately the directions of change.

Table 3.17 shows a rapid growth in civilian employment over the 1970–85 period. While the 1984/5 figure given in the table is almost certainly an overestimate (see the note to the table), it is clear that there was a many-fold increase in the numbers. The balance of employment between the different sectors changes over the period, with the share of agriculture declining substantially (from 40.4 per cent in 1970 to 10.0 per cent in 1984/5), and those of most of the other non-government sectors growing. By the end of the period, 41.3 per cent of the workforce were employed in private services (trade, finance, hotels, transport, etc.), and 30.2 per cent in other producing sectors (much of this in construction). 8.1 per cent were in manufacturing. The numbers employed in the oil industry remained low, at little more than 1 per cent of the workforce, while the share of government services rose in the mid-1970s (from 10.2 per cent in 1970 to 14.1 per cent in 1975) and then fell again in the early 1980s (to 9.0 per cent in 1984/5). Rising oil revenues had made possible the expansion of government ministries, but the enhanced governmental expenditure ultimately had a bigger impact on employment elsewhere.

The employment balance between Saudis and non-Saudis shifted substantially over these years, with the Saudi part of the workforce now becoming a minority. As shown in Table 3.18, Saudis made up only 40.2 per cent of the workforce at the end of the period, as opposed to 71.7 per cent at the beginning. By 1984/5, according to these figures, the Kingdom was hosting a foreign labour force of 2,660,000, whereas the number had been only 494,000 in 1970. A substantial increase in

Table 3.17 Civilian employment by economic activities, 1970, 1975, 1980 and 1984/5

	1970		1975		1980		1984/5[a]	
	000's	%	000's	%	000's	%	000's	%
Producing sectors except oil and gas								
Agriculture	445.8	40.4	695.0	39.8	545.6	18.0	538.0	10.0
Manufacturing industries	36.1	3.2	74.4	4.2	170.4	5.6	424.1	8.1
Other producing sectors	167.4	15.1	191.8	11.0	708.2	23.4	1,586.4	30.2
Service sectors								
Private services	329.8	29.9	511.2	29.3	1,157.7	38.3	2,168.3	41.3
Government services	112.7	10.2	246.7	14.1	399.4	13.2	469.1	9.0
Oil and gas	12.0	1.1	27.4	1.6	44.7	1.5	58.7	1.1
Total	1,103.8	100.0	1,746.5	100.0	3,026.0	100.0	5,244.6	100.0

[a] The figure for 1984/5 was an initial estimate that can be found in the *Fourth Development Plan*, published in 1985. Unlike later figures, a revised number was never published. The estimate, however, is almost certainly excessive, as it is substantially different from the total employment by nationality figure given in Table 3.18. A revised number for the latter was provided, in the *Fifth Development Plan*.

Sources: Khayat, Dina (2005) 'Female Employment in Saudi Arabia' unpublished PhD thesis, University of Exeter. All figures from Kingdom of Saudi Arabia, Ministry of Planning (1975–90) *Development Plans*. Riyadh: Ministry of Planning.

Table 3.18 Civilian employment by nationality, Saudi/non-Saudi, 1975, 1980 and 1984/5

	1975		1980		1984/5	
	000's	%	000's	%	000's	%
Saudi	1,253.0	71.7	1,493.2	49.3	1,786.0	40.2
Non-Saudi	494.0	28.3	1,532.8	50.7	2,660.0	59.8
Total	1,746.5	100.0	3,026.0	100.0	4,446.0	100.0

Sources: Khayat, Dina (2005) 'Female Employment in Saudi Arabia' unpublished PhD thesis, University of Exeter pp. 30, 44. All figures from Kingdom of Saudi Arabia, Ministry of Planning (1975–90) *Development Plans*. Riyadh: Ministry of Planning.

foreign labour had been envisaged by the first two development plans, which perceived a need to facilitate the import of labour and foreign expertise so as to ensure that development projects could be completed effectively. Although there was also a concern with Saudi labour, there was little expectation that this could temper the need for foreign labour in the short term.

By the time of the Third Development Plan, however, there was a clear governmental intention to reduce or at least stabilise the level of employment of foreign labour. There seemed, moreover, a strong basis on which to do this: the major infrastructural projects were now being completed, and the numbers of Saudis emerging from schools and universities was much more substantial than before. The plan's objectives, however, were not achieved. The plan envisaged that foreign labour would grow by no more than 0.2 per cent annually, whereas the figures of actual growth in foreign labour given in the Fourth Plan put it at 11.7 per cent (KSA-MOP 1985a: 12). Looney cites a 1996 World Bank Development Report stating that over the third plan-period the Saudi labour force grew at an average annual rate of 3.7 per cent (Looney 1990b: 33).

In practice, very little Saudi labour was going into the productive sectors of the economy. This should not be surprising: migrant labour was cheaper than Saudi labour, and was also more flexible and efficient. There was at this stage no incentive for the private sector to absorb Saudi labour. The need for labour was also increased by the declining productivity of the labour which was available. The Fourth Development Plan (KSA-MOP 1985a: 36) noted that over the period of the Third Plan, productivity declined at an average annual rate of 2.7 per cent.

3.9   Conclusion

The 1970–85 period saw a major transformation in the Saudi economy, carried through with a vision of development which had a number of key components: developing the oil industry and gaining control of the full benefits from oil production, building up a substantial industrial base through utilising hydrocarbon resources and energy for petrochemicals and downstream industries, promoting agriculture and a measure of agricultural self-sufficiency through the spread of irrigation, and creating the social and physical infrastructure of a modern state. The state was to be the instrument not only shaping the vision but also implementing it. The private sector would provide the consumer needs of the population, and also play a significant role in agriculture and the diversification of the economy through service provision and petty manufacturing.

It would, however, not be central to achieving the major industrial objectives.

While oil revenues were rising, the coherence and feasibility of the vision were easy to accept. At the very end of this period, however, confidence in the state's ability to solve all the country's problems began to weaken. The implications and effects of this will be the concern of the next chapter.

4   Constrained development, 1985–2000

4.1   Introduction

The 1985–2000 period was characterised by the fading of the transformative vision which had underlain development policy in the previous period. To some extent this was because the major objectives of the early development plans had now been achieved: major petrochemical industries had been put in place, the education and health services had been expanded, the country's physical infrastructure was now reasonably strong, and the level of oil-producing capacity had been greatly enhanced.

Yet the most critical factor which was shaping economic perspectives in the mid-1980s, and continued to do so through to the end of the 1990s, was the level of oil revenues. Oil revenues remained substantially below the 1980–2 level throughout the 1985–2000 period, and were subject to abrupt falls as well as occasional spikes. It was increasingly apparent that the Kingdom could no longer count on a continuing upward drift in oil prices, nor on their stabilisation at a high level.

The government's reaction to falling and unstable levels of oil revenue revolved around three different lines of policy. The first was to avoid substantial cuts in expenditure in the hope that the level of oil prices and production would improve. This involved running deficits in the governmental accounts (which in practice held for most of this period) and financing this by selling foreign assets and raising loans on the international financial market. The size of the deficits in governmental accounts, moreover, was kept down by delaying payments for services rendered and contracts fulfilled. Invoices from private-sector organisations were not settled quickly, sometimes remaining unpaid for months or even years. The second line of policy was to seek some reductions in overall expenditure. The third, following from the reduction of governmental expenditure, was to rely on a rise in private-sector investment to compensate for falling public-sector investment.

The government's approach became increasingly unsustainable as time passed. The assumption that oil prices and production would soon recover, and debts could then be repaid and the level of foreign assets rebuilt, gradually ceased to appear realistic. Although there was some recovery of prices in the second half of the 1980s, and a new price spike following the Iraqi occupation of Kuwait in August 1990, the general trend was not one which promised a resolution to the underlying financial problem.

The government increasingly had to rely, therefore, on two other approaches: controlling and limiting governmental expenditure, and counting on the private sector to increase its investment. Yet these approaches also were problematic. The impact of cutting governmental expenditure was bound to depend greatly on the fields in which cuts were made. The least damaging cuts to the economy would have been in the defence sector, which accounted for about 30 per cent of all governmental spending through the late 1980s and 1990s. The value of this expenditure was, in any case, doubtful: the acquisition of weaponry did not give Saudi Arabia the ability to defend its interests successfully, as was apparent in the crisis which followed the Iraqi occupation of Kuwait. The official figures covering the defence budget, moreover, do not reflect the reality of defence-related expenditure. Most of the cost of the 1991 Gulf War, for example, was borne by Saudi Arabia, and the major part of this was in the form of subventions to the US, the UK and other countries in the coalition, which confronted Iraq. This expenditure, however, was not included in the defence budget; it took the form of direct government-to-government transfers. There was, over the period covered by this chapter, no significant reduction either in the absolute amount of defence-related spending or in its share of overall expenditure. The Saudi government was seeking to play a role in global and regional politics as a partner of the US (initially in countering the Soviet Union and then in containing Iraq and Iran), and the high defence expenditure was deemed necessary to pursue that objective.

In practice, the cuts in expenditure which the government made tended to weaken and undermine the productive base of the economy. Physical infrastructure was not developed and expanded so as to keep pace with needs, the maintenance of existing infrastructure was neglected so that services and facilities deteriorated, and there was insufficient funding for human resource undertakings which could produce the skills that the economy needed.

As for the expectation that private-sector investment could make up for falling governmental investment, there was no doubt a vast potential: the holdings of Saudi citizens abroad probably stood at a value of some $500 billion at the end of the 1990s. If a significant part of this had been brought back into the country, or even if the flow of the assets abroad had been halted, private-sector investment could have played the part envisaged by the government. However, while domestic private investment in the Kingdom did increase substantially over the 1985–2000 period, the level of private Saudi assets abroad continued to grow. The conditions under which the private sector operated were simply not good enough to enable private investors to drive forward the country's development, particularly where investment would bring long-term benefit rather than short-term profit. Downstream petrochemicals production provided the main opportunity here.

Much of the writing which covers the development of the Saudi economy at this time criticises the government for having failed to introduce and implement reforms in the economy. This was the line taken by IMF reports (e.g. IMF 1999). No doubt the criticism is valid, but it has often rested on a simplistic assumption. This is that the state's withdrawal from effective economic management of the economy—with the sell-off of public sector corporations and the removal of restrictive legislation on private-sector activities—would through the inherent dynamics of the economic process create an invigorated economy capable of satisfying the needs of the population.

Such an outcome, however, was unlikely. The falling and unstable oil revenues were not the only problem confronting economic development in Saudi Arabia in the late 1980s and 1990s. The economy had become dependent on a large foreign labour force, raising social as well as economic issues. The private-sector was expanding mainly on the basis of foreign rather than Saudi labour, with the latter looking to public-sector employment rather than replacing foreign labour and expertise in private companies. The education system, and the structure of entitlements from which Saudis benefited, were not facilitating the changes in the composition of the labour force which the government desired. The private-sector, moreover, had a natural inclination to the more risk-averse sectors of commercial activity and real estate development than developing the country's industrial base. The country's social structure, furthermore, was characterised by increasingly sharp divisions between rich and poor. No doubt the safety nets of subsidies, which had been introduced and expanded through the 1970s and 1980s, protected the poorest parts of the population from absolute penury, but the inequalities were massive and growing. Some of the major gains in wealth came from corruption, adding an extra edge to the resentment and rancour felt by those who had been left behind.

The sale of public corporations, in an environment where massive wealth was in the hands of a small number of individuals, could have given those individuals a stranglehold over the economy. The further expansion of the private sector would have intensified the demand for foreign labour, which was cheap and competitive, without necessarily increasing the employment of Saudis. Removing controls over foreign investment could have weakened critically the domestic private sector, perhaps subordinating it to foreign capital before it had developed the ability to compete internationally. The benefits from the heavy public investment of the 1970s and early 1980s, then, could have accrued to foreign rather than Saudi business. It is worth recalling, moreover, that the imbalance in governmental finances could have been resolved through other means than limiting the governmental role in the economy.

An economic strategy which would have benefited the Kingdom at this time was one inspired by the model of state-sponsored capitalism. The state still needed to be the primary engine of growth, acting positively to promote rapid industrialisation in areas of comparative advantage and creating conditions conducive to a socially balanced and diversified economy. But the character of its involvement in the economy needed to change. The rigidities of the command economy had to be abandoned and use made of the channels of incentive and support to carry a new economic strategy forward. The emphasis had to be on the facilitation of procedures and the promotion of skills, mechanisms and opportunities to shape new social and economic conditions. State involvement in the economy, therefore, would not diminish but would change in character. The population had to be mobilised and motivated for the task ahead, with the state providing the funds to identify and create the necessary skills and directing productive investment towards carefully selected sectors of the economy. The private sector would play a central role, but within a framework where it served national needs.

The development plans which cover this period provide some hints of such a state-sponsored capitalist approach. There was considerable emphasis on enabling the private sector to participate in sectors critical to the economy's development, investing in training and education, and facilitating the conduct of business.

Yet the Saudi state at this time had neither the political will, nor the structural effectiveness, administrative capacity or social base, to carry forward a programme of this nature. In short, it did not have the characteristics of a developmental state, and that is what the state-sponsored capitalist approach required. Economic decisions often rested on political compromises between powerful princes guarding their ministerial territories, rather than on coherent strategy. Predatory behaviour, with corruption present at the highest levels of the state, distorted economic rationality. The award of contracts was often influenced by the private interests of state personnel, not by the intrinsic qualities of the bids. Business operations remained bound up in administrative obstacles, benefiting those who had the contacts and influence to break through the entanglement. Much of the expenditure on human resources was used to satisfy political objectives, whether through strengthening the influence of religious leaders over the population or absorbing potential youth unemployment, rather than on creating the skills needed by the economy. Education, indeed, tended to mould intellectual straitjackets rather than fostering the creativity needed for innovation and high levels of productivity. Reform was badly needed, but not one which simply involved measures of economic liberalisation. A new social contract would have been necessary for the state-sponsored capitalist approach to succeed.

In practice, the Saudi state attempted some reforms over the 1985–2000 period but brought about relatively little change. The role allotted to the private sector in developing the economy was more substantial than before, and more was done to support the private sector in this role, but this did not constitute a serious attempt to fashion a globally competitive private sector. The economy moved towards state-aided capitalism, but with the state still controlling the key decisions. There was a significant level of bureaucratic obstruction and predatory behaviour. The policy pursued cohered well with the interests of those who were prominent in the political and administrative structure of the state. They could invest their resources in fields which were clearly profitable as a result of state expenditure, they had the personal links which enabled them to have a favoured position in bidding for contracts, they could protect themselves against competition through the continuing existing controls, their schemes were not open to competition from elsewhere, and they could gain access to the credit institutions for the support of their projects. The dynamic for reform within the system, therefore, was limited.

While there was talk of privatisation, joining the World Trade Organisation and reforming the economy, therefore, the reality was that no structural change was envisaged or carried out. Elements within the business elite were unhappy with the framework within which they had to operate, but there were also many who benefited from it. Much of the business elite lacked confidence in the ability of their companies to withstand competition in an open market. This was a time, moreover, when Saudi Arabia was under little pressure internationally to reform its economy. Western governments were rather more intent on ensuring that they secured a major element of arms contracts, and that their companies were able to export to the Kingdom and gain contracts through partnerships with local companies, than they were on opening up the system to competition.

The policies pursued at this time were not conducive to any significant reduction in foreign labour. The private sector needed foreign labour, in so far as it was cheaper, more adaptable, and could more easily be dismissed than local labour. The government ministries were loath to restrict labour imports, partly because their objective was to encourage the private sector, and partly because individual government servants often had personal links with parts of the private sector whose interests were at stake.

Some differences between the analysis given here and other literature covering the Saudi economy at this time should be noted. Publications written in the early 1990s tended to see the years between 1983 and 1986, when oil revenues fell abruptly, as years of recession followed by gradual recovery (e.g. Chaudhry 1992; Okruhlik 1992). It is true that oil revenues were higher in the late 1980s than they had been in the mid-1980s, and underwent a spike following the Iraqi occupation of Kuwait. In retrospect, however, the whole of the period from 1983 to 1999 can be seen as characterised by resource-based constraints on development. The constraints were created not only by low oil revenues but also by the burdens of defence and strategy-related expenditure which the government took on. In the two years prior to 1985, the impact of falling revenues was softened by the surpluses built up in 1980–2.

Works written on the economy around the turn of the millennium (e.g. Champion 2003) project an image which is misleading in a different way. They correctly describe the whole period from 1983 to 1999 as one of resource-based constraint, but see this as undermining and perhaps erasing the oil rentier characteristics of the economy. In fact this was not true even at the time: oil revenues still accounted for at least 50 per cent of governmental revenues when prices and production were at their lowest, and averaged more than 70 per cent over the whole 1985–2000 period. The years since 2003, moreover, have seen a rapid rise in the price of oil, with significant rises in production at the same time. The result has been surpluses which have surpassed those of the 1980–2 peak. Prices and production may fall (and have fallen), but there is no indication that prices will return to pre-2003 levels.

4.2 Governmental revenues and foreign assets, 1985–2000

4.2.1 *Oil revenues and other sources of governmental income*

As can be seen from Table 4.1, the price of oil and the level of production and exports were variable throughout the 1985–2000 period. In 1985, Saudi Arabia was still acting as the swing producer in the oil market, keeping

Table 4.1 Saudi crude oil prices, production and exports, 1985–2000 (million barrels)

Year	Nominal price (Arabian Light 34 API)	Total	% change	Daily average	Total exports
1985	27.52	1,158.80	−22.38	3.17	780.72
1986	13.73	1,746.20	50.69	4.78	1,190.02
1987	17.23	1,505.40	−13.79	4.12	973.12
1988	13.40	1,890.10	25.55	5.16	1,245.49
1989	16.21	1,848.50	−2.20	5.06	1,217.50
1990	20.82	2,340.50	26.62	6.41	1,642.42
1991	17.43	2,963.00	26.60	8.12	2,382.11
1992	17.94	3,049.40	2.92	8.33	2,408.98
1993	15.68	2,937.40	−3.67	8.05	2,296.92
1994	15.39	2,937.90	0.02	8.05	2,275.27
1995	16.73	2,928.54	−0.32	8.02	2,296.13
1996	19.91	2,965.45	1.26	8.10	2,236.01
1997	18.71	2,924.28	−1.39	8.01	2,257.33
1998	12.20	3,022.27	3.35	8.28	2,332.48
1999	17.45	2,761.10	−8.64	7.56	2,087.68
2000	26.81	2,962.60	7.30	8.09	2,282.38

Sources: Prices from World Bank (1985–2000) *Commodity Trade Price Trends.* Washington: World Bank. Other data from Saudi Arabian Monetary Agency (various years) *Annual Surveys*. Riyadh: SAMA.

prices high by reducing its own production. Early in 1986 this policy was abandoned, resulting in a substantial increase in Saudi oil production and a sharp fall in the price of oil. At no stage in the subsequent years, through to the end of the period, did the oil price regain the level it had stood at in 1985, and for much of the period it was less than half what it had been in 1980–1. Production grew significantly through to 1992, but then remained at a plateau (within the limits of Saudi Arabia's OPEC quota at that time) through to 2000.

The oil price fluctuations through this period were significant on a year-by-year basis. 1986 saw the biggest fall in the price (from an annual average of $27.52 per barrel to $13.73), with a small recovery in 1987. In 1988, however, it fell to a new low of $13.40 per barrel. The Iraqi occupation of Kuwait in August 1990, which occurred at a time when the Soviet Union's oil production was in decline, pushed the price up to a briefly held peak of $40 per barrel, with an annual average of $20.82 for that year. Thereafter there was a gradual drift downwards through to 1994 when it stood at $15.39. Prices over the 1995–7 period were stronger, reaching $19.91 in 1996, but in 1998 fell to $12.20–the lowest level recorded since 1976.

Table 4.2 Governmental revenues, 1985–2000 (SR million)

Year	Oil revenues	Other	Total revenues
1985	88,425	45,140	133,565
1986	42,464	34,034	76,498
1987	67,405	36,406	103,811
1988	48,400	36,200	84,600
1989	75,900	38,700	114,600
1990	118,142	36,579	154,721
1991	123,999	37,880	161,879
1992	127,027	38,373	165,400
1993	106,000	35,500	141,500
1994	95,460	33,540	129,000
1995	105,700	40,800	146,500
1996	136,000	43,100	179,100
1997	160,000	45,500	205,500
1998	80,000	61,600	141,600
1999	98,000	49,000	147,000
2000	214,424	43,641	258,065

Source: Saudi Arabian Monetary Agency (2005) *Forty-First Annual Report*. Riyadh: SAMA.

Thereafter they rose again, standing at $26.81 per barrel in 2000. Production, as mentioned earlier, followed a steadier trend, growing through the late 1980s, and stabilising at a relatively high level after 1991. Production had been increased to make up for the shortfall in production created by Iraq and Kuwait, and once that level was established it was maintained. At no stage, however, did it reach the production levels of 1979–81, and only in 1992 did it exceed (marginally) production levels over the 1976–81 period.

The impact of changing levels of oil prices and production on oil revenues can be seen in Table 4.2. Total oil revenues in 1986 came to little more than 12 per cent of what they had been in 1981 ($42.5 billion as against $328.5 billion). Revenues remained low until the 1990–1 Kuwait crisis. In 1990 they rose to $118.1 billion, increasing further in 1991 and reaching $127.0 billion in 1992. Over the following years they fluctuated between $80 billion and $160 billion, and finally rose to a peak of $214.4 billion in 2000.

The apparently favourable resource base in the early 1990s was in reality not as favourable as it seemed. Saudi Arabia was having at this time to spend large sums of money on supporting the coalition confronting Iraq in the First Gulf War. There have been a variety of estimates of the cost of the war to the Kingdom. Azzam (1993: 130) estimated it at $55 billion, equivalent to 56 per cent of GDP in 1991. Other estimates have been higher. Kanovsky (1994: 69) puts the cost at no less than US$65 billion. The 'emergency expenditures' incurred by the Kingdom at this time covered, in addition to its own army mobilisation costs, the local costs of allied forces on Saudi territory, much of the overall cost of US, UK and French involvement, and loans, grants and debt-forgiveness to some other countries to gain their support for the war. Saudi Arabia also increased its overall defence spending as a result of the war. While the war led to increased resource coming in from oil revenues, therefore, it also led to an outflow of resource. It is significant that government finances were in substantial deficit over this period (see Table 4.7).

At the beginning of the period, government revenues still benefited from income from the state's holdings of foreign assets. As the assets were being drawn down to meet the budget deficits, however, this element soon ceased to be significant. Income from the assets was also declining due to the falling interest rates prevailing on international markets in the mid-1980s. These factors explain the substantial fall of non-oil revenues between 1985 and 1986 (from SR45.1 billion to SR34.0 billion). The combined effect of falling oil revenues and falling non-oil revenues drove the overall revenue received by the government in that year alone, down from SR133.6 billion to SR76.5 billion–a level which was lower than in any year since 1973.

Overall, then, the period between 1985 and 2000 was one where the government's resource base was such that it could not act with the same assurance of rising income, as had been the case in the previous period. Nonetheless, for most of the period the reduced level of revenue was not sufficient to force a major restructuring of the economy. The revenue from oil was still substantial enough to enable the government to believe that it could maintain existing policies, with the extra dimension that an expanding private sector would carry through the diversification of the economy and enable the large numbers of young Saudis emerging from the educational system to find employment. The backing of the oil revenues, indeed, created a certain inertia: radical change seemed unnecessary and fraught with difficulty, while there was an expectation that the level of oil revenues was bound to rise in the longer term and thereby enable the country to pay off debts incurred through budget deficits.

4.2.2   *Foreign assets and reserves*

As can be seen from Table 4.3, Saudi Arabia's foreign assets fell steadily over the years between 1985 and 1995. The government was using its

Table 4.3 Foreign assets, 1985–2000 (US$ billion)

1985	87.7
1986	73.7
1987	68.9
1988	63.3
1989	60.5
1990	56.7
1991	55.8
1992	52.3
1993	49.2
1994	47.1
1995	44.0
1996	50.4
1997	56.8
1998	45.3
1999	37.8
2000	47.5

Sources: Calculated from data in Saudi Arabian Monetary Agency, (various years) *Annual Surveys.* Riyadh: SAMA; and International Monetary Fund (various years) *International Financial Statistics.* Washington: IMF.

foreign assets to meet the gap in its finances. From $87.7 billion in 1985 they fell to $44 billion in 1995. There was a small recovery in 1996 and 1997, as a result of the higher oil prices and the finishing of payments from the First Gulf War, but they plunged to $37.8 billion in 1998–lower than at any time since 1974.

It is worth contrasting here the different ways in which Saudi Arabia and Kuwait, a fellow-beneficiary of oil wealth, handled their foreign assets at this time. In the case of Kuwait, the government operated a 'fund for future generations'. A portion of the earnings from oil revenues was placed in an investment fund which was intended to provide finance for Kuwait's survival and development once the oil depleted. Neither the assets in this fund nor the earnings from it could be used for present expenditure (although this had to be lifted during the Iraqi occupation). In the case of Saudi Arabia, there was no such fund. Such foreign assets as were held by the government could be drawn down for present expenditure, and the earnings from the assets could also be used for the same purpose. It could be argued that Saudi Arabia, being a larger country with a wider range of resources to exploit, had more opportunity and need to use its oil wealth for domestic development than did Kuwait. Yet this strategy also had disadvantages, encouraging a more relaxed attitude to controls on expenditure than was warranted.

4.3   Development strategy: overall targets and objectives

After 1985, the government was no longer concentrating on mega-projects aimed at economic and social transformation. This, indeed, constitutes a theme which all of the development plans of the 1985–2000 period articulate: the major expenditure on physical infrastructure and construction which was necessary in the first three plans was no longer necessary, and the task of government was now to develop the productivity of the economy. The emphasis in the Fourth, Fifth and Sixth Development Plans, therefore, was on maintaining and developing the state-run programmes and operations which were in being, promoting human resource development so as to create a well-trained and employable Saudi workforce, and promoting economic diversification. The latter was seen as requiring the private sector to take the major role. This strategy was articulated clearly in the Fifth Plan:

> This stage of infrastructural development in the Kingdom is largely ended, and with the emergence of a new phase both the government and the private sector are adopting new roles. The need for economic diversification and greater mobilisation of private capital will require the private sector to assume a more leading role for future development. The principal driving sectors of the economy in the Fifth Plan – manufacturing, finance, construction and agriculture – are all firmly in the private domain. To facilitate a stronger and more diversified private sector, the government will create a positive environment for private sector activity, implement a wide range of policies and incentives to support the private sector, and establish new institutions to further private sector interests.
>
> (KSA-MOP 1990: 140–1)

Despite the considerable emphasis given to promoting the private sector, relatively little attention was given to privatising the major public-sector corporations which dominated the economy. This topic was effectively ignored in the Fourth and Fifth Plans, although the latter envisaged some of the service provision of state and municipal corporations being put in the hands of the private sector. The Fifth Plan did mention the privatisation of corporations, but this was mainly in the context of initiating consideration of how it might be done. There was no indication that this was a target which the government was expected to pursue urgently. The strength and centrality of the public sector was in practice not greatly changed in 2000 from what it had been in 1985. However, under the

Sixth plan the private sector was expected to move into significant areas which had previously been controlled exclusively by the government. Private investors were now invited to play a greater role in financing, building and operating key facilities in the fields of basic infrastructure and economic and social services (KSA-MOP 1995: 47).

A concrete strategy for privatisation was, for the first time, put forward in the Sixth plan. Three mechanisms for privatisation were put forward. The private sector would, in particular instances, be able to:

- undertake build, operate and transfer (BOT) schemes for the public sector;
- take up equity participation in subsidiaries of public companies, such as downstream petrochemical industries; and
- take over ownership of some public-sector operations.

Another theme which formed part of all of the development plans was the opportunity now available to reduce dependence on foreign labour, and the need to do so. With the completion of the heavy infrastructural projects and the increasing number of Saudis emerging from the educational system, it was said, the economy no longer required so much foreign labour and expertise. The Fourth Plan boldly predicted that the numbers of foreigners in the labour force would decline by 22.6 per cent over the plan-period (KSA-MOP 1985a: 50–1), and the subsequent plans also envisaged severely reduced numbers. All of the plans refer to the 'qualitative improvement' of the Saudi workforce which would be brought about through the acquisition of new skills through education and training, and saw this as leading naturally to a change in the balance of Saudis and non-Saudis in the labour force.

The overall expenditure envisaged in the plans was substantially less than that which had been set for expenditure in the Third Plan. The latter had set an expenditure target of SR698.1 billion, while the projections for the Fourth, Fifth and Sixth Plans were SR500.0 billion, SR394.8 billion, and SR413.0 billion, respectively. Expenditure, then, was to decline significantly under the Fourth Plan, but with a further substantial reduction in the Fifth Plan, and increasing by a fairly small margin in the Sixth Plan. The trend was, of course, in keeping both with the contention that major infrastructural construction had been completed and with the declining oil revenues. Expenditure targets in the Fourth Plan were kept at a higher level than was perhaps justified by some unrealistic assumptions on likely movements in the oil market and the price of oil. The planners predicted that the demand for Saudi oil would increase by some 30 per cent in the later part of the

1990s, with the price per barrel averaging some $28 a barrel (Kanovsky 1994: 24).

With regard to sectoral allocations, it should be noted that Saudi development plans after 1985 were different in character from the earlier ones in two respects. The first is that they do not include the detailed breakdown of intended governmental expenditure, which can be found in the earlier plans. The information which they provide shows how governmental expenditure will be divided between the main sectors of Economic Resource Development, Human Resource Development, Social Development and Physical Infrastructure, but not how each of these sectors is subdivided – e.g. how much of Economic Resource Development expenditure will be devoted to agriculture and how much to manufacturing, how much of Human Resource Development expenditure will be for general education as against higher education, etc. There are detailed sections covering development in each of the sub-divisions, and sometimes indications of how much different projected developments will cost, but no figures showing overall expenditure in each. The assumption seems to have been that greater flexibility was needed than before, rather than tying up all of the funding from the outset.

The second aspect in which the post-1985 plans were different than the earlier ones was in their seeking a more holistic approach to the economy. All of them have substantial chapters on the private sector, with detailed descriptions of the contribution which the private sector is expected to make to the country's overall development in the period concerned. To some extent this stemmed from the greater prominence which the government was now giving to the private sector in the development of the economy, but it also represented a change in the philosophy of development planning. The approach was now referred to as indicative planning, where the emphasis was on how the whole economy would develop rather than how the government would handle its own role.

As can be seen from Tables 4.4, 4.5 and 4.6 (taking account, also, of Table 3.6), there was over this period a steady trend in the allocation of expenditure away from economic resource development and physical infrastructure, and towards human resource development. The proportion of allocated expenditure going to economic resource development declined from 37.5 per cent of the total in the Third Plan to 26.1 per cent in the Fourth, 18.5 per cent in the Fifth and 10 per cent in the Sixth. The changes in the actual amounts allocated to economic resource development were even more dramatic, as can be seen from the tables. Whereas the allocations had stood at SR261.2 billion in the Third Plan, they had declined to no more than SR41.6 billion by the Sixth Plan. Physical infrastructure allocations declined from 35.5 per cent of the total in the Third Plan to 28.9 per cent

Table 4.4 Fourth Development Plan, 1985–90: projected
　　　　　financial allocations (SR billion)

Development sector	Total	% of total
Economic resource development	130.7	26.1
Human resource development	135.3	27.1
Social development	89.7	17.9
Physical infrastructure	144.3	28.9
Overall total	500.0	100.0

Source: Kingdom of Saudi Arabia, Ministry of Planning (1985) *Fourth
Development Plan 1985–1990*. Riyadh: Ministry of Planning, Tables 5.1
and 5.2.

Table 4.5 Fifth Development Plan, 1990–5: projected
　　　　　financial allocations (SR billion)

Development sector	Total	% of total
Economic resource development	73.0	18.5
Human resource development	139.9	35.1
Social development	66.1	16.8
Physical infrastructure	115.8	29.3
Overall total	394.8	100.0

Source: Kingdom of Saudi Arabia, Ministry of Planning (1990) *Fifth
Development Plan, 1990–1995*. Riyadh: Ministry of Planning, Table 5.9.

Table 4.6 Sixth Development Plan, 1995–2000: projected
　　　　　financial allocations (SR billion)

Development sector	Total	% of total
Economic resource development	41.6	10.0
Human resource development	222.2	53.8
Social development	74.2	18.0
Physical infrastructure	75.0	18.2
Overall total	413.0	100.0

Source: Kingdom of Saudi Arabia, Ministry of Planning (1995) *Sixth
Development Plan, 1995–2000*. Riyadh: Ministry of Planning, Table 5.6.

in the Fourth Plan, rising slightly to 29.3 per cent in the Fifth Plan, and then falling to 18.2 per cent in the Sixth. The actual amounts allocated declined from SR247.3 billion in the Third Plan to SR75.0 billion in the Sixth Plan. Human resource development allocations, on the other hand, were increasing both in proportion to the total and in absolute amounts. The proportion rose from 18.3 per cent in the Third Plan to 27.1 per cent in the Fourth, 35.1 per cent in the Fifth and 53.8 per cent in the Sixth. The absolute amount allocated rose from SR128.3 billion in the Third Plan to SR222.2 billion in the Sixth. The proportion of expenditure allocated to social development was higher over the 1985–2000 period than it had been before (rising from 8.7 per cent in the Third Plan to 17.9 per cent in the Fourth), but there was relatively little change in the proportion through the Fourth, Fifth and Sixth Plans. The absolute expenditure was not very much higher in the Sixth Plan than it had been in the Third: SR75.0 billion in the Sixth as against SR61.2 billion in the Third.

The pattern of sectoral allocations was consistent with the rhetoric of the plans. The reduction of projected spending on economic resource development was a reflection, on the one hand, of the completion of the major state-owned petrochemical projects, and on the other of the expectation that investment in economic resource development would now come from the private rather than the public sector. The decline in planned physical infrastructure spending also sprang from a perception of completion–that the communications networks were now in place, so that less expenditure than before was needed. It should be noted, however, that the reduction of expenditure in this sector was less sharp than that in economic resource development. Some recognition was clearly being given to the need to maintain the infrastructure in good repair. The substantial expenditure on human resource development constituted a key means whereby the government could reduce the foreign workforce (in addition to the natural decline in numbers which would follow from the ending of the major economic and infrastructural projects). Educated and trained Saudis would take the place of foreigners.

4.4   The articulation of development strategy and economic policy

4.4.1   Factors shaping the articulation of policy

Two factors were important in determining how the government's economic plans were given practical effect over these years. The first was the constraint of an unreliable and at times declining resource base. Contrary to the 1970–85 period, the revenues available for development between 1985 and 2000 tended to be no more than–and often less than–that which was predicted in the plans. Revenues did increase dramatically in 1990–2 after the Iraqi occupation of Kuwait, but this was matched by the need to raise non-developmental expenditure. Massive spending had to be undertaken in the military confrontation with Iraq and all that accompanied it. Whereas in the earlier period expenditure could be allowed to expand in excess of what had been planned, there was less room for this after 1985. Actual developmental expenditure fell significantly short of the projected allocations in the Fourth and Fifth Plans, exceeding allocations by a small margin in the Sixth Plan (see Tables 4.4, 4.5, 4.6 and 4.8). Governmental finances were in deficit throughout this period with the exception of 2000. The confidence that the country's economic problems could be solved through rising oil revenues, therefore, gradually diminished. The need to find new ways of saving governmental resources and yet developing the economy was more pressing than the plans envisaged.

The second factor was the influence exerted by global economic developments, and in particular the moves towards the liberalisation of international markets. The latter took institutional form with the creation of the World Trade Organisation in 1994. All states were now faced by the choice of whether to join this organisation and thereby accept the rules of a liberalised international trading regime, with its requirements aimed at ensuring free competition in particular spheres, or to stay aloof from the grouping and therefore outside the framework of economic relations which was coming to dominate the global economy. The choice was difficult for those countries which had not previously been members of the General Agreement on Tariffs and Trade (the trading framework which had preceded the WTO). The opening up of markets inevitably brought disadvantages as well as advantages. On the one hand, some economic undertakings which were unable to compete would disappear. On the other, WTO membership created the prospect of expanded markets for those undertakings which were internationally competitive.

For Saudi Arabia the decision was particularly difficult. Substantial changes would be needed if the Kingdom were to gain WTO membership. All aspects of Saudi economic life were shaped by subsidies and by regulations and practices which limited competition. Significant interests were at stake if subsidies were removed and protected sectors opened up to international competition. Initially, however, there seemed no urgency for the Kingdom to commit itself to membership. While it wanted and needed to form part of the international trading network, and WTO membership would also enhance its profile in the post-Cold War economic and political order, the basis of Saudi economic wealth would not be affected by WTO membership. Trading in oil was not subject to WTO rules, and Saudi oil exports and revenues would therefore not be affected one way or the other. The major gains which Saudi Arabia could expect from access to foreign markets were in the field of petrochemicals, where the country's industries had a clear comparative advantage. Here, however, it was unclear whether the governments of the developed Western countries would accept to reduce their tariffs. Claims were being made that competition from Saudi Arabia would be unfair, given that the energy and feedstock for Saudi petrochemical production were supplied at cost price to the industries concerned.

In practice, the Kingdom indicated at an early stage its interest in joining the WTO, but did not initially press its case strongly or urgently. The Saudi application for membership first reached the General Agreement on Tariffs and Trade (prior to the WTO's formation) in 1993, and a Working Party on Saudi membership was formed in the same year. The initial round of discussions between Saudi and WTO negotiators in the Working Party, however, did not take place until May 1996. These discussions covered trade in goods. A second round was held in November 1996, focusing on trade in services and intellectual property rights (Malik 1999: 133). Over the three years which followed, a further five meetings of the Working Party were held, directed at defining the conditions under which Saudi membership would be possible.

The discussions no doubt added to the pressure on the government to give serious consideration to economic reform. Governmental opinion nonetheless remained divided and ambiguous as to whether membership would in fact be in Saudi Arabia's best interests. The WTO team conducting the discussions was insistent that Saudi Arabia would have to dismantle some of its subsidies, especially those which enabled the petrochemical industry to obtain raw materials and energy at discounted rates from ARAMCO. Questions were also raised about the interest-free loans for industrial and agricultural enterprises provided by the Saudi Industrial Development Fund and the Agricultural Bank, and the artificially low prices charged for utilities and energy. The government was aware that without these subsidies many businesses would not be able to compete. While there was new pressure for economic reform coming from the WTO discussions, therefore, this was not sufficient to bring about major substantive change. Some reforms did, however, ensue.

4.4.2   Changes in the regulatory framework

The government's need to limit expenditure and the new context created by the structuring of the global economy led to some policy changes. First, there was an attempt to reduce the level of subsidies. Moves to achieve this were put in hand from the late 1980s, and the Sixth Plan gave the reduction of subsidies as one of its objectives (KSA-MOP 1995: 109). Governmental figures show a reduction in the level from about 3 per cent of GDP in the mid-1980s to little more than 1 per cent in 1998 (IMF 1998a: 39). Subsidies for wheat production, for example, were reduced by 60 per cent in 1996 (EIU 1997: 15). Most of the reductions in subsidies occurred in the second half of the 1990s (Malik 1999: 132).

The elements of subsidy included in governmental figures, however, do not give a full picture of the subsidised dimension of Saudi economic life. The government figures cover the grants provided to support particular activities or sectors of the population, such as payments for food and animal feed, production subsidies for wheat and barley, agricultural inputs subsidies and social relief payments. There are, however, many elements of subsidy in the Saudi economy which are outside of these specially targeted categories. These involve the supply of goods and services to the population, by public-sector organisations, at rates which are below what would be charged commercially. Ever since the beginning of the oil economy, the rates charged for electricity, water, telephone services, petroleum products and many other goods and services were effectively subsidised by the government. From 1995 there was some attempt to reduce these elements of subsidy. In the 1995 budget, charges for the supply of water, petroleum products and electricity were raised, the price of airline tickets was raised to economic levels, and the cost of telephone services also rose. The retail price of petrol sold locally was increased from 60 to 90 *halalah* (24 US cents) a litre (Malik 1999: 132). These were the first sizeable increases in charges for services for Saudi citizens and seemed to constitute the first stage in eliminating the state subsidisation of prices, as had been advised by the World Bank and the IMF. However, the budgets which followed this in the late 1990s did not introduce any new measures to reduce costs or increase revenues, to the disappointment of the IMF (IMF 2001). The only additional measures which were brought in were in 1998, when there was a modest increase in first- and business-class airfares on domestic routes, departure taxes on international travel airline were introduced, and there was some restructuring of electricity tariffs (*MEED*, 27.11.98). A major part of the generalised structure of subsidies, therefore, remained in place.

Second, the government moved slowly towards the privatisation of state corporations. This involved little actual privatisation but rather the creation of institutional arrangements which could make privatisation possible. On 6 August 1997 the Council of Ministers issued a 'decision' identifying eight objectives for privatisation. They were: encouraging private-sector investment; enlarging the productive assets of

Saudi citizens; encouraging domestic and foreign capital to invest locally; increasing employment opportunities; providing services to citizens and investors; rationalising public expenditure and reducing the burden of the government budget; and increasing government revenues (KSA-CM 1997). These, and the description given of the policies needed to achieve them, were clearly well conceived. However, the elaboration of the detailed legal framework, which was needed to make the statements of principle operational, was slow in coming. The IMF noted at the end of 1999 that the legal framework for privatisation, and the elaboration of the steps needed to implement the process, were still being developed (IMF 1999: 26).

Some practical measures towards loosening state control of the economy were nonetheless taken. The Public Investment Fund (PIF), the government investment arm, was entrusted with the task of preparing case studies for privatisation, undertaking the evaluation of assets and the formulation of restructuring programmes (Malik 1999: 130). Among the major corporations which were investigated and assessed at this time were Saudi Arabian Airlines (SAUDIA) and the Saudi Arabian Mining Company (MAADEN).

As a first stage towards privatisation, some previously publicly managed operations were converted into companies – albeit with the shares still owned 100 per cent by the government. In December 1997 the Council of Ministers determined that all of the activities of the Ministry of Posts and Telecommunications, except for those relating to the Ministry's regulatory role and its operation of the partly subsidised postal services, should be hived off to form a separate company which would in due course be sold to private investors (*FT*, 8.5.98). A decree was duly issued in 1998 establishing the Saudi Telecommunications Company (STC), which would take over the running of the Saudi telephone and telegraph system (SAMA 1998: 65). In the same year, the management of the Saudi Port Authority was turned over to a private company (Malik 1999: 131). The *Middle East Economic Digest* reported one year later that the volume of goods handled by the largest port, Jiddah Islamic Port, had increased by 11 per cent since privatisation (*MEED*, 5.12.99). At the end of 1998 the government announced plans to unify the ten regional electricity companies into the Saudi Electricity Company (SEC) as a first step towards privatising the sector (*Arab News*, 1.12.98). Local authorities were also turning their attention towards privatisation at this time, contracting out the operation of some of their facilities, largely so as to contain costs (*MEED*, 27.11.98). Jiddah municipality, for example, contracted out the management of its wholesale fruit and vegetable market. There were frequent reports that the government was planning to sell off part of its shareholding in SABIC, perhaps reducing its holding from 70 per cent to 25 per cent. This, however, did not materialise.

An attempt was made to increase the role of the private sector in the supply of power. The plan was to bring private-sector financing into the financing of a power plant at Shuaiba where the private investor would build, own and operate the plant (the arrangement known as BOO). At this stage, however, the attempt was unsuccessful. The *Middle East Economic Digest* noted that while there was strong pressure at government level for constructing the plant on a BOO basis, the Saudi Consolidated Electricity Company for the Western Region (EWR) successfully blocked the initiative, fearing a diminution of its authority (*MEED*, 27.11.98).

4.4.3 Changing patterns of governmental expenditure

Despite significant cuts in the government's development spending, governmental finances remained heavily in deficit throughout this period except for the final year. Table 4.7 shows the changing balance between revenue and expenditure. The government's statistics covering 1990 and 1991 combine the expenditure totals for these two years into one global figure, presumably because revenue and expenditure stemming from the crisis over Kuwait are best treated as a composite straddling the two years. As a ratio to GDP, the deficit was highest in the late 1980s, reaching 25 per cent in 1987. It remained high (in excess of 14 per cent) through to 1993, then declined gradually through to 1997 when it stood at 2.9 per cent (SAMA 1998: 125). The relatively small deficits of 1996 and 1997 could in fact have been surpluses if the government had not taken the opportunity of high oil prices to repay some its debts. Most of the domestic debt was paid off at this time, and the backlog which had built up on payments to farmers, contractors and medical suppliers was closed (*MEED*, 21.3.97). The same was done with part of the foreign debt which had been acquired at the beginning of the decade. The *National Commercial Bank Economist* (*NCB Economist* 1997: 1) noted that Saudi Arabia was able to repay $1.8 billion out of the $4.8 billion of its external loans from 1991. Similar factors apply to the financial balance in 2000. In this case the surplus could have been yet higher if not for the repayment of debt. Higher revenues, therefore, were not being used immediately to boost levels of expenditure.

Tables 4.7 and 4.8, taken together, reveal that the development sectors were not the major cause of government overspending between 1985 and 2000. Development expenditure was cut more extensively than other fields of expenditure. This can best be seen in the perspective of changes since the Third Plan (1980–5). In the latter period (see Table 3.8) development

Table 4.7 Budgeted and actual revenues and expenditures, 1985–2000 (SR million)

| | Revenues | | Expenditures | | Surplus/deficit |
	Budgeted	Actual	Budgeted	Actual	Actual
1985	200,000	133,565	200,000	184,004	−50,439
1986	106,926	76,498	159,646	137,422	−60,924
1987	106,926	103,811	159,646	173,526	−69,715
1988	105,300	84,600	141,200	134,850	−50,250
1989	N/A	114,600	140,060	149,500	−34,900
1990/1	118,000	316,639	359,601	457,477	−140,838
1992	151,000	169,647	181,000	211,340	−41,693
1993	169,150	141,445	196,950	187,890	−46,445
1994	120,000	128,991	160,000	163,776	−34,785
1995	135,000	146,500	150,000	173,943	−27,443
1996	131,500	179,085	150,000	198,117	−19,032
1997	164,000	205,500	181,000	221,272	−15,772
1998	178,000	141,608	196,000	190,060	−48,452
1999	121,000	147,454	165,000	183,841	−36,387
2000	157,000	258,065	185,000	235,322	22,743

Note: The figures for 1990 and 1991 are combined in the official statistics due to the character of the expenditure incurred during the First Gulf War. It was not easy to separate out such expenditure by year. Official statistics do not give a budgeted revenue figure for 1989

Sources: Pre-1990 figures taken from Saudi Arabian Monetary Agency (1991) *Twenty-Seventh Annual Report*. Riyadh: SAMA. Post-1990 figures taken from Saudi Arabian Monetary Agency (2005) *Forty-First Annual Report*. Riyadh: SAMA.

Table 4.8 Breakdown of governmental expenditures in the Fourth, Fifth and Sixth Plan periods

		Economic resources development	Human resources development	Social and health development	Infrastructure development	Total
Fourth Plan	SR billion	71.2	115.1	61.9	100.7	348.9
	%	20.4	33.0	17.7	28.9	100.0
Fifth Plan	SR billion	34.1	164.6	68.0	74.2	340.9
	%	10.0	48.0	20.0	22.0	100.0
Sixth Plan	SR billion	48.2	216.6	87.5	68.1	420.4
	%	11.5	51.5	20.8	16.2	100.0

Source: Kingdom of Saudi Arabia, Ministry of Planning (2000) *Seventh Development Plan 2000–2004*. Riyadh: Ministry of Planning.

spending came to SR625.2 billion, while total government expenditure stood at SR1,212.6 billion. As a proportion of total spending, then, development expenditure constituted about 52 per cent. In the Fourth Plan period total governmental expenditure (i.e. the totals for 1985, 1986, 1987, 1988 and 1989 in Table 4.7, combined) came to SR779.3 billion, of which the developmental sectors accounted for SR348.9 billion. The proportion had declined to 45 per cent. In the case of the Fifth Plan period, development spending accounted for an even smaller part of total expenditure: SR340.9 billion as against SR1020.5 billion. The proportion now stood at 30 per cent. This low figure is explained mainly by the extensive non-development spending made necessary by the Gulf War. In the Sixth Plan the share of development spending was rather higher, SR420.4 billion as against SR967.2 billion, constituting about 43 per cent. The major changes in expenditure, therefore, were taking place outside of the developmental fields.

The decline in government spending on development was not simply a result of the major development projects in the country having been completed. A comparison between the targets of development spending in the three plans (see Tables 4.4, 4.5 and 4.6) and the actual expenditure over the three periods (see Table 4.8) shows that actual spending fell far short of projected spending in the Fourth and Fifth Plan periods, and only marginally exceeded the projected target in the Sixth Plan period.

Clearly it was non-development spending which the government was having most difficulty in controlling. The governmental machine was being allowed to operate much as before, but with fewer resources given to the economic and social development of the country. The strategy was based on political realities and choices. While the government machine was overstaffed and beset with inefficiencies, and substantial savings could have been made by cutting wasteful practices and sinecure employment, it was easier and less contentious to cut back on development expenditure. The public payroll had been used as an instrument to maintain social stability in the country. The large numbers of young Saudis emerging from the expanding educational system had to be offered jobs, despite frequently being underemployed in the posts to which they were appointed. The National Guard was also growing in number, a move deemed necessary to maintain the loyalty of the traditional tribal peoples at the heart of the country.

Another substantial reason for the continued heavy non-developmental expenditure was the spending on defence needed to maintain the outgoing strategic posture adopted by Saudi Arabia over this period, especially during the 1990–1 Kuwait crisis. The 1991 Gulf War was financed largely by Saudi Arabia, with some $60 billion being put towards supporting the war effort (most of this money going to the US, followed by Britain), providing grants and loans to key allies which needed to be brought into the coalition, operationalising its own armed forces, and repairing the damage done to Saudi installations by the Iraqi missile and ground attacks on Saudi territory. While security-related expenditure was particularly high in 1990–1, it was substantial throughout this period. Defence generally made up some 30–35 per cent of budgeted expenditure in the years between 1985 and 2000 – rather more than the share it occupied in the early 1980s (Cordesman 2003a: 77).

While it could be said that the government was achieving some success in curbing expenditure in response to the sharply reduced revenue, then, the means by which and the extent to which it was achieved was not so positive. Expenditure was being reduced most sharply in areas critical to economic development; some of the reduction in expenditure came from the government postponing payment on, or even failing to honour, its debts (especially domestically, to Saudi-owned companies); and there was a continuing deficit in the government's finances, leading to borrowing on the international market and some reduction in Saudi Arabia's foreign assets (see Table 4.3). All three of these aspects of policy had damaging effects on the long-term effectiveness and health of the economy. Moreover, there was a slight decline in expenditure on 'operations and maintenance', which should have been rising so as to cover the upkeep of the projects which had been brought into existence.

4.5 The record of achievement in economic and social development

4.5.1 The growth and composition of GDP

Over the 1985–2000 period, GDP at constant prices did not reach the targets which had been set in the development plans. This was hardly surprising. The economic environment was not conducive to growth: government expenditure for economic purposes was substantially less than that which the plans had envisaged, foreign investment was given little encouragement, and the private sector was still operating within a relatively regulation-bound environment.

The period is often portrayed as one where the economy was gradually shrinking, at least relative to the level it had achieved in the early 1980s. This is true if the measure is in current prices. As can be seen from Tables 3.9 and 4.9, GDP at current prices in 1986 had declined to little more than one-half what it had been in 1981. While it grew through most of the rest of the 1980s and 1990s, it only regained the 1981 level in the year 2000. In the meantime, of course, there had been population growth as well as

Table 4.9 Growth in Gross Domestic Product, 1985–2000 (current prices, SR million)

Year	Total GDP[a]
1985	372,408
1986	318,775
1987	318,775
1988	322,283
1989	350,325
1990	430,334
1991	484,853
1992	484,853
1993	485,630
1994	485,630
1995	526,004
1996	581,873
1997	608,802
1998	536,635
1999	593,955
2000	697,007
Total	759,8142

Note: [a] Total except import duties.

Source: Kingdom of Saudi Arabia, Central Department of Statistics (1985–2000) *Statistical Abstracts*. Riyadh: Ministry of Planning.

the shrinkage in GDP, and inflation had lessened the purchasing power of the dollar. GDP per capita stood at $18,039 in 1981, and in 1998 came to no more than $7,181 (World Bank 1999).

The current prices measure of GDP, however, is not a useful measure of the overall strength of the economy. The decline in GDP at current prices after 1981 simply reflected the unprecedented heights to which oil prices had risen in the early 1980s, and the sharp falls thereafter. In constant prices the pattern was different. Here also there was a decline after 1981, but the trends over the 1985–2000 period have a more positive appearance. The year 1985 constituted a low point, due to the fall in oil production and the impact of cuts in government expenditure on development in all sectors. Thereafter, there was a gradual improvement over the remainder of the decade, and a more substantial rise in the early 1990s (see Table 4.10). By 1992, GDP in constant prices had surpassed the peak reached in 1981. It remained on this plateau for three years before rising again in the final years of the decade. Government plans over these years gave emphasis to the contribution which the private sector was now making to the growth of the economy. The Fifth Plan, for example, noted that the economy had

Table 4.10 GDP by kind of economic activity, 1985–99 (producers' values, constant prices at 1999 SR million)

	1985	1986	1987	1988	1989	1990	1991	1992	1993	1994	1995	1996	1997	1998	1999
Industries and other producers except producers of government services:															
Agriculture, forestry and fishing	17,865	20,551	23,919	26,498	28,356	29,150	29,991	31,796	32,912	32,157	32,476	32,371	33,354	33,676	34,443
Mining and quarrying	74,306	111,086	95,953	120,089	117,536	148,381	187,485	192,896	185,957	186,132	185,748	188,126	185,677	191,915	175,566
(a) Crude petroleum and natural gas	72,649	109,475	94,378	118,496	115,888	146,733	185,760	191,176	184,155	184,186	183,599	185,913	183,332	189,476	173,102
(b) Other	1,657	1,611	1,575	1,593	1,648	1,648	1,725	1,720	1,802	1,946	2,149	2,213	2,345	2,440	2,464
Manufacturing	35,565	37,439	37,534	38,940	38,657	40,560	40,692	42,187	43,772	46,119	49,312	56,268	58,839	60,191	62,800
(a) Petroleum refining	12,868	15,378	15,547	16,295	15,110	17,392	16,029	16,781	17,007	17,094	16,400	18,612	17,921	18,101	18,021
(b) Other	22,697	22,061	21,987	22,645	23,547	23,168	24,663	25,406	26,765	29,025	32,912	37,656	40,918	42,090	44,779
Electricity, gas and water	3,624	3,820	4,046	4,290	4,509	4,564	4,925	5,219	5,736	6,362	6,649	6,938	7,138	7,511	8,174
Construction	39,489	34,612	33,629	31,951	31,784	31,483	32,255	31,706	32,477	34,140	37,021	39,666	39,610	40,406	39,437
Wholesale and retail trade, restaurants and hotels	33,633	32,354	31,791	31,475	31,160	31,535	33,019	34,520	35,462	35,745	35,157	35,505	38,073	42,394	45,992
Transport, storage and communication	21,666	21,076	20,568	20,774	20,880	21,492	22,363	26,803	28,858	29,342	24,472	24,840	26,152	27,186	27,893

Finance, insurance, real estate and business services	81,509	68,888	67,415	68,604	69,437	68,491	67,032	69,099	67,573	66,707	65,261	68,093	70,354	70,020	73,824
(a) Ownership of Dwellings	53,722	44,483	42,551	42,500	42,500	41,193	41,491	41,060	39,409	38,230	37,871	40,795	42,092	40,682	42,221
(b) Other	27,787	24,405	24,864	26,104	26,937	27,298	25,541	28,039	28,164	28,477	27,390	27,298	28,262	29,338	31,603
Community, social and personal services	17,604	16,891	16,687	17,217	17,482	17,648	17,597	17,830	18,353	18,935	19,100	19,511	20,218	20,620	21,377
Less imputed bank services charge	7,332	8,542	9,379	9,505	9,728	9,655	9,333	9,796	10,199	10,660	10,674	10,470	10,669	11,493	12,340
Sub-total	317,928	338,175	322,163	350,335	350,072	383,650	426,025	442,261	440,899	444,982	444,522	460,848	468,747	482,426	477,166
Producers of government services	86,757	86,991	86,590	86,857	89,166	92,575	94,973	100,464	102,028	102,818	105,441	106,702	113,690	115,728	116,789
Import duties	4,289	4,627	3,917	9,415	7,648	7,881	7,179	9,899	9,842	8,649	7,603	8,883	8,940	9,987	9,634
Gross Domestic Product (GDP)	408,974	429,792	412,670	446,608	446,887	484,106	528,178	552,625	552,769	556,448	557,566	576,433	591,378	608,141	603,589

Source: Kingdom of Saudi Arabia, Ministry of Planning (2000) *Achievements of the Development Plans*. Riyadh: Ministry of Planning.

exhibited considerable resilience between 1985 and 1990 despite the cuts in public spending, such that the economy had become less dependent on government spending as its driving force (KSA-MOP 1990: 25). This had been one of the goals of the Fourth Plan. There is some truth in the contention, although in practice the sectors which experienced the greatest growth were those which benefited most from government support.

Nonetheless, it is true that the growth targets put forward in the plans were attained only in the Fifth Plan. Rather than increasing at 2.9 per cent, 3.2 per cent and 3.8 per cent respectively in the Fourth, Fifth and Sixth Plans (KSA-MOP 1985a, 1990, 1995), GDP at constant prices rose by only 1.0 per cent over the Fourth Plan, by 4.5 per cent in the Fifth Plan and by 1.6 per cent in the Sixth Plan (calculated from the data in Table 4.11). Growth, moreover, was heavily influenced by factors in the external political environment. Of key importance here was the Gulf War of 1991. GDP at constant prices grew by 8.33 per cent and 9.10 per cent respectively in 1990 and 1991, as a result of the spending boom created by the arrival of the Allied troops and Kuwaiti refugees. All of these had to be housed and fed. Considerable profiteering was rife over these years, as companies took advantage of the urgent demand for supplies (Wilson and Graham 1994: 190). This had a negative impact subsequently, however, due to the increase in the Kingdom's budget and current account deficits and the level of debt. With cuts in public expenditure, the growth rate flattened out. The average growth rate of the GDP between 1992 and 1995 was 1.38 per cent (see Table 4.11) and most sectors saw sluggish growth.

Crude petroleum and natural gas continued to make the most substantial contribution to GDP, although remaining substantially below the level reached in 1981. 1985 marked the low point, with the contribution in constant prices standing at little more than one-third of what it had been in 1981. Thereafter there was a gradual increase in the late 1980s, with a higher level being reached and maintained through the 1990s. Given that the measure here is in constant prices, the fall and rise in the contribution reflects largely the changing levels of production – both of crude oil and natural gas.

The most substantial growth in any of the major sectors, besides crude petroleum and natural gas, was recorded by the agricultural sector. This stemmed mainly from the extensive development of irrigated schemes in the late 1980s and early 1990s, and the benefit which the sector drew from the expanded local demand for food during the Kuwait crisis. The level of production, therefore, was significantly higher than that which had existed at any time during the 1970–85 period. The growth was heavily dependent on government subsidies. Rather than reducing Saudi Arabia's dependence on oil, therefore, the buoyancy of the agricultural sector highlighted the

Table 4.11 Percentage growth in sectors of the Gross Domestic Product, 1986–2000 (constant prices at 1999)

	1986	1987	1988	1989	1990	1991	1992	1993	1994	1995	1996	1997	1998	1999	2000
Agriculture, forestry and fishing	15.03	16.39	10.78	7.01	2.80	2.89	6.02	3.51	-2.29	0.99	-0.32	3.04	0.97	2.28	3.91
Mining and quarrying	49.50	-13.62	25.15	-2.13	26.24	26.35	2.89	-3.60	0.09	-0.21	1.28	-1.30	3.36	-8.52	7.23
(a) Crude petroleum and natural gas	50.69	-13.79	25.55	-2.20	26.62	26.60	2.92	-3.67	0.02	-0.32	1.26	-1.39	3.35	-8.64	7.30
(b) Other	-2.78	-2.23	1.14	3.45	0.00	4.67	-0.29	4.77	7.99	10.43	2.98	5.96	4.05	0.98	2.15
Manufacturing	5.27	0.25	3.75	-0.73	4.92	0.33	3.67	3.76	5.36	6.92	14.11	4.57	2.30	4.33	4.77
(a) Petroleum refining	19.51	1.10	4.81	-7.27	15.10	-7.84	4.69	1.35	0.51	-4.06	13.49	-3.71	1.00	-0.44	3.55
(b) Other	-2.80	-0.34	2.99	3.98	-1.61	6.45	3.01	5.35	8.44	13.39	14.41	8.66	2.86	6.39	5.26
Electricity, gas and water	5.41	5.92	6.03	5.10	1.22	7.91	5.97	9.91	10.91	4.51	4.35	2.88	5.23	8.83	4.73
Construction	-12.35	-2.84	-4.99	-0.52	-0.95	2.45	-1.70	2.43	5.12	8.44	7.14	-0.14	2.01	-2.40	5.88
Wholesale and retail trade, restaurants and hotels	-3.80	-1.74	-0.99	-1.00	1.20	4.71	4.55	2.73	0.80	-1.64	0.99	7.23	11.35	8.49	4.76
Transport, storage and communication	-2.72	-2.41	1.00	0.51	2.93	4.05	19.85	7.67	1.68	-16.60	1.50	5.28	3.95	2.60	4.02
Finance, insurance, real estate and business services	-15.48	-2.14	1.76	1.21	-1.36	-2.13	3.08	-2.21	-1.28	-2.17	4.34	3.32	-0.47	5.43	3.69
(a) Ownership of dwellings	-17.20	-4.34	-0.12	0.00	-3.08	0.72	-1.04	-4.02	-2.99	-0.94	7.72	3.18	-3.35	3.78	2.26
(b) Other	-12.17	1.88	4.99	3.19	1.34	-6.44	9.78	0.45	1.11	-3.82	-0.34	3.53	3.81	7.72	5.59
Community, social and personal services	-4.05	-1.21	3.18	1.54	0.95	-0.29	1.32	2.93	3.17	0.87	2.15	3.62	1.99	3.67	5.15
Less imputed bank services charge	16.50	9.80	1.34	2.35	-0.75	-3.34	4.96	4.11	4.52	0.13	-1.91	1.90	7.72	7.37	8.78
Sub-total	6.37	-4.73	8.74	-0.08	9.59	11.05	3.81	-0.31	0.93	-0.10	3.67	1.71	2.92	-1.09	5.40
Producers of government services	0.27	-0.46	0.31	2.66	3.82	2.59	5.78	1.56	0.77	2.55	1.20	6.55	1.79	0.92	3.00
Total except import duties	5.06	-3.86	6.96	0.47	8.42	9.40	4.17	0.04	0.90	0.40	3.20	2.62	2.70	-0.70	4.93
Import duties	7.88	-15.34	140.36	-18.77	3.05	-8.91	37.89	-0.58	-12.12	-12.09	16.84	0.64	11.71	-3.53	0.83
Gross domestic product (GDP)	5.09	-3.98	8.22	0.06	8.33	9.10	4.63	0.03	0.67	0.20	3.38	2.59	2.83	-0.75	4.86

Source: Calculated from data in Saudi Arabian Monetary Agency (1986–2000) *Annual Surveys*. Riyadh: SAMA.

critical role of oil-generated government expenditure. Subsidies were progressively reduced through the 1990s, due in part to the realisation that the falling water-table was causing environmental damage. With this reduction the growth rate of the sector slowed considerably in the mid- and late 1990s.

Manufacturing also recorded substantial growth over this period, only slightly less than that of agriculture. The sector expanded steadily, achieving levels of production well above those of the previous period. Some of this expansion occurred in the refining sector, but the more substantial growth occurred elsewhere. The growth of non-refining manufacturing seems to have been evenly split between the petrochemicals industry and non-petrochemical manufacturing. Given the huge investment which the government had put into petrochemicals developments, this is perhaps surprising. Part of the reason appears to have been that Saudi petrochemicals had not yet achieved sufficient market access internationally. Petrochemical prices in the 1980s, moreover, had slumped, and the profitability of the petrochemicals industry was affected by this. Auty (1990: 152) points out that the total project investment of SABIC in 1985 came to more than double the $6 billion total assets of the company. Yet SABIC was only barely making a profit in the late 1980s. Higher profit margins were available in the more downstream petrochemical operations, such as plastics, but these had not yet developed significantly. Nonetheless, with the rise in petrochemical prices in the 1990s this sector became increasingly profitable. Production and profitability improved over these latter years.

The construction sector accounted for a declining share of GDP, and also a lower absolute level relative to the early 1980s. The contribution in 1985 came to only about 65 per cent what it had been in 1981, falling still further in the late 1980s and early 1990s, before rising again in the mid- and late 1990s. At the end of the period the absolute value of the sector's contribution, in constant prices, was little more than what it had been in 1985.

The trade and services sectors did not perform well over this period. Finance and real estate ended the period with a lower level of activity than at the outset. Wholesale and retail trade declined steadily through the 1980s after 1983, before resuming some growth in the early 1990s. It was, however, not until 1997 that it had regained the level of 1983. The transport, storage and communication sector saw little growth between 1983 and 1991, a rather higher level of activity between 1992 and 1994, and then a decline before growth started again in 1997. Community and personal services experienced relatively little change in the level of activity from year to year, although at the end of the period the level was higher than at the beginning.

Overall, then, while the industrial and agricultural sectors were benefiting from the increased investment which the government was putting into these fields, whether through direct investment or subsidised credit facilities, the sectors which were sensitive to the overall level of governmental expenditure in the economy were not growing.

4.5.2 The strengthening of infrastructure and social provision

Despite the cutbacks on infrastructural and social expenditure in the late 1980s and a limited level of expenditure through the 1990s, there was nonetheless some increase in social provision for the population and an expansion of the physical infrastructure. The expansion was not on the multi-fold scale seen in the previous period, but rather took the form of slow and sometimes unsteady growth. The needs of the growing population, and the requirements of a private sector attempting to broaden and deepen its activities, were in practice outstripping the facilities and services which were available.

Physical infrastructure certainly followed this pattern of slow expansion, with the benefits spread rather unevenly over the country. Of the major cities, Riyadh experienced a more substantial improvement in its physical infrastructure than did Jiddah. In the latter, water and electricity supplies, the sewage system and the airport were all becoming overstrained by the growth of the city. Nationally, the length of paved roads in the country grew by about 50 per cent between 1984 and 1999, and the volume of cargo handled in the ports by about 25 per cent. The numbers of passengers handled in the country's airports, however, barely increased. The number of telephone lines operating increased by some three-fold, from a low base. Electricity supply grew almost three-fold, and the supply of desalinated water by about 50 per cent (KSA-MOP 2006: 70–89).

The expansion of educational provision followed a similar pattern, with growth taking place. The output, however, was not always sufficient, in the right specialisations, or of good enough quality to satisfy the needs of the economy. Educational enrolment more than doubled over the period, with particularly strong growth at the elementary, intermediate and secondary school levels, and especially in girls' education. The number of teachers expanded at a similar rate, with the number of female teachers exceeding that of male teachers by the end of the period. Although development plans referred to the need to expand technical and vocational education, the growth in these sectors was limited. In 1999 the total number of graduates emerging from technical educational schools and institutes was less than 10,000, and the number of graduates of vocational training institutes was about 6,000 – approximately the same as it had been at the beginning of the period.

If education was to be the channel through which an effective Saudi labour force was to be created its development over the 1985–2000 period was neither adequate nor appropriate to the given purpose. Quality was important as well as quantity. The private and public sectors both needed Saudi employees with the specialisations, initiative and problem-solving capacity required by a modern economy. In practice, the educational system was not producing the necessary skills or the spirit of initiative. There had been no reform of educational syllabi, and a substantial proportion of the time of school students, in particular, was being spent on subjects which were not of direct use in employment. The major expansion in the universities was occurring in the Islamic universities, and while these covered many of the same subjects studied in the main national universities, the scope of study tended to be more limited and the level of graduates was lower. The quantitative measures of educational development, therefore, do not show how significant the contribution was to the country's development and to the ability of Saudi labour and expertise to replace that of expatriate labour and expertise (KSA-MOP 2006: 9–14).

Health provision grew some three-fold between 1984 and 1999, as measured by the number of hospital beds, but by less than twice when measured by the number of personnel working in this field. Social security payments at the end of the period were running at a level more than twice what it had been at the start. This perhaps reflected the increasing numbers of people in need of support, rather than an increase in governmental generosity. The government was, however, achieving considerable success in bringing into its social insurance framework Saudis who were not in public-sector employment. Only a small number subscribed to this scheme at the start of the period, but it covered some 1.5 million at the end (KSA-MOP 2006: 14–19).

4.5.3   Balance of payments

Movements in the balance of payments over this period were similar to those in the deficit/surplus position of Saudi budget, and for the same reason: oil prices and the level of oil production were the determining factors. Whereas the Saudi balance of payments had been characterised by massive surpluses at the beginning of the 1980s, the overall balance was heavily in deficit by the mid-1980s. Changes in the value of exports were dramatic, with goods exported (mainly oil) falling from a peak of US$112 billion in 1981 to a low of US$20 billion in 1986. Although the value of exports increased substantially during and after the 1990–1 crisis in the Gulf, the impact of this was offset by other factors. Small surpluses in the balance of payments were achieved in 1992 and 1994, and rather larger ones in 1996 and 1997, but there was no sustained or stable surplus at any stage during the 1985–2000 period (see Table 4.12).

Despite the large increase in oil revenues which resulted from the 1990–91 crisis in the Gulf, the overall impact of the crisis on Saudi Arabia's balance of payments was negative. Non-oil commodity exports were depressed over these years, but more significant was the large increase in 'payment for services' which came about. Imports also rose sharply. The increases in these two elements were caused by the need to cater for the requirements of the foreign military forces present in the Kingdom, to pay for the additional weaponry which was needed, and to meet much of the overall cost of the foreign involvement in the Gulf. The current account balance was in deficit for most of the period covered here, apart for the years 1996, 1997 and 1999. The deficit reached a peak of $27.6 billion in 1991.

Another crucial change affecting the current account at this time was the increase in workers' remittances. In 1986, as can be seen in Table 4.12, these stood at $4.8 billion. In 1994 they reached $18.1 billion. In the years which followed, through to the end of the period, they were rather lower, but still remained around $15 billion annually. Clearly the government's strategy of reducing dependence on foreign labour was not achieving the results which had been anticipated. The resulting drain on the country's foreign exchange holdings was considerable.

The balance of payments was, however, helped over this period by significant private capital movements into the Kingdom. In the late 1980s this seems to have stemmed from Saudi citizens moving resources back into the country to make up for losses in their domestic businesses caused by the economic recession. More substantial inward private capital movements took place in 1991 and 1992, and were clearly associated with the Gulf War. Saudi businessmen were using their external assets to take advantage of the investment opportunities opened up by the influx of foreigners into the country, the need for services and facilities supporting the military operations, and the reconstruction which was necessary once the war was over. Increased government expenditure, made possible by the higher oil revenues, was fuelling the business expansion. In the last three years of the period covered in this chapter, however, more private capital was moving out of the country than was entering it.

Another encouraging development reflected in the statistics was the growth of non-oil exports over this period. Starting at $1.5 billion at the beginning of the period, they had reached $6.6 billion by the end. In 1998, a year when the value of oil exports was low, the non-oil side

Table 4.12 Balance of payments, 1985–2000 (US$ billion)

	1985	1986	1987	1988	1989	1990	1991	1992	1993	1994	1995	1996	1997	1998	1999	2000
Current account																
Exports and incoming transfers																
Oil exports	25.8	18.0	20.4	20.1	24.0	40.0	43.5	46.4	38.5	38.0	43.4	54.1	53.2	32.5	44.7	70.7
Other commodity exports	1.5	2.1	2.8	4.2	4.3	4.3	4.1	3.8	3.8	4.5	6.5	6.5	7.4	6.3	5.8	6.6
Investment income	12.4	11.3	10.5	10.5	10.4	9.2	8.7	7.4	6.2	4.0	5.0	5.1	5.6	5.8	5.8	3.3
Service exports	3.6	2.7	2.6	2.4	2.6	3.2	3.1	3.6	3.4	3.5	3.6	2.9	4.4	4.8	5.5	5.0
Total	43.5	34.1	36.2	37.1	41.3	56.5	59.2	61.2	51.9	50.0	58.5	68.6	70.6	49.4	61.8	85.6
Imports and outgoing transfers																
Commodity imports	21.9	19.2	21.5	24.0	23.5	25.8	30.0	34.0	29.5	25.8	32.1	31.8	33.7	33.7	31.5	34.3
Payments for services	29.3	21.9	19.6	13.9	18.9	23.7	43.0	31.5	24.0	16.9	15.1	21.2	21.9	13.8	16.3	
Workers' remittances	5.2	4.8	4.9	6.5	8.5	11.2	13.8	13.4	15.7	18.1	16.6	15.5	15.0	15.0	14.0	15.0
Total	56.4	45.9	46.0	44.4	50.9	60.7	86.8	78.9	69.2	60.5	63.8	68.5	70.6	62.5	61.8	71.3
Current account balance	−12.9	−11.8	−9.8	−7.3	−9.6	−4.2	−27.6	−17.7	−17.3	−10.5	−5.3	0.7	0.3	−13.1	0.4	14.3
Capital movements																
Oil sector and government capital transactions (net)	0.4	0.9	−1.2	−0.3	−0.6	1.9	0.2	−0.8	1.4	0.4	−1.9	−1.1	3.0	4.3	−0.8	−1.9
Private capital movements (net)	3.9	4.2	8.8	5.2	8.0	2.6	26.4	13.8	9.4	8.5	4.1	11.5	1.1	−1.9	−9.5	−1.0
Commercial bank movements (net)	−0.8	−2.7	−1.4	−2.2	0.5	−2.4	0.6	4.8	−0.4	4.1	0.2	−2.5	3.8	2.8	0.7	1.0
Total	3.5	2.4	6.2	2.7	7.9	2.1	27.2	17.8	10.4	13.0	2.4	7.9	7.9	5.2	−9.6	−1.9
Balance of payments surplus/deficit	−9.4	−9.4	−3.6	−4.7	−1.7	−2.1	−0.4	0.9	−6.9	2.5	−2.9	8.6	8.2	−7.9	−9.2	12.4

Source: Saudi Arabian Monetary Agency (1970–2006) *Annual Reports*. Riyadh: SAMA.

made up 16.3 per cent of total exports. The increase in the exports of petrochemicals and light manufactured goods was approximately equal, while agricultural exports now figured for the first time in the total (IMF 1998b: 14). The latter was composed mainly of wheat grown on the new irrigated schemes.

4.6 The contribution and composition of the private sector

As shown earlier, government plans over this period gave emphasis to the growing role of the private sector. In view of the reduced level of oil revenues and the need to employ more Saudis, the private sector was to become more central to the process of economic development. In particular it was to be the key instrument in achieving greater economic diversification, which itself was crucial for creating more labour opportunities for the population. The Sixth Plan, reflecting on the development of policy since the Fourth Plan, described the line of policy which had developed since 1985 as follows:

> The Fourth Development Plan (1985–1990) saw a greater role for the private sector. In a change from previous plans, economic diversification was amongst key goals and objectives. This was to be carried out by the private sector. The government created an environment that was conducive for the private sector, encouraging it through financial measures and through encouraging joint ventures with foreign firms. The private sector was also seen to have grown in maturity and resilience due to its ability to stand up to the declining oil revenues and the subsequent fall in government expenditure.
>
> (KSA-MOP 1995: 43)

Journalistic writing at the time gave some emphasis to the shift which had been taking place. A report in *Business International* (1985: 181), for example, argued that a major change in the relationship between the private sector and the government was taking place, not only in Saudi Arabia but throughout the Gulf region:

> Businessmen have looked to their rulers for wealth and favours, in the form of contracts, land and concessions, and the government has been happy to enrich business as part of its general policy to spread its oil revenue in society.
>
> Now the Arabian relationship is changing to something more like the Western pattern, the government for the first time is starting to

make demands on the private sector, and the businessmen are starting to make counter-demands.

The business community's view of developments at this time was not so positive, as will be shown in Chapter 5. For many Saudi businessmen the years between 1982 and 1989, in particular, were dark years with large numbers of bankruptcies. As well as the cuts in expenditure, the government also implemented a variety of cost-cutting measures which damaged private businesses. Particularly harmful was the late payment for contracts fulfilled, which could cover months or even years. In addition to this, the government halved the advance payments to contractors (Wilson and Graham 1994: 182–3). Many contractors experienced severe cash flow problems as a result of this. The delayed payments reached billion-dollar levels in the later 1980s. Wilson and Graham (ibid.) noted that the Korean Embassy estimated that its contractors were owed at least US$4 billion in 1986; a similar amount was owed to French contractors. Saudi companies were often worst hit as they had no outside body through which to seek recompense.

Nonetheless, the private sector did grow in strength over the 1985–2000 period. There was a steady albeit slow increase in the private sector's contribution to Gross Domestic Product (at constant prices) between 1987 and 2000. This can be seen from Table 4.13. Although 1985 and 1986 had seen falling private-sector output, continuing a trend which had been present since 1983, the fall was relatively limited in comparison to that in overall GDP between 1983 and 1987 (see Tables 3.13 and 4.13). The private sector's share of total GDP was higher in 1985 than it was in 2000, but the 1985 figure covered a freak year: oil production was abnormally low due to Saudi Arabia's role as a swing producer (a policy which was abandoned in 1986). What is more significant is that the private sector retained a share of GDP between 38.5 per cent and 46.5 per cent of the total for the remainder of the period. This was substantially higher than the level prior to 1981 (when the swing producer role had first begun to reduce Saudi oil production).

It was largely in agriculture and manufacturing that the main growth in private-sector output occurred at this time, with very modest rates of growth in the services (see Table 4.14). The increase in agricultural output was mainly in the Fourth Plan period. Much of this stemmed from the sub-sidised agricultural loans for irrigated agriculture which had been readily available in the early 1980s. The high rate of growth tailed off when the loans became more difficult to acquire, and concern spread over the detrimental environmental effects caused by irrigated agriculture. Most of the growth in manufacturing, on the other hand, came at the end of the period.

Table 4.13 Private-sector share in the Gross Domestic Product, 1985–99 (constant prices at 1999, SR million)

	Private sector	% of total	Oil sector	% of total	Government sector	% of total	GDP
1985	208,543	51.5	92,525	22.9	103,617	25.6	404,685
1986	190,879	44.9	131,162	30.8	103,125	24.3	425,166
1987	190,081	46.5	116,103	28.4	102,568	25.1	408,752
1988	193,481	44.3	140,769	32.2	102,942	23.5	437,192
1989	196,827	44.8	136,966	31.2	105,445	24.0	439,238
1990	197,041	41.4	170,076	35.7	109,108	22.9	476,225
1991	200,866	38.6	207,911	39.9	112,222	21.5	520,999
1992	208,908	38.5	214,109	39.5	119,709	22.0	542,726
1993	212,868	39.2	207,491	38.2	122,568	22.6	542,927
1994	215,719	39.4	207,889	37.9	124,191	22.7	547,799
1995	217,644	39.6	206,972	37.6	125,346	22.8	549,963
1996	228,397	40.2	211,879	37.3	127,274	22.4	567,550
1997	238,705	41.0	208,724	35.8	135,008	23.2	582,438
1998	244,891	40.9	215,357	36.0	137,905	23.1	598,154
1999	255,200	43.0	198,988	33.5	139,767	23.5	593,955

Source: Kingdom of Saudi Arabia, Ministry of Planning (2000) *Achievements of the Development Plans.* Riyadh: Ministry of Planning.

Table 4.14 Percentage growth in private-sector fields of activity, 1985–2000, by plan-period (compounded, at current prices)

	Plan IV average	Plan V average	Plan VI average	Average of the 3 plans
Agriculture, forestry and fishing	11.67	1.43	1.22	4.77
Mining and quarrying	−0.68	0.65	2.06	0.68
Manufacturing	1.98	1.95	3.86	2.60
Electricity, gas and water	5.55	3.78	2.7	4.01
Construction	−2.95	3.22	1.34	0.54
Wholesale and retail trade	−1.03	0.85	1.1	0.31
Transport, storage and communication	−0.33	1.13	1.3	0.70
Finance, insurance, real estate	3.02	0.18	0.68	1.29
Community, social and personal services	2.38	0.73	1.64	1.58

Source: Kingdom of Saudi Arabia, Ministry of Planning (2000) *Achievements of the Development Plans.* Riyadh: Ministry of Planning.

Table 4.15 Gross fixed capital formation by sectors, 1985–2000 (current prices, SR million)

Year	Govt (non-oil)	% of total	Private sector (non-oil)	% of total	Oil sector	% of total	Total
1985	32,775	42.95	35,236	46.18	8,303	10.89	76,313
1986	25,184	38.07	32,033	48.43	8,927	13.50	66,144
1987	27,402	42.03	31,047	47.62	6,753	10.36	65,202
1988	24,029	42.22	31,642	55.59	1,247	2.19	56,918
1989	26,285	43.51	32,590	53.95	1,534	2.54	60,409
1990	42,491	56.80	28,078	37.54	4,234	5.66	74,803
1991	45,201	52.25	36,804	42.54	4,505	5.21	86,510
1992	32,289	34.36	54,686	58.19	7,000	7.45	93,975
1993	30,029	30.50	60,421	61.37	8,000	8.13	98,450
1994	23,969	28.46	52,084	61.85	8,154	9.68	84,207
1995	25,168	26.90	53,619	57.31	14,768	15.79	93,555
1996	12,914	12.56	81,398	79.14	8,536	8.30	102,848
1997	16,102	14.74	83,846	76.75	9,293	8.51	109,241
1998	12,437	11.01	89,056	78.84	11,466	10.15	112,959
1999	12,958	10.96	92,091	77.91	13,147	11.12	118,196
2000	16,353	13.26	92,953	75.37	14,018	11.37	123.324

Source: Saudi Arabian Monetary Agency (1986–2000) *Annual Surveys*. Riyadh: SAMA.

The private-sector construction industry underwent changes which reflected government spending: declining in the Fourth Plan period when spending was cut, growing strongly in the Fifth Plan period as a result of the 1990–1 Gulf crisis, and then expanding at a slower pace during the Sixth Plan period. The supply of electricity, gas and water by private-sector companies grew significantly. In the latter fields, however, the private sector did not occupy a role of any great significance at this stage.

The figures on private-sector investment over this period suggest a more positive trend than do the output figures. They provide evidence that the balance was shifting away from the public sector and towards the private sector (see Table 4.15). Although private-sector gross fixed capital formation in the late 1980s and in 1990–1 was mostly lower than at the beginning of the 1980s, it increased rapidly after 1992. By 2000 it was almost three times as high as it had been in 1986. As a proportion of total investment, moreover, it accounted for more than three-quarters of all gross fixed capital formation in the country between 1996 and 2000. Over the 1970–85 period it had on average accounted for only about one-third. The sharp rise after 1996 appears to have been encouraged by the government paying off some of its debts to the private sector which had accumulated over the previous decade (*NCB Economist* 1997: 2).

Table 4.16 Number of establishments by sector, 1985–2000

Year	Private	Government	Total
1985	12,020	1,367	13,387
1986	12,174	1,337	13,511
1987	11,926	1,353	13,279
1988	11,970	1,313	13,283
1989	12,046	1,325	13,371
1990	12,006	1,326	13,332
1991	12,131	1,290	13,421
1992	14,269	1,307	15,576
1993	15,487	1,329	16,816
1994	16,508	1,340	17,848
1995	17,234	1,174	18,408
1996	17,972	1,181	19,153
1997	18,623	1,185	19,808
1998	22,850	1,176	24,026
1999	25,506	1,152	26,658
2000	28,396	1,173	29,569

Source: Kingdom of Saudi Arabia, General Organisation for Social Insurance (1985–2000) *Annual Statistical Reports*. Riyadh: GOSI.

The growth in the number of private-sector establishments over this period also suggested that the private sector was preparing for an expanded role in the economy (see Table 4.16). The pattern, indeed, was similar to that of gross fixed capital formation. There was little or no increase in the number between 1985 and 1991, and initially some decline in number as some businesses were going bankrupt as a result of the fall in government spending. Thereafter the number increased steadily, reaching a high point in the final three years of this period. It is significant that on this occasion the number of establishments continued to increase strongly through 1998, even though oil revenues had fallen sharply and government expenditure was being cut back. In 2000 there were 28,396 private establishments in the country, whereas in 1985 there had been only 12,020.

4.7   The social dynamics of the private sector

The developments which will be covered here form a continuum with those which had developed over the 1970–85 period. While the rate of expansion of the private sector was slower after 1985 than before, the social trends which had emerged in the earlier period were further developed in the later one. Private-sector investment, as mentioned earlier, was growing again strongly after 1990. The lower levels of the late 1980s, therefore, can be seen as more of a hiatus than a change of direction. The social dynamics of the private sector continued to be characterised by some lessening of the role of the long-established (largely Hijaz-based) merchant families, and an increasing role played by businesses close to the centre of government and administration in Riyadh: Najdi-run companies established since the beginning of the oil boom, enterprises involving royal family members, and some undertakings run by resourceful individuals (often of foreign origin) who enjoyed close relations with key members of the royal family.

Chaudhry sees the developments at this time as the displacement of one business elite by another: the new Najdi businessmen rising to pre-dominance while the old Hijaz-based merchant elite declined. This, she contends, had a critical impact on government policies, given that the new business elements had close links with Najdi administrators in the ministries. She sees these personal links as ensuring that reforms aimed at creating a more open and competitive market were not adopted. There is some truth in this, but it is also misleading. It exaggerates the decline of the Hijaz-based merchant families, and also leaves out of account some signi-ficant business undertakings which were neither Hijazi nor Najdi. The old Hijazi-based businesses retained an important stake in the economy. On the other hand, Chaudhry's approach underestimates the extent to which all aspects of business were characterised by common character-istics: heavily dependent on the government for the contracts, licences and commercial protection which they needed, and yet often frustrated by the bureaucratic hurdles placed before them and the predatory behaviour of some of those in positions of power or influence. This is shown in the analysis of business attitudes given in Chapter 5.

Three sets of data throw some light on the composition of the busi-ness elite in the 1990s. The first looks at the wholesale trading houses which existed at that time, the companies which they owned, and the brands and products which they traded. Chart 4.1, which is taken from information gathered in the early-1990s, presents this data (Azzam 1993: 158–61). The identification of the companies according to their regional origin has been added by the author of this book. Wholesale trading was the field of activities where the old Hijazi merchant establishment had developed its wealth, so it is not surprising that they retained consider-able strength here. Yet the continuance of this commercial predominance is worth noting. The wholesale commercial sector generated consider-able wealth, and the Hijazi trading houses continued to benefit from this. A number of the trading houses were also involved in banking and man-ufacturing, but the focus here is exclusively on their wholesale trading activities.

Chart 4.1 Leading wholesale trading houses in Saudi Arabia, early 1990s

Name of family	*Major companies, establishments, affiliates and subsidiaries*	*Selected agencies and activities*
Alireza (Hijaz)	Haji Husein Alireza and Co. Ltd; Kitchen World; Transcontinental Corporation; Rezatrade Marketing and Development; Husein Jamil and Rezatrade; NEC Saudi Arabia Ltd; Wexico Systems and Services; Xenel Industries Ltd; Dakhakhni Bookshops; Saudi Electronics and Trading Co.; Rezayat Trading Co.; ICI Trading and Rezatrade.	Mazda; Goodyear; Gerber; Lister; Arby's ICIT Pools; NEC; Westinghouse; Havana Cigars; Ford; Mercury; Kia; Rolm; Fujitsu. Activities cover the entire range of commercial sectors in the Kingdom.
Binzagr (Hijaz)	Binzagr Co.; Wahib S. Binzagr & Brothers; Arabian Stores Co.; International Agencies Ltd; Binzagr International Trading Co.	Avon Products Inc.; Advanced Linen Services; Unilever Exports; British American Tobacco; Brown and Williamson International Tobacco; Imperial Tobacco; Lipton Exports, HJ Heinz; Kelloggs; UB (Biscuits) Uncle Ben's; Royal Foods; Hershey International, Dr Pepper Co.; Wilkinson Sword; Dunlop; General Tire.
Buqshan (Hijaz)	Abdullah Said Buqshan & Bros; Buqshan Trading Co.; Saudi Bazaar; Buqshan Pharmacy; Ahmad Sulaiman Buqshan and Co.; Ali Abdullah Buqshan Showroom; Salim Ahmad Buqshan.	Perfumes: Christian Dior, Georgio, Clarins, Muko, Kent; also clothing; jewellery; automobiles and spare parts; books; furniture; carpets; processed foods; shoes; household appliances; and electrical goods.
Algosaibi (Eastern Province)	Abdulrehman Algosaibi General Trading Bureau; Ahmad Hamad; Algosaibi & Bros; Algosaibi Grandmet Services Ltd; Algosaibi Hotels; Algosaibi Trading & Contracting Co.; Khalifa A. Algosaibi Group of Companies.	Mitsui; White Westinghouse International Co.; Sumitomo; Fiat; RC Cola; and a range of other from the US, UK, Germany, France, Italy, Belgium, Switzerland, Austria, Denmark, Sweden, Spain, Pakistan, Jordan and Japan.
Jamjoom (Hijaz)	Jamjoom Group of Industries; Jamjoom Vehicles and Equipment; Chemtech Industries; Jamjoom General Agencies; Dar al-Shorouq Publications, Distributing and Printing; Yahya Jamjoom Establishment; Delicatessen Hanaa, Al Madina; Modern Commercial Establishment; Modern Vehicle and Equipment; Saudi Marketing Establishment; Radwa Trading Co.; Al-Sharafiah Hotel, Trading and Construction World Jamjoom Corporation for Commerce and Industry; Jamjoon Foremost Ltd.	Widely diversified international range that has included Pfizer; Ceiba-Geigy; Peugeot; Hino trucks; Kleber Tyres; Continental Pharma; Sans Souci; and Allercan.

Continued

Chart 4.1 (continued)

Name of family	Major companies, establishments, affiliates and subsidiaries	Selected agencies and activities
Juffali (Najd, although based in Hijaz)	The Juffali Group of Companies; National Electric & Products Co.; Saudi Business Machines; EA Juffali & Bros.	Daimler-Benz; IBM; Kelvinator; Michelin; Siemens, Sulzer, York; Bosch.
Kaki (Hijaz)	Ahmad and Mohammed Saleh Kaki Group of Companies; Al Kaki Co.; General Establishment for Trade and Contracts; Jeddah Kaki Hotel; National Printing Press.	Concentrating on: industry; contracting; banking; real estate; and technical service; but buys in bulk for projects. Also runs large hotel and restaurant operations, including management services.
Kanoo (Eastern Province)	Yusuf B. Ahmad Kanoo; cable and Wireless Saudi Arabia.	Esso; Exxon; BASF. It has many branches and affiliates throughout the Gulf region.
Olayan (Najd)	Arabian Automotive Co.; General Trading Company; Olayan Saudi Holding Company; Olayan Saudi General Transportation Co.	Jaguar; Rover; Land Rover; General Foods; Kimberly-Clark; Rowntree Mackintosh; Chesbrough Ponds; Unigate; Tulip; Jacob Suchard; Tuborg; Lowenbrau; Borden; Waitaki; Campbells; Pillsbury; Overseas Trading (Lyons Tea); Beechnut; National Cheese; National Cheese; Société des Eaux Minérales (Sohat); Colgate Palmolive; Holland Canned Milk, Imperial Tobacco.
Pharaon (Riyadh-based, Syrian origin)	Saudi Research and Development Corporation; Redec Intertrade Arinco; Saudi Food Suppliers & Supermarkets; Saudi Computer Services Co.; Intermec; Arabian Homes.	Texas Instruments; Memorex; plus interests in BSN Gervais Danone; Industrie Buitoni Perugina; Montedison; Rosenthal Studio Line.
Al Quraishi (Hijaz)	Ali Zaid Al Quraishi & Bros; Saleh Zaid Al Quraishi Establishment for Trading and Contracting; Al Quraishi Distribution Services; Al Quraishi Leisure Services; Al Quraishi Furniture; Al Sabah Trading.	Samsonite; Canon; Sheaffer; AMF Bowling; Westinghouse; Reckitt & Colman; Tobacco Exporters International; Citizen; Swatch; Fabre-Leuba; Cussons; Fisher-Price; Mattel; Lego.
Shaker (Palestinian)	Ibrahim Shaker Co. Ltd; Shaker Trading Co.	General Electric; Electrolux.
Sharbatly (Hijaz)	Saudi Arabian Marketing Corporation; Sharbatly Establishment for Trade and Development.	Importers and distributors of: foodstuffs; furniture; leisure and sporting goods; educational materials; paints and toys.

Chart 4.1 (Continued)

Name of family	Major companies, establishments, affiliates and subsidiaries	Selected agencies and activities
Shobokshi (Hijaz)	Ali and Fahd Shobokshi Group; Al Arousa Furniture Factory, Orient International Agencies; Oriental Company for Trading & Marketing; Shobest Automotive Trading; Shobak Catering Group; Tihama Advertising; Shobokshi Commercial Enterprises; Public Relations and Marketing; General Agencies Corp.; Alphatrans.	Thorn Lighting; Klein Philips BV; MAN; Magirus. The family founded the Arabic daily, *Okaz*, and the English-language *Saudi Gazette*.
Sudairi (Najd)	Arabian Food Supplies.	Mars; Hero; Wellcome International; First Brands; Wrigleys; Green Giant; Ross; Pedigree Petfoods; Tate & Lyle.
Tamimi (Najd)	Tamimi & Fouad; Tamimi & Fouad Foods Co. Ltd.	Owns supermarkets in Riyadh, Dammam and Al Khobar. Originally set up with Safeway Stores of the US but now independently run. Imports, stores and distributes foodstuffs, cosmetics, toiletries and household goods.
Zahid (Hijaz)	Zahid Motors & Importers Co. Ltd; Zahid Tractors & Heavy Machinery Co. Ltd; Zahid Enterprises Co. Ltd.	Renault; Volvo; Caterpillar; Mannesman Demag; Pirelli Tyres. Has also represented General Motors, Pignon and GMODC (Isuzu). Imports and sells clothing, dairy foods, paints and car care products.

Source: Azzam, Henry (1993) *Saudi Arabia: Economic Trends, Business Environment and Investment Opportunities.* London: Euromoney Books.

The chart indicates that nine of the 17 major wholesale trading houses were owned by Hijazi families (and had in each case developed in the Hijaz). Of the remainder, three were owned by families from the Eastern Province, three by Najdi families (one of which based most of their trading activities in the Hijaz) and two by families with a recent Syrian or Palestinian origin. One of the latter was based mainly in the Hijaz, and the other mainly in Najd. In wholesale trading, therefore, Najdi businesses had not taken over a significant position, let alone predominance.

A rather different picture of where wealth lay in the private sector, however, comes from a second set of data. This covers the background and ownership of the 100 top companies in Saudi Arabia in the late 1990s. Listings of the top 100 companies can be found on the website of the *Arab News* (www.arabnews.com), and the analysis which follows is based on the data for 1996. The companies concerned were involved in a wide range of business: banking, industry, agribusiness, services, trading and 'diversified activities'. Not all can be identified with a specific part of the country or a particular social group. In some cases the major shareholding of the listed companies comprised investors from different regional and social backgrounds. Regional/social identification, therefore, was not fundamental to all private-sector activity. Some listed companies, moreover, were wholly or majority-owned by the state, so that their regional/social identification was not relevant. Among the latter was SABIC, by far the largest company.

Nonetheless, there are some 73 companies in the listing where the predominant shareholding can be identified with a particular family/ region/grouping. In the case of a company operating as a partnership between a foreign company and one or more Saudi investors, only the latter shareholding has been taken into account. Of the 73 companies, the largest single contingent comprised those with strong Najdi connections, totalling 32. The distribution of the remainder was: Hijaz 14, Eastern Province 9, royal family 8, Saudis with Syrian/Palestinian backgrounds 7, Asir 3. These figures, however, underestimate the Najdi connections, and also the extent to which Riyadh had displaced Jiddah as the business capital of the country. Most of the companies where royal family members held majority shareholding were based in Riyadh, as also was the preponderance of those owned by Saudis of Syrian and Palestinian origin. The latter have been treated as a category by themselves here, both because the owners were relatively recent incomers (post-1948), and because they constitute a significant cluster. Many of the Hijazi companies, moreover, had an administrative presence in Riyadh as well as in Jiddah.

The role of the royal family in business activity is understated by these figures. Much of the investment by members of the royal family was through minority shareholdings and therefore does not figure in the listings. The extent and composition of royal family investment in the private sector is well documented in a work by Sharaf Sabri (2001). This constitutes the third set of data. On the basis of material which covered the years up to the late 1990s, Sabri shows that only about 20 per cent of the undertakings in which royal family members invested were sole proprietorships. The rest were limited liability companies (effectively partnerships, where the royal family member usually held a minority but nonetheless significant shareholding) and joint-stock companies. The distribution of royal family investment across the different forms of ownership can be seen from

Chart 4.2. The significance of royal family business activity, therefore, was substantially greater than that revealed in the analysis of the top 100 companies. The actual value of the stake which members of the royal family had in the private sector, furthermore, was higher than the chart's investment figures suggest. The latter represent the value of the stake at the time of investment rather than actual value at the end of the 1990s.

Another important aspect of the royal family's involvement in the private sector which emerges from the chart is the distribution of activity and investment across different branches of the family. Only a relatively small proportion of royal family investment had come from outside the descendants of King Abd al-Aziz. At the end of the 1990s the companies in which the latter were involved accounted for about two-thirds of the total, and perhaps 98 per cent of the funds invested. They had clearly been able to draw the greatest benefit from their role, privileges and rights within the Kingdom. Those closest in blood to the King, not surprisingly, enjoyed the best access to those in authority and used this to facilitate their business activity. They also gained substantially from grants of land (or land sales at reduced prices), which in due course was sold or resold so as to obtain funds for investment. It is questionable, on the other hand, whether the non-core elements held a significant business advantage over other prominent families within the Kingdom. The one major exception to the latter consisted of some of the descendants of Prince Saud al-Kabir bin Faisal Al Saud, who enjoyed privileges stemming from the ruling group's desire to conciliate a branch whose head had posed as a rival to King Abd al-Aziz in the past.

Despite the privileged channels through which funds were obtained, it should not be assumed that royal family investment was inherently unproductive. On the contrary, much of it was put into the manufacturing, finance and service-provision sectors of the economy, and helped to broaden the economy's productive base. The social dimensions of the development, however, were to deepen greatly the inequalities and social divisions present in the Kingdom.

Overall, then, a significant change in the composition and regional location of the leading business sector had taken place since the beginning of the oil boom. The hub of big business activity had moved to Riyadh, and many of the successful new businesses came from outside the traditional merchant families. This did not mean, however, that the traditional merchant elite was no longer economically significant. They retained a substantial stake in the economy. The social composition of the private sector had been broadened. Most elements, from whatever background, maintained close links with those with governmental authority or influence. As will be shown in Chapter 5, however, they were also developing an

Chart 4.2 The royal family's business interests, late 1990s

Branch	Members involved in commerce			Number of business concerns				Investment(SR)
	Prince	Princess	Total	Joint stock	Sole prop.	Limited liability	Total	
King Abd al-Aziz descendants	217	107	324	49	132	474	655	41,390,341,250
Brothers of King A/A descendants	77	32	109	22	37	161	220	740,116,750
Saud al-Kabir descendants	14	7	21	8	14	29	51	190,258,150
Muhammad, brother of Saud al-Kabir, descendants	29	1	30	10	11	46	67	35,227,500
Al-Farhan branch	23	15	38	7	12	31	50	102,658,000
Al-Turki branch	23	5	28	18	7	28	53	124,152,800
Al-Thunayan branch	5	1	6	1	2	4	7	1,657,500
Al-Jiluwi branch	17	15	32	-	3	11	14	10,412,500
Al-Abdullah branch	7	3	10	3	1	9	13	13,865,000
Al-Faisal branch	1	1	2	4	1	12	17	20,821,860
Total	413	187	600	59	220	765	1044	42,629,511,050

Source: Sabri, Sharaf (2001) The House of Saud in Commerce. New Delhi: I.S. Publications, p. 250.

intra-business ethos which ran counter to governmental interference or bureaucratic obstruction.

4.8 The changing pattern of employment

The development plans over this period gave strong emphasis throughout to the need to replace expatriate labour with Saudi labour. This was a significant change from the earlier plans. Each plan suggested that the size of the expatriate workforce would be reduced over the period of the plan. The major target here was the private sector, the major employer of expatriate labour. Most of the jobs in the public sector were already occupied by Saudis. The Fourth Plan stated boldly that 'for the first time since the First Plan...not only the share but also the absolute number of non-Saudi workers in the Kingdom will decline', noting that this was 'one of the most important targets of the plan' (KSA-MOP 1985a: 50). The private sector was expected to replace 374,000 expatriates by an equivalent number of Saudis. The Sixth Plan projected that 319,500 jobs in the government and the private sector would be Saudiised during the plan, leading to a fall in the number of non-Saudi workers by 1.5 per cent per annum. The expectation was still that the major change would come from the private sector, where 95 per cent of net growth in aggregate employment was expected to occur (KSA-MOP 1995: 173).

The planners were clearly aware, by the time of the Sixth Plan, that the process of Saudisation would not be easy. The plan noted constraints for the private sector in achieving Saudisation (KSA-MOP 1995: 171). First, it stated, Saudis had shown a preference for employment in the government sector, which paid higher wages at middle-level positions and provided greater job security, better working conditions (in terms of working hours), more favourable employment regulations and brighter promotion prospects. Second, the private sector had preferred to recruit foreign workers, whose qualifications, training, wages and flexibility matched their requirements better. Finally, the training costs of upgrading new Saudi graduates were perceived as high.

Tables 4.17 and 4.18 show that the government's objectives were indeed not being achieved, at least as far as Saudisation was concerned. Table 4.17 indicates that the size of the workforce was indeed growing quickly over this period, despite the economy's relatively slow rate of economic growth. This brought new job opportunities for Saudis: the civilian Saudi workforce expanded by about one million between 1984/5 and 1999. The growth of the non-Saudi workforce, however, was even more substantial (see Table 4.18). It increased by almost two million. There was no sign of the 'reduction in absolute numbers' of the non-Saudi workforce which the Fourth Plan had envisaged. Overall the proportion of the workforce made

Table 4.17 Civilian employment by economic activities, 1984/5, 1989, 1994 and 1999

	1984/5[a]		1989		1994		1999	
	000's	%	000's	%	000's	%	000's	%
Producing sectors except oil and gas								
Agriculture	538.0	10.3	393.2	6.5	500.9	7.7	567.1	7.8
Manufacturing industries	424.1	8.1	494.7	8.2	530.9	8.2	638.5	8.8
Other producing sectors	1,586.4	30.2	986.9	16.3	1075.2	16.6	1,236.5	17.1
Service sectors								
Private services	2,168.3	41.3	3,414.8	56.4	3429.5	52.8	3,703.2	51.2
Government services	469.1	9.0	711.2	11.8	860.3	13.3	1,001.2	13.8
Oil and gas	58.7	1.1	48.6	0.8	93.1	1.4	83.8	1.2
Total	5244.6	100.0	6,049.4	100.0	6,489.9	100.0	7,230.3	100.0

[a] The figure for 1984/5 was an initial estimate which can be found in the Fourth Development Plan, published in 1985. See note in Table 3.17. The figure given for employment in the Other producing sectors are clearly unrealistic. They bear little relationship to the trends of employment before or after that period.
Sources: Khayat, Dina (2005) 'Female Employment in Saudi Arabia' unpublished PhD thesis, University of Exeter, pp.30, 44. All figures from Kingdom of Saudi Arabia, Ministry of Planning (1984–99) *Development Plans*. Riyadh: Ministry of Planning.

Table 4.18 Civilian employment by nationality, Saudi/non-Saudi, 1984/5, 1989, 1994 and 1999

	1984/5		1989		1994		1999	
	000's	%	000's	%	000's	%	000's	%
Saudi	1,786.0	40.2	1,981.5	32.8	2,544.8	39.2	2,712.0	37.5
Non-Saudi	2,660.0	59.8	4,067.9	67.2	3,945.1	60.8	4,518.3	62.5
Total	4,446.0	100.0	6,049.4	100.0	6,489.9	100.0	7,230.3	100.0

Sources: Khayat, Dina (2005) 'Female Employment in Saudi Arabia' unpublished PhD thesis, University of Exeter, pp. 30, 44. All figures from Kingdom of Saudi Arabia, Ministry of Planning (1975–90) *Development Plans*. Riyadh: Ministry of Planning.

up by Saudis fell over these years, starting at 40.2 per cent of the total and ending at 37.5 per cent. This was not what the government had planned. A significant part of the new Saudi employment, moreover, appears to have been in the public sector. The share of 'government services' (employment in government institutions) in total civilian employment rose from 9.0 per cent in 1984/5 to 13.8 per cent in 1999.

In the later part of the 1990s the government introduced measures to enforce Saudisation on the private sector. The policy of leaving this to follow naturally from the flow of trained Saudi graduates into the market place was abandoned. Among the new measures were the refusal of government contracts to companies which were failing to move towards Saudisation, and the linking of government-subsidised loans to the rate of Saudi employment within the recipient companies (KSA-MOP 1995: 109). Manpower recruitment offices were banned from hiring foreign workers if they failed to adhere to the rules and regulations regarding Saudisation, and their applications for the transfer and renewal of labour licences were limited to the number of the required Saudis in the company concerned. At this stage, however, the new measures were not seriously enforced. As they went against the interests of private-sector employers, moreover, the latter had a strong inclination to evade the regulatory procedures. Some areas where there had been success in Saudisation were given publicity: ARAMCO and SABIC were cited as having taken an exemplary path, both having achieved over 70 per cent of Saudisation by 1995. It was also stressed that 94 per cent of the 738 employees in the Ministry of Petroleum and Minerals Resources were Saudi at that time (KSA-MOP 1995: 197). These areas of success, however, were ones where the government was able to determine employment practices by diktat.

In the later 1990s there was a growing consciousness within Saudi society that unemployment constituted a growing problem which could pose a threat to social stability. Some Saudi estimates have indicated that on the basis of existing trends, there would be 5–9 million job seekers entering the labour market between the years 2000 and 2005, creating the need to provide at least 600,000 jobs annually. They also forecast that in the early years after 2000 the unemployment rate would reach 13.2 per cent. These figures, moreover, were conservative compared to those suggested by Ghazi Obeid Madani. He suggested in 1999 that Saudi Arabia's unemployment rate had more than doubled since 1993, with the jobless accounting for about 27 per cent of the working-age population, whereas it had been 12 per cent in 1993 (Reuters, 11.4.99). There was little doubt that the rate of unemployment in the late 1990s had increased significantly, especially among high school and university graduates, although no accurate statistics on this were available.

4.9 Conclusion

Oil revenues and government spending remained central to the Saudi economy's performance over this period, despite the government's efforts to diversify the economy. The country remained a rentier state, albeit with a more limited resource base than before.

The oil rentier basis accounted for the government's ability to maintain economic policy and practices without substantive change. While the linkages between government personnel and individual businessmen were a prominent characteristic of the political economy, the underlying reality was that the ruling establishment had no need or inclination to undertake radical reform. Even with the fall in oil revenues there were still sufficient funds to keep the existing bureaucratically restrictive economic framework in place. A simple lifting of restrictions, moreover, would not have solved the social dilemmas which were now looming. These centred on growing social inequality, inadequate employment prospects for the new generation, and a continuing rise in the non-Saudi workforce. Nor would it have necessarily created the conditions for Saudi Arabia to achieve a globally competitive economic role. The state needed to be taking on a new and different role, rather than simply abandoning any attempt to direct the development process. There was no indication at this stage that it had the ability or the will to play such a role.

Nonetheless, the private sector continued to grow over this period and parts of the business elite were now beginning to assert the collective interests of the business community. This will be examined further in the next chapter.

5 Attitudes of the business elite, 1970–2000

5.1 Introduction: the role of the private sector as seen by the business elite

This chapter examines the perceptions of the business elite in the late 1990s. The focus is on how leading businessmen saw the private sector's role in the economy and the state, in terms both of the present reality and the future potential. The objective is to assess the extent to which the private sector was capable of taking the part played by private sectors in developmental states. The necessary elements here, as shown in Chapter 1, are:

- a relationship with the government which is enabling and supportive rather than restrictive and subject to predatory behaviour;
- a corporate structure which is inherently effective and a trading framework which enables it to compete globally; and
- a domestic social, legal and economic environment which facilitates its activities.

The main part of the chapter is divided into three parts, each based on one of these elements. While the business elite's perceptions of its own strengths and weaknesses are not necessarily accurate, their perceptions are bound to be relevant. A private sector which is convinced of its inability to act effectively or competitively will not play a strong role in promoting the development of the national economy.

The material used in the chapter comes from a survey conducted by Monica Malik in 1999 (Malik 1999).[1] Twenty-four leading businessmen were interviewed. Although all the interviews were conducted in Jiddah, the businessmen came from a range of different regional backgrounds and their companies covered most sectors of economic activity: banking, construction, petrochemicals, non-hydrocarbon manufacturing and shipping.

Agriculture, however, was not included. The companies were of many different types: agencies, family-owned businesses, joint-stock companies, and companies linked to the royal family. The interviewees were generally open in discussing their views, even on sensitive issues relating to governmental policies and the royal family. In a small number of cases, however, there was some reluctance to be seen as overtly critical of government.

The analysis given here focuses on general trends of opinion. Rather than recounting the views of individual businessmen or the precise way in which opinion was divided, then, the emphasis is on the way businessmen in general conceived their role and the problems confronting their businesses. Mention will be made of minority views when these are relevant.

There was one other significant survey of business opinion conducted by an academic researcher during the 1990s, besides that by Malik. This was by Mary Okruhlik (Okruhlik 1992). The latter covered some 118 interviewees, spread across the major regions of the country. Both surveys reach broadly similar conclusions. Whereas the survey by Okruhlik was conducted in the early 1990s, that by Malik has the advantage of coming at the end of that decade, in March – November 1998. The businessmen surveyed by Malik, therefore, were able to take into account developments during the decade. Malik's survey, moreover, focused specifically on the most prominent elements in the business community. Where there are significant differences between the surveys, they will be mentioned in the text.

5.2   Perceptions of the business elite: the relationship with government

This section looks at the business elite's views on how governmental activity and policy impinge on the private sector. In the theoretical literature this element constitutes the key factor shaping the state/private sector relationship, determining whether that relationship can enable a developmental state to emerge. Its various dimensions are covered in the sub-sections which follow. The strong relationship between the state and the private sector is vital to the developmental state model. The two sides need to have a high level of communication and a good working relationship. This is not to say, however, that in all cases where there is a good relationship between the two parties a developmental state exists. It is important to look into the dynamics of the relationship. Furthermore, the state has to provide the appropriate framework and infrastructure to promote the private sector in state-sponsored capitalist development. This will be done here by examining businessmen's views on:

- the commitment of the government to the growth and expansion of the sector;
- the effectiveness and utility of the channels of communication between government bodies and the private sector;
- the extent to which the bureaucracy supported or hindered private-sector activities; and
- the degree to which 'crony capitalism' (based on predatory behaviour by personnel in governmental or administrative positions) affected the activities of the private sector.

5.2.1   *The commitment of the government to the growth and expansion of the private sector*

Most of those surveyed believed that the government now intended for the private sector to play a leading role in the economy. There was a feeling that the sector could have played a larger role earlier, and that this would have aided development, but the government had at that stage not taken the possible contribution of the private sector seriously. It was only when the oil prices started falling, and the government was faced by budgetary and financial problems, that the government started promoting the private sector. The government had taken on burdens of expenditure, in subsidies and social and educational services, which could not be sustained from public resources. The strategy, then, was seen as stemming from financial problems and not from faith in the ability of the private sector. While the transition from the early emphasis on large government-funded project to an increasing reliance on the private sector was seen as a natural evolution of economic policy, this was not what was genuinely shaping government policy. Some interviewees believed that if oil prices rose again to the level of the early 1980s, the government's enthusiasm for the private sector would disappear.

This attitude is in fact supported from some of the statements of government policy. The Fifth Development Plan, for example, combines mention of the demonstrated ability of the private sector with the prospect that the sector could take over some of the burdens of service provision from the government (KSA-MOP 1990: 40):

> ... the private sector has demonstrated its willingness and capacity to take on a wider range of economic activities and development responsibilities that are compatible with commercial principles. In the

Fifth Plan period, therefore, the private sector will be able to take
over, on a commercial basis, many of the services provided by the
government.

Government policy on privatisation was regarded with some scepti-
cism by most of those surveyed. For them, there was general agreement
that a move towards privatisation was both justified and necessary. The
state-owned enterprises (SOEs) would, they said, be more effective and
efficient under private ownership. Most believed, however, that it was not
likely to happen in the near future. The government was seen as committed to retaining most of the SOEs. The grounds of the government's
commitment were that the SOEs constituted important assets for the state,
necessary both for raising money and for controlling the economy. Owing
to the lack of a coherent tax system, the state was critically dependent
on them for income. The undertakings in which private investors would
be most interested in buying a stake were the successful and profitable
operations like SABIC, yet the government needed those most as a source
of finance.

The social role of the SOEs was also seen as a reason why the government would be reluctant to privatise them. Many of them were providing
goods and services to the population at subsidised prices. If they were to
be privatised, such practices would have to be abandoned, with damaging
effects on the poorer parts of the population. Such an outcome would not
be acceptable politically. The government would therefore have to devise
a whole new structure of social welfare provision before privatisation could
move ahead. The SOEs had, moreover, provided an important source of
employment for Saudis. The favourable and protected conditions under
which they operated, and their subjection to political and administrative
pressures to absorb unemployed graduates, had led them to being severely
overstaffed. This social role could also not be continued in a commercially run enterprise. There was also the danger of increasing inequalities
through further enhancing of wealth of the richest elements in society.
One interviewee suggested that, unless there was an effective stock market, the SOEs would be bought by the 20 or 30 leading business families
in the country.

The private sector would require significant changes before businesses could contemplate investment in privatised SOEs. The latter would
need to be reorganised and restructured (with some being broken up) to
make them economically viable, decisions on what would happen to their
debts would have to be taken, ownership rights to the land on which SOE
undertakings operated would have to be clarified, the regulations governing the activities of the privatised companies would have to be determined,

and the obligations of some of the companies under international treaties would have to be clarified (especially in the posts and telecommunications sector). Among the SOEs regarded as most problematic was Saudi Arabian Airlines (SAUDIA). The latter was seen as critically dependent on subsidies and on its position of privileged monopoly, without which it would not be profitable. Members of the royal family had, moreover, been able to use the airline for their own purposes, often without payment.

At the time when the survey was conducted, some moves were of course already being taken towards developing the strategies and policies advocated by the business elite. The slow pace of these developments, however, appears to have convinced the interviewees that nothing substantial was likely to be forthcoming in the near future. There was, moreover, an expectation that the form of privatisation envisaged might not be productive. It was unclear, for example, whether the private sector would be free to manage the privatised companies independently. The object of privatisation, interviewees stressed, should not be to raise money for the government but to create companies which could be run on a proper commercial basis. One interviewee gave the instance of governmental discussions about the privatisation of the postal services, where an assurance had been given that none of the current staff would lose their jobs. An article in the *Arab News* (4.12.98) at about this time indicated that jobs would also not be lost in the electricity sector:

> The Industry and Electricity Minister Dr Hashim Abdullah Yamani yesterday dispelled anxiety of the future of the existing staff of the merged electric companies by stressing that the new company will be needing the experience and the expertise of the existing staff.

Other interviewees suggested that the management of the companies was likely to remain bound by government managerial practices as it was being proposed that the government should retain a majority of the shareholding in the privatised companies. The government shareholding was justified on the government side by the contention that the financial market in Saudi Arabia was not big enough to absorb the full equity (*Financial Times*, 8.5.98).

5.2.2 The effectiveness and utility of the channels of communication between government bodies and the private sector

Most of those, surveyed indicated that many and varied channels of communication existed between the private sector and the government.

There was recognition, however, that it was largely the big companies, and the key individuals within them, who were able to use the most critical channels. Smaller companies were seen as having relatively little contact with government bodies or personnel.

Three principal channels of communication were mentioned. First, meetings with the King and senior princes. Top business figures were able to meet with members of the royal family, from the King down. In particular, the door of the then Crown Prince, Abdallah, was seen as being open to the private sector. Such contact was seen as an effective way in which business interests could be promoted. One interviewee recalled that when the plan to impose taxes on expatriates was introduced, senior businessmen took their concerns to the King and the plan was cancelled. More often, however, meetings at that level were used to promote specific interests rather than those of the wider business community.

Second, meetings with government ministers and top officials. There was a feeling that access to ministers, in particular, had become more useful. Ministers now listened to the representations made to them rather than simply dictating government policy. This is consistent with pronounced government policy, publicly promoted since the late 1980s. Ministers had been under instruction to interact effectively with the business sector, bringing it proactively into consultation on policy rather than waiting for businessmen to approach the government. Interviewees mentioned having been part of discussions on Saudi Arabia joining the WTO and participating in trade delegations visiting foreign countries. Nonetheless, there was also a feeling that the contacts did not necessarily lead anywhere. One of the interviewees maintained that 'the government is still not that responsive to the feelings and the needs of the private sector … it feels that the private sector is only interested in its own personal gain – and that it only pursues profit'. Such governmental attitudes do not appear to have changed much since the beginning of the decade, when Soufi and Mayer referred to ministers 'fumbling in their new role of seeking out the business sector rather than waiting for businessmen to come to them' (Soufi and Mayer 1991: 121).

Third, the chambers of commerce. While most saw these as useful, and appreciated the extent to which they served as focal points for the business community, the overall feeling was that they did not necessarily constitute the best channel to influence governmental opinions or actions. That could be done better by direct contacts, at least for those businesses which enjoyed a reasonable level of access to decision-makers. The work of Okruhlik, undertaken at the beginning of the decade, suggested that a new generation of businessmen were taking over leadership in the chambers, and that 'there has been re-assertion of the identity of the private sector ... the business community has articulated a new agenda that includes increased privatisation, the integration of small and medium size businesses, and an organisational framework for the business environment' (Okruhlik 1992: 321). This is an accurate reflection of what was happening in the chambers of commerce at that time, and through the 1990s, but there is little evidence that they were able to operate as an effective partner of government in constructing economic policy.

5.2.3 *Bureaucratic support and hindrances*

'Bureaucratic support', as used here, covers not only the efficiency of the bureaucratic machine but also the extent to which it implements regulations and practices which are helpful to the private sector. Overall, the attempt here is to assess the extent to which, and the manner in which, the bureaucratic structures are seen as enabling and/or hindering the private sector's operations.

Most of those surveyed believed that the private sector was wasting money and losing efficiency due to unnecessary bureaucratic practices and inappropriate regulations. Regulations were in some cases seen as excessive and burdensome and in other cases as inadequate for ensuring an effective and competitive market. Some felt that bureaucratic ineptitude and red tape were the major factors inhibiting the sector's expansion, describing the private sector as 'shackled' by bureaucracy. The government's policy of hiring people for social reasons was seen as a major factor contributing to the problem. The effect of this policy was to encourage the bureaucracy to maintain administrative procedures which justified its inflated size, while employing individuals to perform them who were unsuited to the tasks required. One interviewee attributed the rising level of corruption to the government's employment policy. Public officials could not be rewarded properly for their work as government expenditure was strained by the rapidly growing number of employees. They needed to accept bribes to maintain a reasonable standard of living.

In some areas, as noted, there was over-regulation while in others there was under-regulation. Among the examples given of excessive bureaucracy, inefficiency and an inadequate framework of regulatory support which were mentioned were the following:

- It took three to six months just to register a company. The procedures were seen as being tedious, with the need to liaise with a number of different ministries and departments, in particular the Ministry of Commerce and the Ministry of Industry. All required different sets of paperwork. One interviewee pointed out that a company could be established over the phone in Dubai. The difficulty in registering companies in Saudi Arabia was cited as one of the main reasons why Saudis invested abroad.

- Applying for licences to operate a business also took about six months, with no guarantee that the licence would be given. Often licences were not granted on the grounds of there being other companies operating in the same field. This meant that some companies survived through bureaucratic protection rather than competitive efficiency. Information gathered through licensing and registration processes, moreover, was not used to good effect. It did not form the basis of governmental projections on the industrial sector's need for water, electricity and other services. Licences for exports also took a long time to obtain, despite the governmental rhetoric on the need for the private sector to boost its exporting activities.

- The services necessary for operating a business were often difficult to obtain, at least within an acceptable time frame. Acquiring a new telephone line could take six months, and one interviewee suggested that in some cases it had taken two to three years. Government departments, it was said, were not service-oriented and had little understanding of the needs of the private sector. They had a tendency to treat the private sector as if they were doing the businessmen concerned a favour. Even when businesses offered to pay all the costs in extending services to a new area, the requests were frequently turned down.

- The labour laws, originating from the 1960s, were seen as out of date and unsuited to the needs of running a business. They were not a suitable basis on which to regulate or manage the workplace, and they made it difficult for employers to dismiss ineffective employees – especially if they were Saudis.

- Regulations covering financial organisation and operations were inordinately restrictive, inadequate or absent. Lack of clear procedures on mergers, for example, meant that most companies were too small to operate effectively at the global level. Companies were, moreover, frequently unable to raise capital by going public, as the rules governing the latter process were not transparent and the procedure could take years. The capital market itself was subject to manipulation. Among the various business sectors, the insurance sector was seen as particularly poorly regulated. An article in a Saudi-based bank journal towards the end of the decade articulated the latter view cogently:

> ... Saudi Arabia has no legal framework to regulate and supervise the insurance business. Disputes between the insurance

companies and policyholders are currently handled by the ad hoc committees formed by the Chambers of Commerce and the Ministry of Commerce. The Saudi court system does not legitimise insurance activities and, accordingly, does not handle insurance conflicts.

(*NCB Economist* 1998b: 7)

- Regulations governing foreign direct investment made it difficult to bring in foreign investors to support domestic industries. The areas where foreign investment was permitted were restricted, and in the permitted areas the conditions which governed it and the taxation to which it was subject were discouraging. There was, furthermore, a range of practical difficulties which deterred investors. Among the latter was the difficulty in obtaining visas, especially for women, and the need for the investor to rely on a Saudi sponsor to obtain basic services (such as acquiring a telephone line, travel permission, etc.). The inadequate protection given to intellectual property rights, moreover, made investors reluctant to share their technology with domestic investors.

The provision of the basic information which business needed was also seen as deficient: macro-economic information was not sufficiently in-depth; employment and demographic figures were out of date and unreliable; little market information was available; and business directories scarcely existed. The late arrival in Saudi Arabia of the internet, which was officially launched on 1 February 1999 (although accessible through Bahraini channels before that), was a further ground of complaint. Nonetheless, it was acknowledged that there had been considerable improvement in the quality of statistical and other governmental data in the later part of the 1990s.

5.2.4   *Crony capitalism*

The term 'crony capitalism' is used here to refer to business decisions being shaped by the personal connections among the decision-makers – whether within the business sector or between government and business personnel. It was given prominence internationally at the time of the 1990s financial crisis in Thailand and some other Far Eastern and South-East Asian countries, where the crisis was attributed to a business milieu in which it 'mattered more who you knew than what you knew' (Krugman 1998: 28). Banks lent money not because the projects funded had been shown to be viable but because the lender and the bankers were cronies.

Usually there was a government dimension to the relationship also. In the case of Saudi Arabia it has been suggested that the phenomenon could best be termed *'asabiyah* capitalism, referring to the importance of the family, kin and tribal bases of key business relationships (Champion 2003: 10–12; Niblock 2006: 76–7).

While the assumption must be that decisions made on personal rather than business grounds are likely to be flawed, it is also worth noting that the *wastah* (privileged contact which brings gain) has the advantage of cutting through bureaucratic obstacles (Cunningham and Sarayrah 1993: 15). Strong personal contacts with other businessmen or with government personnel, therefore, are often seen in Saudi Arabia as essential to running a business. The same applies in many other countries. In some business operations it may indeed work simply as a lubricant to the smooth running of the business, and may not be seen pejoratively either by those involved or by wider society. Nonetheless, the practice does have costs. At the lower level (payments to relatively junior officials to speed up administrative processes) it adds to the costs of business activity, while at the higher level (payments or resource transfers of other kinds to senior personnel to secure contracts, etc.) it can seriously distort rational economic decision-making. The impact may not be simply on the businesses directly involved. The quality and content of national economic policies can also be affected. Predatory behaviour of this kind, furthermore, tends to concentrate wealth in a narrowly based and tightly configured business/government elite, with damaging effects on social cohesion and the welfare of the wider population.

Chaudhry, based on material gathered in Saudi Arabia at the beginning of the decade, wrote:

> It is widely believed that princes and politically important persons were the main beneficiaries of the sectoral development programmes, and the most colourful examples of instant riches in Saudi Arabia do suggest the importance of personal contacts with the royal family. Yet the size and breadth of the new middle and upper class bespeaks a much broader involvement of the bureaucracy.
>
> (Chaudhry 1997: 161)

Malik's survey suggests that a similar pattern existed at the end of the decade. The beneficiaries of deals shaped by personal contacts, however, appear to have come from a narrower range of influential individuals than before. Most of those interviewed suggested that major government tenders depended on 'who you know and not what you know', while the lesser contracts were allocated by openly competitive bids. Members of the royal family were seen as being the most crucial channels of influence and, as a result, the main beneficiaries. A businessman would turn to a prince for help in securing a contract, and the prince would then be given a share of the undertaking or of the profits. In some cases the project would involve the prince/princess investing some of his/her own resources in a project, perhaps through the use or sale of land of which the prince/princess had acquired ownership (by land grant from the King). A royal role in promoting the project, and securing the necessary governmental approval, could then be assured.

Parts of the business elite were clearly unhappy with the strong royal involvement in private-sector activity. It was seen as undermining the establishment of an achievement-oriented culture, which was what the country needed if a successful private sector was to develop. The quotations which follow come from two of the businessmen in Malik's survey:

> Interference and competition from the royals is one of the main challenges faced by the private sector. They compete in every sector and not as equals. They get better privileges due to their status – it is not fair competition.
>
> (Malik 1999: 240)

> Royalty and patronage takes away from ... private sector development and the culture required for sustainable development. They are limiting factors. The royal family controls the critical economy. Mega-businesses such as contracting and the port authority see a lot of government and royal family involvement. Big postage couriers are all linked to the royal family and contracting projects often go to them.
>
> (ibid.)

5.3   Perceptions of the business elite: the strength of the private sector and its ability to meet international competition

If the private sector was to become the main agent of economic development, as Saudi developments plans envisaged, it clearly needed to have the strength and capacity appropriate to the allotted role. The first sub-section which follows focuses on the business elite's overall attitude to this issue – whether the private sector did indeed have the ability to assume a leading role in the country's economic development. The later sub-sections look at more specific issues, all covering aspects of the strength or weakness of the private sector. The issues given attention here are:

- The effectiveness of the management of Saudi companies.
- The ability of the sector to compete internationally and the likely impact of WTO membership.
- The efficiency and capacity of family businesses, which constitute a key element of the Saudi private sector.

5.3.1   *The overall strength and capacity of the private sector*

Those interviewed were convinced that the private sector was becoming stronger. There was a perception that it had taken up the challenge of changing conditions and had begun to restructure and reorganise so as to compete internationally. The Gulf War had opened up new opportunities for the private sector, and a number of new businesses had developed from that. The recessions of the late 1980s and late 1990s had eliminated the least efficient companies, making those which remained more competitive. They had been forced to become less dependent on subsidies and were consequently now more competitive in the global market place. The subsidies which remained were mainly indirect (such as the subsidisation of energy, feedstock and water prices, and of industrial loans), whereas historically companies had benefited from direct subsidies – especially in the agricultural sector. Business had also become less dependent on government contracts. Some companies, indeed, now deliberately avoided such contracts, in part because they were not as lucrative as before, and in part because they entailed bureaucratic hindrances and obstruction. All interviewees were convinced that the private sector was considerably more efficient and effective than the public sector.

Despite this optimistic perspective on their sector, however, only a minority of the interviewees were prepared to assert that the private sector was now effectively free of dependence on the state and capable of taking a lead in developing the economy. The remainder were split between some who attributed the level of continued dependence to the inherent weaknesses of the sector, and others who believed that the environment still constituted the main problem. Among the aspects of internal weakness identified in the private sector were the following:

- It lacked sufficient experience, in particular with regard to issues of national economic policy. In part this was because the government had not brought business into effective consultation.

- It remained heavily dependent on factors outside its control or influence. Of key importance here was government spending, which gave the public sector a powerful influence on the market place. Parts of the sector, moreover, were still dependent on government contracts, especially those in construction, operations and maintenance, and servicing. The sector was also very reliant on outside sources for technology, and through that on foreign partners.
- It suffered from low productivity (albeit higher than that of the public sector) and managerial inadequacy. The low productivity stemmed from a failure to adapt to changing economic conditions. The poor management was reflected in weak procedures for planning, organising, controlling, reporting and ensuring accountability.
- It retained a culture of dependence. Many companies sought to keep the preferential and protected status which government policy had afforded them in the past. It was, then, not only a matter of the government being prepared to give up control but also of the private sector allowing it to. One interviewee stated:

One of the greatest challenges faced by Saudi Arabia is that the government has to learn to let go and it is very important for the private sector to allow the government to let go and to stop relying on protectionism. If the private sector allowed the government to do this then the capability of the private sector would greatly improve.

(Malik 1999: 200)

Such private-sector resistance to liberalisation is a phenomenon present in many other countries besides Saudi Arabia. Cragg noted that in the case of India one-third of the private sector seemed resistant to the privatisation and liberalisation wave that started in 1990s (Cragg 1996: 6). The businesses that were resisting were those which depended on winning licenses or were protected by high tariff barriers. Ayubi noted a similar point for the Middle East in general:

Although always pushing for increased privatisation, the business community may not necessarily opt either for full economic liberalization or for ultimate autonomy from the State. To start with, its members will always ask for as much State subsidy, protection and support as possible.

(Ayubi 1992: 52)

Those interviewees who identified the surrounding environment as the reason for the private sector's inability to play a lead role viewed the inherent strength of the sector much more positively. They saw the sector as capable of achieving substantial growth and creating a self-sustaining path of economic development for the country. This, however, was held back and frustrated by inadequate governmental regulation, excessive bureaucracy and poor infrastructure (social as well as physical). In a number of areas, it was claimed, the private sector had the potential to play a significant role but was blocked from doing so by government regulations and agencies. The private sector could have benefited the population by providing services in fields where the government was not active, but this had been refused. Royal interference in the private sector was also seen as a complicating and debilitating factor.

5.3.2   The effectiveness of management

A relatively small number of companies were seen by the interviewees as effectively managed. These used sophisticated management techniques and employed highly specialist and capable personnel who were used to the best strategic effect. As a result the companies concerned attained high levels of productivity.

Overall, however, the perception was that most companies were poorly managed. Management had improved over time and with the expansion of education, but it was not up to international standards. One interviewee said that if his own company was run in the same way in Europe or in the US it would not survive. Management, then, was seen as a major issue. Some believed that the underlying problem was the traditional foundations from which many Saudi businesses had emerged. Others attributed it to the factors which had contributed to a company's growth, suggesting that too much stemmed from personal connections and too little from entrepreneurial flair. Illustrating the significance of personal connections, an interviewee commented: 'You always have to look for the name behind the name' (Malik 1999: 215). Among the aspects which reflected bad management were the following:

- The absence of long-term plans, goals and strategies. The emphasis was on the short term and on prospects for immediate profit-making. Often projects were initiated without feasibility studies being undertaken first.
- The reluctance of the companies to change or to operate in an entrepreneurial manner. There was a trading and agency-based mentality rather than one appropriate to industrial expansion.
- Absence or weakness of accountability within the companies. When the desired results of a business undertaking were not achieved,

no one could be held accountable. Some joint-stock companies were performing badly yet the boards of directors did not change. The auditing of accounts was inadequate, and the financial statements and reports produced were not well grounded.

- Skewed recruitment processes. Appointments were often made on a basis of personal favour rather than qualification.

5.3.3 International competitiveness and Saudi membership of the World Trade Organisation

Assessments of the gains and losses which would stem from Saudi Arabia becoming a member of the World Trade Organisation are bound to be linked to the international competitiveness of Saudi companies. If the latter are not considered competitive or deemed capable of becoming so, they would clearly be damaged or eliminated by the key requirements of WTO membership: the removal of high tariffs and the reduction of subsidies. The two issues, therefore, are covered here in the same sub-section.

Most interviewees were of the opinion that the private sector was not yet globally competitive, despite the fact that companies had become more efficient. There was, nonetheless, a perception among some that the best Saudi companies were more competitive internationally than their counterparts in other Arab countries (including those in the Gulf). One estimate was that there were some ten internationally competitive private companies, among them those in the Abdel Latif Jameel, Zamil, Bin Laden and Kingdom groupings. These had shown their competitiveness by winning contracts around the world, competing with many of the world's leading companies.

One reason for a lack of global competitiveness in some areas of business activity was deemed to be the nature of the domestic market. Profits could easily be made domestically, reducing the need to compete globally. Businesses could be inefficient and still be commercially successful. Tariff protection and subsidies were seen as further factors depressing competitiveness. They had been used not to nurture a sector until it had grown strong enough to compete, but rather as a substitute for competitiveness. This was particularly true of the agricultural sector, which was highly inefficient by international comparison. SIDF loans also had the tendency to encourage practices which were not competitive internationally. Some interviewees believed that competitiveness could be improved not only by removing subsidies and protection but also by allowing foreign companies to compete more effectively in the domestic market.

The implications which the size of companies had for their efficiency and global competitiveness was seen as double-edged. On the one hand, companies needed to be large enough to compete with foreign companies which operated on the global market. On the other hand, some of the larger companies were considered over-bureaucratised and inefficient. Smaller operations, controlled by an owner who would follow through all aspects of activities, could be more effective. Merchant operations benefited from a situation where, to quote one interviewee, 'the merchant tends to have perfect knowledge of their product, market, etc., and this is what they respond to' (Malik 1999: 212).

Opinion on the advantages and disadvantages of Saudi Arabia joining the WTO were mixed, and indeed polarised. Roughly one-half of those interviewed believed that the Saudi private sector was strong enough to withstand the impact of joining the WTO, while the other half believed that membership would bring manufacturing in the Kingdom to an end. Among those who were optimistic about the prospects, the justifications given differed widely. Some had a simplistic faith that the government would not move in a direction that harmed that which it had helped to create. Others thought that the increased competition which came with membership would be intrinsically beneficial: the inefficient companies would close, while those with genuine potential would adopt global modes of business conduct. The most competitive businesses would thrive, forge alliances with foreign companies, enter new markets and establish themselves in the global market. Saudi products were seen, by those promoting the latter views, as being of high quality and capable of attracting substantial demand. Some of the companies from which these interviewees came were already active globally, operating in strategic alliances with foreign companies. Speaking of the overall possibilities, one interviewee said:

> Many in the private sector are worried that their businesses won't survive. But this is not true–the WTO will put in place a code of conduct that will make sure that every one will play at the same level. It should not hurt as long as we move slowly and adjust internally. We have to look at the global scheme–we have to market not only in Saudi Arabia but also in the world. We have to create a market outside–so we have to take strategic partners. Saudi companies have to merge so as to become bigger to be more effective internationally. There is a very weak manufacturing structure as it is very fragmented.... Import substitution industry has reached its limits in Saudi Arabia– most of the big projects have been built and there is a small market. Therefore mergers and restructuring is very important especially to compete globally.
>
> (Malik 1999: 261)

Nonetheless, the need for the government to ensure that the regulatory framework was appropriate prior to WTO membership was stressed. Some interviewees, indeed, envisaged WTO membership as an instrument to bring in a better regulated economy, especially with regard to the regulation of international property rights and of banking and insurance services. The private sector itself would need to make necessary preparations, instituting training, improving management and carrying through some mergers. The period of transition granted to new WTO members should be used to enable a process of restructuring and reorganisation to take place.

The more pessimistic grouping saw WTO membership as the biggest challenge which the private sector had faced, and questioned whether the government knew what it was doing. The perception was that ARAMCO and SABIC would gain from Saudi Arabia's membership, but others would not. Few companies, it was pointed out, had carried out feasibility studies on how they would be affected, and did not have the managerial capacity to adapt effectively. All producers of non-branded, non-MNC consumer goods would be hard hit. There were predictions of greater unemployment, less possibility of Saudisation, and substantial prospects of recession. Saudi producers still needed government protection from competition and the 'dumping of cheap products'. The range of fears is brought out in this quotation from an interviewee:

> I am not convinced the government knows what it is doing. It could be from a consumer's point of view—i.e. they will benefit through cheaper imports. ... Private sector industry will suffer. At the moment industry is very fractured. Manufacturing is too fragmented—it has not reached a level of sustained comparative advantage. If companies merge some will survive—if there are mergers then there may be a group big enough to compete regionally. Most manufacturing will collapse. Coca-Cola will move into the region and put in a lot of money to gain market share. The market will be dominated by and will oscillate between Coca-Cola and Pepsi—between 30–70 per cent. Others in the fizzy drinks industry will not survive. Soaps and skin products will be dominated by Unilever and by Procter and Gamble. The others won't survive. ...
>
> (Malik 1999:292)

There was disagreement between the interviewees as to which sector would be the hardest hit. Some believed that companies producing small and medium non-branded products would be the first to disappear. Others thought that it would be the large Saudi companies that would encounter the greatest difficulty, as these were the ones competing with MNCs. Agents for foreign companies would go out of business as there would no longer be any need for them.

Overall, there was agreement among all interviewees that Saudi companies did need to become more competitive, whether the Kingdom joined the WTO or not. They needed to introduce the most modern technology and to become conversant with international trends. Mergers would be needed if the objective of greater competitiveness was to be met. In practice, some mergers were already taking place at this time. The merger between the Saudi American Bank (SAMBA) and United Saudi Bank (USB) was seen positively in this regard, as also that between Savola and the Saudi al-Aziza Company (Malik 1999: 264).

5.3.4   Family businesses

The prominent role played by family businesses in the Saudi private sector has, clearly, been a key aspect of the sector–almost to the extent of defining its character. Business perceptions on the value and effectiveness of this form of economic organisation, and its significance for the future development of the Saudi economy, are therefore important.

Many interviewees saw substantial advantages in family businesses. At their best, they were effectively led, tightly organised, and elicited high levels of commitment from employees and partners (especially family members). The family leader knew the market well, kept himself aware of changing circumstances, and followed through all aspects of the business's activities. Nevertheless, family businesses were also seen as having potential weaknesses. Among the potential weaknesses were the following:

- If the family was large, the company management could become overloaded and divisive. One interviewee commented:

> When there are many brothers, normally one is the major worker. Many may not be suitable or capable. ... The non-capable brother wants to be a major decision-maker, money does not satisfy him, and he wants to take the top position. Some have a poor work ethic and a large ego. There is the example of one leading family business that was torn apart due to family rifts. They were money-changers and wanted to move in to banking, where they would be regulated by SAMA. Four very close brothers ran the business, with 30 sons and daughters below them. The family pushed the government to allow the money-changing business to become into

a bank. They sold 40 per cent to the public and kept 60 per cent between the brothers. Within one year they all became enemies because of their children. The children started to complain that uncle was giving his cousin a better position than he had. ...

(Malik 1999:217)

- If the father left no succession plan, in-fighting in the family and therefore also within the company could result. A power struggle for the top position could debilitate the company.
- Delegation of responsibilities was often deficient. Too many decisions were dependent on one man. One result of this was that the children of business owners did not acquire sufficient managerial experience in the running of the company, and were not sufficiently well prepared to take over the leadership. They lacked understanding of the company and the business culture. In some cases they also had not been educated or trained to the appropriate level needed for the operation of a modern business.
- If senior members of the family began losing interest in the company, the impact on the company's operation could be very severe.
- Without a separation between ownership and management, there was a tendency for family businesses to be resistant to change. Company decisions and strategies rested on the same individual, dependent on the same coterie of advisers, over a prolonged period. There was not a natural process whereby new ideas entered the business through new personnel at the top.
- Women would often inherit a major part of the business, and then be able to affect business decisions, but often they had not had any previous business experience or knowledge of company activities.

Some interviewees believed that a reasonable way of resolving these problems was for family companies to go public, with a listing on the stock exchange, after transforming themselves into joint-stock companies. This could ensure that multi-million-riyal companies could remain in being but with a rather broader shareholding. They would then be able to raise new resources and have a basis for forging strategic mergers, thereby raising their international competitiveness. One example of this being done occurred at the time the survey was conducted. In early May 1998, the Al-Zamil Group announced that it had combined the areas of air-conditioning, steel buildings and glass operation and had applied for a licence to the Ministry of Commerce for a closed joint-stock company. This was the first step for them to go public, which would take place two years later. The *Middle East Economic Digest*, reporting on a statement by Mohammed Al-Zamil, described the rationale and the process as follows:

> Al-Zamil contends that going public will guarantee the continuation of the group's activities after the family's second generation departs. He also argues that by accepting new partners, the company will be in a stronger position to compete regionally and globally, especially in the current climate of international mergers and acquisitions. With a larger capital, the company will be able to step up investments in training of the national workforce, the introduction of new technology and marketing that in turn can only benefit its export sales. 'I believe turning these activities into a public company with wider ownership is a positive step towards expansion.'
>
> (*MEED*, 2.6.98)

Another example of family businesses going public was that of the Fitaihi Company, a jewellery maker and retailer, which was converted into a SR200 million closed joint-stock company (*MEED*, 31.7.98). The National Commercial Bank (NCB), where the Bin Mahfouz family held a predominant stake, had also initiated a similar process. In 1997 it widened its ownership to 20 investors (*Arab News*, 1.4.97), and two years later announced that its shares would be traded on the Saudi stock market. The intention of the Gazzaz Company, a leading perfume and cosmetics retailer, to convert the family business to a closed joint-stock company, prior to making the company public, was announced early in 1999 (*MEED*, 19.2.99).

Despite this, many of the interviewees who came from family businesses did not see going public as their best option. They believed that it would be a personal loss and that families often had the experience to run businesses better than others. With a good business strategy and a capable family member running the business, there should be no need to go public. Separating management from ownership was another viable option. In the case of businesses which operated mainly as agents for foreign companies, there seemed no possibility of going public, given that contracts would have to be renegotiated or abandoned. Government regulations, moreover, were seen as making it difficult for companies to go public. Although the regulations were loosened in 1999 from what had been in force before that, they were still regarded as being obstructive. Companies applying for conversion to public status had to have assets of SR50 million, a substantial level of profitability in the year prior to application (previously the requirement was for 10 per cent profitability over five years), and three years of audited balance sheets (*MEED*, 29.1.99).

5.4   Perceptions of the business elite: the business environment

Government plans, as indicated in earlier chapters, envisaged a rapid increase in private-sector investment, with the latter making up for falling or unstable oil revenues. The Fifth Plan gave this as one of its key aims. Saudi private funds needed to be invested in productive schemes within the country rather than flowing abroad for investment elsewhere. The plan stated:

> Although the private sector has accumulated substantial financial assets as a result of strong economic growth in the past, only a relatively small fraction has been invested within the Kingdom. This has been a natural response to the general availability of funding for private sector activities from government sources, and to the difficulties of finding viable new investment opportunities, given the relatively small domestic market. However, private sector capital represents a very important under-utilised resource for the Kingdom, and the success of future economic development depends on introducing a much greater deployment of this resource in the Saudi and GCC economies.
>
> (KSA-MOP 1990: 141)

The attraction of private investment in any country depends in part on the quality of the business environment, and how it compares with that elsewhere. World Bank reports often list the elements deemed important by international financial circles. One such report suggests that the following elements need to be present:

- A supportive (or 'enabling') business environment consisting of a stable macro-economic setting, economic incentives that promote efficient resource allocation by the private sector, and laws and regulations that protect the public interest but do not necessarily interfere with private initiative.
- The services in infrastructure and human resource development necessary to permit private-sector enterprises to function efficiently.
- A financial system that provides the incentives and institutions needed to mobilise the allocated financial resources efficiently (World Bank 1989: vii).

This section covers these elements, giving the perceptions of the business elite as to whether they were in place at the end of the 1990s in Saudi Arabia. Overall, the view was mixed. On the positive side, interviewees noted that there were many opportunities available, access to subsidised loans was beneficial, inflation had been kept low, and considerable liquidity was present in the Saudi market. The government's active promotion of Saudi exports, through trade agreements (such as with Iran) and the despatch of trade delegations around the world, was also seen as beneficial to private investors. On the negative side, the overriding perception was that government policies were not focused sufficiently on gaining and exploiting competitive advantages. Social and economic conditions needed to be shaped more effectively to cater for the needs of the sector. One interviewee expressed the range of his frustrations as follows:

> We are always late on macroeconomic policy. For example, we do not have a Free Trade Zone, as many of our competitors do. If we are always behind, then we will lose our competitive advantage. The government does not have the basic business vision. The government says they want to liberalise the economy but the foreign investment law is outdated, which is not conducive to attracting foreign investment. They all go to Jebel Ali where 100 per cent equity is allowed. The government wants to get Saudis into the employment pool and this is not happening. The education system is not suited to the needs of the private sector, the private sector will need to change and be more involved in training but they need the prerequisites for that. For example if you want an accountant – you can train him but he needs the basic skills and knowledge, this is not happening. And work ethics are a big problem. The levers are not with the private sector but with the government.
>
> (Malik 1999: 227)

5.4.1   *Educational qualifications of the Saudi labour force*

The business environment will inevitably be affected by the work ethic, adaptability, skills and qualifications of the population. The social dimensions are combined here with the educational as they are clearly closely related.

Almost all of the business elite surveyed saw the educational system as characterised by serious failings. Some of the words used to describe it were 'disaster', 'obsolete', 'discourages innovation' and 'a major handicap'. Improvement of the educational system was seen as particularly pressing due to the government's Saudisation policy. The competitiveness of the private sector was now critically affected by the competitiveness of Saudi labour. As a result of the deficiencies the private sector had to spend much time and money on retraining graduates, which had a negative impact on profits and efficiency. The only educational institution which was consistently complimented was the King Fahd University for Petroleum and Minerals. Among the criticisms made were the following:

- The education system was backward and outdated. Some students left school without being able to read, write or communicate effectively. Very few had computer skills. The system of rote learning, moreover, was inimical to students thinking freely or developing an internally driven work ethic.
- Too little attention was given to technical, vocational and scientific courses, and too much to religious education. This point had also been given attention in the work of Osama in the second half of the 1980s Abdel-Rahman (1987), He showed that nearly half of the students graduating at that time were specialised in religious-related subjects.
- The universities were making too little contribution to research and development.

The criticisms made by the private sector were acknowledged in the reports of some official Saudi bodies. One prepared by the Saudi Development and Training Company in 1996, for example, stated that:

Most employers seek good standards of literacy, numeracy, an appreciation of technology and a foreign language capability, usually English. Numeracy and English tend to be the problem areas–these are what the private sector runs on. ...

... There is a perception, often murmured about but only recently surfaced in the *Majlis al-Shura* (the Consultative Assembly), that the Saudi education system does not fit candidates too well in to work. Streaming takes place in the majority of Saudi schools into literary and scientific streams ... the vast bulk of students follow these two routes with a tendency of the majority to follow the Literary Section. ... Whereas English and Arabic appear in the scientific syllabus, some corresponding form of Mathematics or Technology does not appear in the literary section certificate. ... Not only do the syllabi cause employers concern, the general methodology of teaching that favours imitation and rote learning as against experimentation or empiricism is also perceived as a difficulty–mainly because many of the employers find difficulty in subsequently putting into operation the knowledge that they have acquired in school. It is not that Saudis do not learn English. It is generally taught as a dead language. Saudi students do learn English but in many cases they do not have the strategies to operationalise and use what they have learnt.

(Saudi Development and Training Company 1996: 12–16);

(Italics not in original)

5.4.2   *The legal system*

The legal system in Saudi Arabia is based on the Islamic *shari'a*. Some secular codes, however, have been introduced for commercial activity such as distributorship agreements, company laws and government contracts. These are subject to 'Regulations' and 'Implementing Rules', which are decreed or issued by the Council of Ministers and the various government ministries. Commercial disputes can be handled by special committees such as the Board of Grievances, SAMA's Committee for Banking Disputes or the Commission for Labour Disputes (Turck 1998: 416). Issues of jurisdiction, however, are not distinct. As Al-Hejailan notes:

> The jurisdiction of the commercial courts in Saudi Arabia is not yet well defined. Sometimes commercial cases are presented to the Board of Grievances in a rather narrow application of the term 'commercial', and sometimes to the Shari'a Court which has a very broad jurisdiction.
>
> (Al-Hejailan 1998: 6–7)

This was another area where most interviewees felt that the existing structure was not suited to the needs of the business community, describing it as a significant hindrance. The commercial codes were generally seen as lacking and out of date. A more comprehensive set of civil and commercial laws or regulations were needed, they believed. In matters of leasing or lending, for example, it was difficult to retrieve money or a product if the borrower reneged. Problems over the sale/purchase of cars by instalment were frequently cited as an example of this. The point is illustrated by an article in the *Arab News*, which quoted a car distributor as saying:

> ... it is not very lucrative since the chance of the customer defaulting on payments is high. There is no security for us because official rules require the transfer of ownership immediately after down payment ... if he stops paying we can not do anything. The legal process is time consuming and produces little result.
>
> (*Arab News*, 3.8.98)

In some cases, people in need of money would put down an instalment on a car, sell the car cheaply and retain the profit. There was no centralised data bank on those who had defaulted payments, and no clear legal base on which to pursue them. The difficulty in recovering money from a debtor also made it difficult for a mortgage market to develop. Nor were there explicit regulations dealing with bankruptcy.

Another area where interviewees identified a legal inadequacy was with regard to labour. The labour laws, covering labour relations, workers' rights and employers' rights, dated from 1969. They made it difficult for an employer to dismiss or to terminate the contracts of Saudi employees, especially at the managerial level. If such action were taken the dispute would take a considerable time to be resolved, and would end with the Board of Labour requiring the payment of a considerable sum in compensation. The laws encouraged a tendency to allow inefficient staff to remain in place.

There was also a range of other problems raised with regard to the resolution of disputes. These included the following:

- Legal procedures took a long time to process. One interviewee had been fighting a case in the courts for 15 years. Where the judgement might go against an influential individual, courts were reluctant to proceed. Some observers have suggested that the length of the processes was caused by the courts' emphasis on reconciliation rather than delivering judgements (Business International 1989: 22).
- Transparency was lacking. The bases on which judgements were made were left unclear, in part because the codification of regulations was inadequate. It was, as a result, difficult to judge what the outcome of a case might be. As a result of this, contracts with a foreign partner often had to be written under the law of the partner's home country.
- Decisions, once made, were poorly enforced.

5.4.3   *The financial system*

To serve the interests of the private sector, financial systems need to be able to mobilise and allocate financial resources efficiently. They must provide the channels through which the resources required for fixed capital formation are made available. Wilson, writing in the year Malik was undertaking her survey, noted that the Saudi financial markets were underdeveloped when taking into consideration the size of its economy and its banking system. This was partly, he said, a result of the 'historical importance of cash and liquidity in the Saudi financial market, and the fact that until the 1980s the country as a whole funded itself from cash flow reserves …' (Wilson 1998: 233).

Saudi development plans in the late 1980s and the 1990s also emphasised the importance of developing the country's financial structures, with a view to ensuring that more of the personal savings of Saudi citizens were invested within the Kingdom rather than outside. The Fifth Plan stated:

> The opportunity for individuals to invest their personal savings in productive enterprises in the Kingdom rather than in the international money markets or physical assets, such as land and gold, need to be developed. An important step in this direction was taken in the last two years of the Fourth Plan with the issuance of government development bonds, thereby promoting both savings and opportunities for investors to increase their participation in the development process.
>
> (KSA-MOP 1990: 155)

The aims of the Fourth and Fifth Development Plans with regard to the financial sector were summarised well in an article by Wright and Albatel. They were:

- To promote the incorporation of national financial institutions which could facilitate the investment of private funds within the country.
- To encourage private banks to increase their credit facilities for productive activities rather than focusing on import trade.
- To encourage joint-stock companies to undertake a greater number of large projects so that more citizens could find investment opportunities.
- To encourage the exchange of company shares to facilitate investment (Wright and Albatel 1996: 59).

Most interviewees saw the existing financial system as inadequate for their needs. The main areas mentioned were problems linked to the stock market and the need for increased loans for commercial purposes. With regard to the latter, there was a perception that banks tended to favour a few large corporate clients and the government. By focusing on these, the banks could make large profits and be assured of security for their assets. They had little incentive to expand their base. Bank loans, moreover, were predominantly for short-term financing rather than long-term. The problem for smaller companies obtaining finance was often acute, especially as they were not always eligible to apply for government agency loans (such as those from the SIDF). Such concerns were given substance by a report prepared by the Riyadh-based Consulting Centre for Finance Development in 1999, acting under the auspices of the Riyadh Chamber of Commerce and Industry. This revealed that more than 75 per cent of bank loans were being channelled to larger enterprises, and that the recipient companies and departments made up less than 20 per cent of all public- and private-sector establishments (*Arab News*, 16.2.1999). Insurance was another area where the services provided were not adequate for the private sector.

The stock market was viewed yet more critically. Among the problems raised were the following:

- Few companies were listed. This meant that there were relatively few options for those wanting to invest in the country. In particular, there were very few small and medium-sized companies. This was linked to the regulations covering the procedures for a company to go public.
- Even for those companies which were listed, there was little actual trading in shares. Company shares were held by a small number of major shareholders, who mostly were intent on retaining them.
- The stock market was not run professionally. The interviewees mentioned different ways in which the market could be and was manipulated. Company board members would sometimes use their privileged knowledge for their own personal gains and the benefit of their friends. This coheres with a view expressed by Henry Azzam in a report published in 1997:

> One of the major sources of unfair practices in a stock market is insider trading, i.e. the use of privileged information by insiders (executives, directors, large investors) to trade in the market for their own advantage. Such use of privileged information is illegal in Saudi Arabia as in the United States. However, the enforcement mechanism in Saudi Arabia is poor. The penalty for such trading is not specified in the regulation. In practice, an offender usually receives a warning for such violations asking him not to do it again.
>
> (Azzam 1997: 156)

5.4.4 Infrastructure

Despite the efforts of the government to develop the infrastructure, most of the interviewees spoke with considerable frustration about the state of Saudi Arabia's infrastructure. Inadequacies in infrastructure were seen as constituting a significant bottleneck for private business, especially in the industrial sector. Many of the interviewees noted that when the government was building the infrastructure they missed out some key elements, and that the infrastructure created was now a substantial burden on the economy. Massive spending was needed both to maintain the existing infrastructure and to build new infrastructure to keep up with the demands of the economy. Yet the budgetary problems had made this impossible. Some stressed that the private sector could help to resolve some of the problems, if given the appropriate opportunities. Private investors, for example, could be attracted to invest in the ports and airports if they were given management contracts for the operation of the relevant facilities, and they could also play a part in transforming the telephone and electricity services.

The areas which the interviewees found most inadequate for the expansion of their businesses were the following:

- Industrial cities. There were shortages of land, water and electricity in these cities. The shortage of electricity was such that some companies had introduced their own generators to satisfy their needs. Facilities to deal with sewage and waste were seen as inadequate, such that trucks had to be used to remove them. The shortage of land had made some investors seek opportunities elsewhere.
- Telecommunications. As indicated earlier, the shortage of telephone lines was seen as a major problem, as also was the delay in introducing the internet. The mobile network reached Saudi Arabia later than it did elsewhere in the Arabian Peninsula, and mobile charges remained more expensive than elsewhere in the region.
- Railways. These were seen as being too underdeveloped and limited in extent to serve a significant range of business interests.

5.4.5   *Saudisation and the labour market*

All the interviewees mentioned that Saudisation would affect the workings of the private sector in a negative manner, mostly through increased costs and reduced productivity. This did not necessarily mean, however, that they were opposed to the policy per se. A significant number saw Saudisation as necessary for the future and sustainable development of the country, and believed that it was the duty of the private sector to employ Saudis. Others were of the view that the private sector already had sufficient problems, in particular restructuring activities to prepare for globalisation, and that it was unfair of the government to place this extra burden on them. All sides, however, were convinced that part of the solution lay with education and training, and that radical changes were needed in order to create the appropriate educational and training foundation.

The specific problem areas identified related mainly to the higher salaries which Saudis required, the technical skills required by employers, the difficulty in moving Saudi employees to different parts of the country, the regulations governing the dismissal of inefficient employees, and the work ethic. Some of these problem areas, moreover, were interlinked. The shortage of Saudis with appropriate technical skills, for example, meant that there was intense competition for those available. One interviewee suggested that the issue of the work ethic depended on the social background of the individual concerned, with the best-motivated workers coming from the least privileged backgrounds. Companies could, it was suggested, solve some of their problems by acting proactively to foster the careers of such people. He gave the experience of his own company:

> We have to bring in hard working Saudis – these come from families with minimum means, so that they have the motivation. For example the head of purchasing – we trained him, I mentored him, now he is the head of the section and better than anyone else. This is the same for our Head of Human Resources – we gave him the responsibility, the freedom and we sent him abroad for training.
>
> (Malik 1999: 266)

The report by the Saudi Development and Training Company, mentioned earlier, gave a rather similar account of employers' attitudes to that which emerges from Malik's survey. The report states:

> Saudi employers generally believe that Saudi employees are generally more expensive and less productive than the foreigners. They also believe that foreigners are more compliant to their wishes.... In all of these matters there is an element of truth. Saudi employees are more expensive in that they do seek high salaries and also are less productive. Saudi employees are less compliant than foreigners with regards to moving to where the work is–Nejdis wish to stay in the Nejd, Hijazis the Hijaz, etc. This is because it is difficult for Saudis to function socially outside their family circle.
>
> (Saudi Development and Training Company 1996: 12)

The comments by interviewees showed an awareness of the danger that Saudisation, however much needed, might weaken the private sector's potential to take a lead in the economy–or at least delay the time when it could really take effect. The impact of Saudi membership of the World Trade Organisation made the problem more acute, in view of the increased pressure for companies to be competitive and efficient.

5.5   Conclusion

The attitudes of the business elite as conveyed in this chapter suggest a pessimistic view of the private sector's potential at the end of the 1990s to take a lead in the Saudi economy. To conclude from this that the sector was not capable of developing such a role, however, would be misleading. What is revealed is indeed the problems which confronted the sector, but also the clarity of the business sector's conception of what was wrong and how it could be remedied. On some issues, moreover, there was at least evidence of governmental awareness of the problems, and in some areas government policy had begun to change. It remained an open question as to whether the initial indications of change would develop into something more substantial. This is the concern of the chapters which follow.

6 Planning for reform, 2000–6

6.1 Introduction

Over the years since 2000 economic reform has taken practical effect in the Kingdom. Reforms which had been long discussed and considered, were now implemented. Particular attention in this chapter will be given to the regulatory changes which laid the basis for reform. The wider developments in the economy will be traced through a similar range of data as in Chapters 3 and 4, but less space will be devoted to analysing their significance. The analysis and assessment of the developments are the concern of Chapter 7.

The shape taken by Saudi Arabia's political economy since 2000 is similar in some respects to that of the developmental states of East and South-East Asia. The similarity is greatest with respect to the more recent years of the Asian experience, when the most salient features of state-sponsored capitalism have been softened and the dimensions of state-aided capitalism given more emphasis. Economic planning in Saudi Arabia has come to be imbued once more with a transformative vision. Part of this vision involves a return to mega-projects of the kind which had been present in the 1970s and early 1980s. But while the state frames this vision, and creates the framework within which the mega-projects are implemented, the major investments and the management of the new projects are expected to come from the private sector. The leading elements in the private sector, indeed, are central to the conception of much of the vision. It is in these respects that there is a similarity with the Asian developmental states.

In terms of the theoretical framework underpinning this work, the key question is whether the economic reforms, and the overall direction of current economic development in Saudi Arabia, reflect a major change in the dynamics underpinning the country's political economy: whether, in other words, the relationship between the leading business circles and the state has changed, coming to cohere with the embedded autonomy relationship characteristic of developmental states. This chapter will focus on the character of the changes and the factors driving them, leaving a definitive judgement on the theoretical issue to the next chapter.

The initial impetus of the post-2000 economic reform programme was fuelled by financial crisis, accompanied by associated economic and social problems. The financial crisis was that of the late 1990s, when oil revenues sank to a level which had not been seen since the 1970s. Among the dimensions and effects of this crisis were the relatively low level of foreign assets and reserves, the rise of unemployment, the continuing and substantial deficit in the balance of payments, the inadequate facilities available for the population as a result of too little public investment in the social and economic infrastructure, and the worsening of the poverty which still characterised life for some parts of the population. The country had, of course, known financial crises before (especially in the mid-1980s), and the problems facing society and the wider economy were not new. Yet the need to act was greater than before. On the one hand, the problems which faced Saudi society had grown with the expansion in the population, a phenomenon which brought with it new requirements for social and physical provision. On the other hand, the possibility that such a crisis would resolve itself no longer appeared as realistic as before. Oil revenues had been fluctuating, unreliable and generally low since the mid-1980s. Reality now had to be confronted: the combination of oil revenue and a moderately expanded role for the private sector had achieved some growth during the 1990s, but not to the degree needed to solve the country's social problems.

As was shown in Chapter 4, the seeds of economic reform were developing at the end of the 1990s. The guidelines for privatisation were laid down and a new strategy began to be drafted. This continued, and increased in pace, after the turn of the millennium. The central perception was that new sources of investment funding were needed, leading to more substantial economic growth. Some of this investment had to come from outside. Foreign investment was needed in a broad range of different sectors, rather than being restricted to narrowly specified areas where it was unavoidable. Attracting increased involvement by foreign investors would require more explicit legal frameworks and conditions to be developed, of the kind offered to investors elsewhere. There would have to be fewer bureaucratic hurdles, and more possibilities for direct ownership of the operations in which investments were made. Domestic investors also needed to be attracted. These would benefit from the improved legal and regulatory framework introduced for foreign investors, while being encouraged to move into some of the core industrial developments which had previously been beyond their reach. They would find the economic environment more competitive than before, having to compete more directly against foreign firms, but this would have the beneficial effect of improving their efficiency and encouraging them to focus on those areas where they enjoyed a competitive advantage. It was hoped that some of the assets which the private sector held outside of the country would be sold and the proceeds invested within the Kingdom.

While the financial need spurred the new policy on, however, the political context was also more conducive to change than before. Central to this was the rising power and influence of Crown Prince Abdallah. He took over as head of government in November 1995, following the stroke which King Fahd suffered that month. While his exercise of authority was still limited by the power of other senior princes, who sometimes used the reported word of the King to stifle new initiatives, he was able gradually to advance new programmes. He enjoyed three significant strengths in pursuing such ends. First, he was not bound to any vested interests, as he had no significant business involvement of his own (although some members of his immediate family did). He had every reason to give priority to national needs rather than promote dubious deals. Second, he had a reputation for fair dealing and integrity. He was reported to be critical of some of the extravagance and the misuse of state resources by members of the royal family, and was determined to end such practices. This accorded well with popular perceptions and wishes. Third, he maintained close links with senior members of the private sector, whose advice on the economy he deemed important. He was seen by the business elite, as mentioned in Chapter 5, as someone whose door was always open to their representations.

The rising size and strength of the private sector, as documented in earlier chapters, however, was also important in moving the policy forward. With the growing authority of the Crown Prince the sector now had a new channel of influence, but it was also in a better position than before to exert influence. It was a more organised body than before, clearer about its own objectives, and with a stronger sense of its own interests. Organisationally, the Chambers of Commerce had become increasingly effective in articulating these interests. The business elite, as Chapter 5 has shown, had developed some clear ideas of what it wanted to achieve for itself and for the wider economy and society.

Although financial crisis, accompanied by more favourable political conditions, provided the initial impetus, however, the events which follow create a paradox. In practice the financial crisis which had preoccupied attention in the late 1990s, especially in 1998 and 1999, began to fade after 2000. At the very time the reforms were moving from ideas to implemented programmes, therefore, the original impetus behind them was ceasing to be so relevant. Oil prices and oil revenues strengthened after 2000, began to look increasingly strong after 2003, and grew rapidly from the early part of 2005. Whereas prices had fallen to a low point of $10 per barrel in 1996, they were averaging around $25 in 2001 and 2002, reached $60 per barrel in June 2005, and even touched $80 for a brief time in 2006.

The new resources flowing into the country, however, did not, as might be expected, slow the pace of reform. On the contrary, the pace of the practical implementation of reform steadily quickened. Between 2001 and 2003 most of the main regulatory measures needed for economic reform were put in place, and after 2003 the determination with which reform measures were implemented increased.

A number of explanations may be put forward to explain the paradox of why reform advanced just when the immediate financial pressures eased. First, policy changes take time to develop within the Saudi political system, sometimes coming well after the events which caused them. In economic policy in particular, major changes in direction come after a long process of gestation, where a consensus gradually builds up among the interested parties–the ruling family, senior civil servants, and leading elements in the private sector. This had accounted for the relatively slow pace at which the Kingdom moved towards instituting a major development programme under King Faisal, and again the slow movement towards reform in the 1990s. Many of the changes instituted in and after 2000, such as the privatisation programme, were shaped in the late 1990s, but not implemented until there was sufficient consensus in inner circles to carry the process forward. Some of the political dynamic was provided by Crown Prince Abdallah's increasing dominance in decision-making. Although he had been in charge of government business since 1995, his effective authority was initially limited. It was only towards the end of the decade that he was able to carry through significant policy changes. Even though financial conditions had become more favourable after 2000, therefore, the dynamic which had been born of financial crisis still exerted an influence. For some time, moreover, the long-term perspective remained unclear. It was feared that the higher prices and production in the early part of the millennium could still be followed by decline– as had occurred with the prices and production spike in the early 1990s. There was initially, therefore, a cautious attitude to the improved financial conditions.

Second, the new line of policy was very much in tune with the dominant economic philosophy in the global order at this time, and gained reinforcement from that. The Washington Consensus view of the negative dynamics stemming from state control of the economy, and the liberating effects which privatisation and an increased reliance on the private sector had, was influencing policy-makers in the Kingdom just as it was elsewhere. The availability of new and higher revenues, therefore, did not necessarily negate the perceived need to rely primarily on the private sector. Of critical importance in the new dynamic towards economic reform was Saudi Arabia's application for membership of the World Trade Organisation. On the one hand, this constituted a factor driving the process forward; on the other, it was itself a product of the reform process. That is to say, Saudi Arabia needed to carry through substantial economic reforms in order to comply with the requirements of the WTO, but the government's interest in WTO membership was also an outcome of the its acceptance that reform was necessary. Prospective WTO membership, therefore, became a tool which the government could and did use to justify and explain economic reform, and to build up the consensus for reform which it needed so as to carry core elite elements with it. As noted above, the Saudi Arabian government entered into negotiations in 1996. It was not, however, until 2002 that the critical issues impeding membership began to be seriously addressed.

Third, domestic political unrest had become more open and explicit than before, so that the government felt impelled to reshape its policies. Even though oil revenues had risen and the government was reaping the rewards of this, some of the problems facing the population had not eased. Unemployment levels had continued to rise (in part through the high population growth and the large numbers of young people emerging from the educational institutions), the services available to the population were often inadequate, and the living standards of some parts of the population had fallen. Discontent over these conditions was feeding into a growing mood of popular unrest in the country.

Fourth, Saudi Arabia became subject to much greater international pressure than before as a result of the events of 11 September 2001. The US government, in particular, took the view that Saudi Arabia's domestic conditions were feeding the forces of international terrorism. There were both political and economic dimensions to US concern with domestic conditions within Saudi Arabia, but for the Saudi government there was a rationale for prioritising economic reform. It was less controversial and less problematic for the government, and indeed to some extent provided a cover for the failure to pursue radical political reform.

6.2   Governmental revenues and foreign assets, 2000–6

6.2.1   Oil revenue and other sources of governmental income

As can be seen from Table 6.1, the period since 2000 has seen high levels of both oil prices and oil production–relative to the levels which were present over most of the 1985–2000 period. While in the initial years after 2000 the trend took the form of a steady firming of prices and production around the high levels attained in 2000, the period after 2003 saw a rapid increase in prices and some increase in production. The most substantial rises took place between early 2005 and mid-2006. While the price rise was not of the same proportion as those which had taken place in 1973–4 and 1980–1, they were nonetheless very substantial. In some respects, indeed, their significance was greater than on those earlier occasions. The earlier price spikes were cause by 'supply-side problems'–the perception that political events in the major oil-producing countries of the Gulf would disrupt (or in reality were disrupting) the supply of oil to the Western world. In the period after 2004, the dynamic producing upward pressure on prices was related more to the demand side. Rising global demand for oil, much of it stemming from the rapid industrialisation underway in China and India, was forcing up the price. There was every indication that this demand would continue to rise, outstripping the growth of supply.

There were also some supply-side developments affecting the price. The continuing conflict in Iraq, and the possibility that Iran might be targeted militarily by the US in a bid to contain and destroy its capacity for developing nuclear weapons, all raised fears over future supplies. These, however, may explain the spikes in prices (such as the $80 spike

Table 6.1 Saudi crude oil prices, production and exports, 2000–5 (million barrels)

Year	Nominal price (Arabian Light 34 API)	Total	% Change	Daily average	Total exports
2000	26.81	2,962.60	7.30	8.09	2,282.38
2001	23.06	2,879.46	−2.81	7.89	2,203.10
2002	24.32	2,588.98	−10.06	7.09	1,928.89
2003	27.69	3,069.74	18.57	8.41	2,380.85
2004	34.53	3,256.30	6.08	8.90	2,486.77
2005	50.15	3,413.94	4.84	9.35	2,631.24

Sources: Prices from World Bank (2000–5) *Commodity Trade Price Trends*. Washington: World Bank. Other data from Saudi Arabian Monetary Agency (various years) *Annual Surveys*. Riyadh: SAMA.

reached in mid-2006) rather than the overall trend through the 2003–6 period. In September 2006 the price fell back to around $60 per barrel, and it ended the year at about $50 per barrel. The important aspect here, however, was that even after the fall the price remained more than twice what it had been two years earlier. Over the period covered by this chapter, therefore, there was increasing confidence that Saudi Arabia would be able to benefit from a favourable situation on the oil market.

Furthermore, there are indications that the GCC countries as a whole have been more careful this time around with their oil revenues. The spending ratio (i.e. the proportion of additional oil revenue being spent by governments) is now lower than during the boom of the 1970s. The IMF has estimated that governments have on average spent 30 per cent of their extra oil revenue from 2002 to 2005, compared with 75 per cent in the 1970s and early 1980s. Instead, regional oil-exporting countries are running greater external surpluses, paying off debts and building up assets.

As a result of rising prices and production, oil revenues maintained a level significantly higher than at any time since the early 1980s (see Table 6.2). In 2005 and 2006 they increased further, at a dramatic pace, and now reached levels which had not been seen before. Oil revenues, however, are calculated in current prices, so the real resource in the hands of the government must take into inflation account. According to reports from the Saudi media, inflation in the global market place had raised the prices of goods which Saudi Arabia needed by some 90 per cent over the two intervening decades since 1980–2. In practice, then, the revenues accumulating in 2005–6 were of less value than the rather lower sums received at the beginning of the 1980s. Nonetheless, the high levels of revenue put the government in a very different position than before, gradually leading to the realisation that the country could now begin to reconsider its development strategies. The conviction that higher revenues were there to stay took hold particularly strongly, not surprisingly, after 2003.

Table 6.2 Governmental revenues, 2000–5 (SR million)

Year	Oil revenues	Other	Total revenues
2000	214,424	43,641	258,065
2001	183,915	44,244	228,159
2002	166,100	46,900	213,000
2003	231,000	62,000	293,000
2004	330,000	62,291	392,291
2005[a]	491,000	64,000	555,000

[a]Preliminary data and revenues for 2005 are forecasts.
Source: Saudi Arabian Monetary Agency (2005) *Forty-First Annual Report*. Riyadh: SAMA.

Table 6.3 Foreign assets, 2000–5 (US$ billion)

2000	47.5
2001	48.3
2002	41.9
2003	59.5
2004	86.4
2005	150.3

Sources: Calculated from data in Saudi Arabian Monetary Agency (various years) *Annual Surveys.* Riyadh: SAMA; and International Monetary Fund (various years) *International Financial Statistics.* Washington: IMF.

6.2.2   Foreign assets and reserves

Assets did not increase immediately after 2000. Between 2000 and 2002 they maintained a level which was similar to that of the late 1990s (see Table 6.3) despite the much higher revenues. One reason for this was that the government was using the higher level of revenues to pay off international debt. This had been accumulated when oil prices had crashed at the end of the 1990s. After 2003 foreign assets rose rapidly, reaching an unprecedented peak in 2005.

The position after 2003 was in some respects similar to that of the 1970s: the level of foreign assets rose sharply, over a period when spending plans had not had the chance to catch up with increasing revenues. Yet in one crucial respect the situation was different. While government expenditure did increase after 2003, the increase remained well short of the growth of revenues. The government was showing more caution than before in initiating new expenditure. Many of the major projects which were initiated, in any case, were dependent more on private investment than on governmental spending. There was a greater determination than before to avoid wasteful expenditure. The rise in assets, therefore, was more capable of being sustained. As a result of this, the Saudi government appeared likely to benefit from a more substantial and more sustained inflow of investment income from its foreign assets than before.

6.3   Development strategy: overall targets and objectives

As noted earlier, the tone of the development strategy at the beginning of this period was set very much by the large deficits in the government's finances at the end of the 1990s. A number of speeches by Crown Prince Abdallah in 1999 set the agenda. The theme was that the dependence on the state which had characterised Saudi economy and society in the past was no longer useful or feasible. Saudis had to move away from an expectation that the state would provide for every aspect of their lives. In one speech, on 19 January 1999, Crown Prince Abdallah stated: 'We must all get used to a different way of life, which does not stand on total dependence on the state' (Reuters, 19.1.99). The national budget of 1999 had, according to Taecker (1999: 13), imparted the same message: 'The economic role of Saudi Arabia's government is shrinking, and the private sector–which by outward measures still appears healthy–must become stronger in order to take over the leading role as the nation's engine for future economic growth'.

The Crown Prince also stressed, in his January 1999 speech, the need to create more employment opportunities for Saudis, and the role which the private sector should play in that. There was a clear realisation that the public sector was no longer in a position to do this on a substantial scale. As part of this strategy, a tougher policy on Saudisation would have to be pursued, although not without due preparation: 'The private sector has to reduce its dependence upon non-nationals within the context of a practical and well-studied programme' (Reuters, 19.1.99).

The Seventh Development Plan (2000–2004) marked a substantial change in the content, form and style of Saudi development planning. The plan was, for the first time, set within the context of a long-term strategy for the development of the economy. This strategy comprised a coherent vision of the country's development, identifying with some accuracy the central problems, outlining the policies which should be pursued if these problems were to be remedied, and outlining the shape of economy and society which Saudi Arabia might have in 2020 if the correct strategy was pursued (KSA-MOP 2000: section 3.2). The key elements covered by the long-term strategy were:

- Population growth and its expected socio-economic impact. It was estimated that the number of Saudi nationals would grow from an estimated 15.7 million in 1999 to 29.7 million in 2020. The Saudi labour force would rise from 3.17 million in 1999 to 8.26 million in 2020. There would, as a result of these increases, be substantially increased demands for municipal water, housing, electricity, telecommunications and transportation.
- Structural changes in the economy. Strong emphasis was now placed on developing those areas where there was comparative advantage, and on enhancing competitiveness. Economic policy over the long term would focus on the development of three specific industrial sectors: petrochemicals, other energy-intensive industries, and

capital-intensive and advanced technology industries. It was recognised that 'international competitiveness of Saudi export industries can be enhanced through an improved regulatory and institutional environment for private business, the provision of modern infrastructure, and a broad base of qualified and productive Saudi manpower' (KSA-MOP 2000: section 3.2.2).

- The development of human resources. Sustainable development and the ability to face international competition, it was recognised, had to be based on 'the accumulation of human capital through education and training of highly skilled manpower that can keep abreast with recent scientific developments through the effective transfer and adaptation of technology' (ibid.: section 3.2.3).
- The future position of the Kingdom in global energy markets. Careful monitoring was required due, in particular, to the growing impact of environmental and technological policies on world energy markets.
- Economic stabilisation and the diversification of government revenues. The scale of development which was now required meant that new sources of revenue were needed. The structures for taxation, customs duties and service charges would all have to be adapted to this end.
- The management of water. Rising demand for water made necessary 'an integrated strategy for conservation and optimal utilisation of water resources' (ibid.: section 3.2.6), in order to meet ongoing industrial, agricultural and domestic needs.
- The role of science, technology and information technology. A 'comprehensive future vision for science, technology and informatics' was needed, so as to reduce the technological gap between the Kingdom and industrialised countries and acquire strategic technologies.

These themes infused the 5-year strategy of the Seventh Plan as well as the 20-year perspective beyond it. The private sector was portrayed not just as an instrument for economic diversification and the provision of employment, but the potential driving force of the economy. Over the 2000–4 period, it would play a central role in 'increasing the Kingdom's capacity to adjust flexibly to rapidly changing technological and economic conditions at the global level', and in 'raising the overall level of efficiency of the national economy through more efficient use of resources'. 'Intensive efforts' would be exerted so as to bring about privatisation (KSA-MOP 2000: sections 5.1 and 7.3). For the first time the plan gave projections of the level of private investment which was expected over the five years and the fields in which that investment was needed. Private investment was evidently no longer an add-on contributing to the all-round development

Table 6.4 Seventh Development Plan, 2000–4: projected financial allocations (SR billion)

Development sector	Total	% of total
Economic resource development	54.0	11.1
Human resource development	276.9	56.6
Social development	95.8	19.7
Physical infrastructure	61.5	12.6
Overall total	488.2	100.0

Note: The above figures for Seventh Plan allocations differ marginally from those given in the Seventh Plan itself. The reason is that the distribution between Economic Resources and Physical Infrastructure changed as a result of ministerial responsibilities being rearranged during the plan. The revised figures are consistent with the pattern of responsibilities in the Eighth Plan, and therefore make comparison between the two plans more accurate.
Source: Kingdom of Saudi Arabia, Ministry of Planning (2005) *Seventh Development Plan 2005–2009*. Riyadh: Ministry of Planning, Table 1.4.

of the economy but was now a key element at the heart of the economy. Over the period covered by the plan, 71.2 per cent of all investment would come from the private sector.

The plan was prepared at a time when the scale of resources available for governmental development spending over the coming five years remained unclear. The immediate objectives for government spending were therefore fairly modest–at least relative to that which was to occur in the Eighth Plan. Nonetheless, as can be seen from Table 6.4, spending projections for the Seventh Plan were higher than those for the Sixth Plan. Total planned expenditure stood at SR488.2 billion, as against the SR413.0 billion of the Sixth Plan. The distribution of the allocations, moreover, was significant. The priority given to human resources development, which had already been marked under the Sixth Plan, gained even greater emphasis. Spending in that sector was to increase from SR222.2 billion to SR276.9 billion, making up 56.6 per cent of the total as against 53.8 per cent in the Sixth Plan. There were also modest increases in the proportions devoted to economic resource development and social development, with a decline in that allocated to physical infrastructure. One reason for the latter decline, from 18.2 per cent to 12.6 per cent, was the expectation that private-sector investment would play a bigger role in physical infrastructure provision.

The Eighth Development Plan (2005–9) was framed at a time when the planners could be more confident of the high level of oil revenues continuing. There was now a conviction that substantial resources would be available for spending, and therefore a willingness to envisage more ambitious short-term objectives than before. The transformationist vision which was put forward in the 20-year strategic plan (adapted in the Eighth Plan to cover the years through to 2024) now informed the five-year objectives more clearly. Indeed, the plan states that the Eighth Plan represents 'the first stage of the long-term strategy for development of the Saudi economy' (KSA-MOP 2005: section 3.5). Significantly, most of the main chapters of the plan have a section entitled 'Future Vision', where a perspective on the transformation intended for the sector is provided. GDP at constant prices was expected to grow by 4.4 per cent annually, with the private-sector element of this increasing by 5.7 per cent annually. Gross fixed capital formation in the private sector would grow by 10.45 per cent annually. The unemployment rate, it was predicted, would fall from 5.6 per cent to 2.4 per cent for men, and from 15.9 per cent to 4.4 per cent for women (ibid.: section 4.2.1).

The 'strategic bases' outlined in the plan covered a wider scope than before, emphasising the close links between economic development and social development. For the first time, the role of women found a place in the listing of strategic bases, with the commitment to 'place emphasis on the welfare of women, upgrade their capabilities and remove the constraints which impede their participation in development activities'. The 'management and reduction of poverty' also figured in the strategic bases for the first time. The need to carry forward the privatisation policy was now accompanied by a statement that 'consideration should be given to raising citizens' share in the ownership of assets within the framework of competition and transparency'. Education and training systems should not only be upgraded but should 'keep abreast of advancements in knowledge and technology, and pay attention to the promotion and dissemination of culture' (KSA-MOP 2005: section 2.3.2).

The new transformationist vision was structurally different from that which had shaped developments through the mid- to late 1970s and early 1980s. The role of government was portrayed more as the facilitator of transformation than the sole instrument through which transformation could be achieved. The private sector was now to play a pivotal role within the core economic developments, whereas previously it had been there as an accompaniment – adding some diversification to the economy, supplying the population with consumer goods and light-manufactured products, and absorbing some of the new graduates coming onto the jobs market.

The spending projections for the Eighth Plan were substantially higher than those of the Seventh Plan (see Table 6.5). Total spending rose from SR488.2 billion to SR614.6 billion. The Eighth Plan total brought the level of projected government spending back up to the level reached in the Third Plan. Whereas previously the governmental expenditure was intended to constitute the motor driving development forward, it was now meant to fill the more limited role of facilitation. The distribution

Table 6.5 Eighth Development Plan, 2005–9: projected financial allocations (SR billion)

Development sector	Total	% of total
Economic resource development	71.0	11.55
Human resource development	347.6	56.56
Social development	116.5	18.96
Physical infrastructure	79.5	12.94
Overall total	614.6	100.0

Source: Kingdom of Saudi Arabia, Ministry of Planning (2005) *Eighth Development Plan 2005–2009.* Riyadh: Ministry of Planning, Table 4.3.

of projected allocations between the different sectors remained very close to what they had been in the Seventh Plan. Most importantly, the proportion taken by human resources still accounted for more than half all projected development spending, with the actual sum rising from SR276 billion to SR347.6 billion.

6.4 The articulation of development strategy and economic policy

6.4.1 Factors shaping the articulation of policy

As noted earlier, the pattern of expenditure which followed the post-2003 oil-generated boom in Saudi Arabia was rather different from that pursued after the oil price rises of the 1970s. In the 1970s development expenditure had grown rapidly, substantially exceeding that projected in the First and Second Plans. This was done by adapting and inflating the annual budgets, thereby enabling significantly more development spending than previously envisaged. In the post-2003 boom, development expenditure remained within the limits set by the plans. The annual budgets did not expand the sums available for expenditure. Indeed the budgeted spending over the Seventh Plan fell a little short of the planned projections, as can be seen by comparing Tables 6.4 and 6.7.

The disinclination to raise development spending beyond the planned allocations reflects the central dynamic of economic policy at this time. The reform strategy, which had been adopted to cure a financial crisis survived the disappearance of the crisis. Policy did not depart from the framework of 'state retreat': dismantling elements of the command economy, limiting the state's direct investment in and management of the productive sectors of the economy, and encouraging the private sector to play a role at the centre of the industrial and mining development of the Kingdom (in addition to the services, contracting, light manufacturing and commercial areas where the private sector had been active before). There was, therefore, no cause for a sudden and rapid expansion of public expenditure on development.

The factors which brought about this commitment to continue with economic reform have already been discussed. The significance of Saudi Arabia's negotiations for membership of the World Trade Organisation requires particular emphasis. The shape of the reform measures was clearly moulded through the process of application for WTO membership and the negotiations which led up to admission. It could be argued that the pursuit of WTO membership itself stemmed from the reform agenda which Crown Prince (later King) Abdallah and some key Saudi ministers and influential businessmen and advisers were seeking to institute. Whatever the dynamic, however, the negotiations determined the form and much of the content of the economy's new regulatory framework.

From the beginning of this period (or marginally earlier), the government was creating new administrative structures geared to promote and implement reform. Although the bodies created were the instruments of specific reform agendas, they also tended to become pressure groups within the structures of government, advocating and pressing the case for wider reform. Their formation, therefore, was of considerable importance to how economic policy was formulated, and constituted a factor shaping the articulation of policy. The development of the new structures began in August 1999 with the creation of the Supreme Economic Council (KSA-SEC). This was given responsibility for evaluating economic, industrial, agricultural and labour policies to assess their effectiveness. The focus of the KSA-SEC was to be on opening up Saudi markets and attracting investment.

The year 2000 saw the formation of a series of organisations covering economic policy in areas which were critical to the process of economic reform. In January of that year the Supreme Council for Petroleum and Minerals (SCPM) was established, with responsibility for policy-making on the exploitation of the Kingdom's hydrocarbon resources. The Council was to give particular attention to the attraction of international investment into this field, starting with the natural gas sector. In April 2000 the establishment of the Supreme Council of Tourism (SCT) was announced, with responsibility for fostering tourism and encouraging investment in this sector. The notion that the Kingdom should actively encourage tourism in different parts of the country and encourage international investment in new projects, rather than simply respond to the annual flood of pilgrims to the holy places, marked a significant new departure for the Kingdom. The Secretary-General of the new Council announced a 20-year plan for the development of tourism in September 2003, which envisaged that by

2020 there could be as many as 2.3 million Saudis employed in tourism (AMEINFO 2003).

April 2000 also saw the establishment of the Saudi Arabian General Investment Authority (SAGIA), which was given the task of promoting foreign investment and serving the interests of the business community as a 'one-stop shop' for licences, permits and other administrative procedures relevant to business. SAGIA was to work closely with the KSA-SEC and the SCT, playing a mediating role between investors and the government (SA-IR 2005).

The introduction of new institutional structures for privatisation was also highly significant, making it possible to move on from the stage when privatisation was little more than a slogan to one where it could actually be implemented. The new phase was marked by the decision, in February 2001, to give the Supreme Economic Council responsibility for supervising the privatisation programme, determining which activities were to be privatised, developing a strategic plan and timetable for the privatisations, and monitoring the implementation. In August 2001 the Supreme Economic Council created a Privatisation Committee to take charge of the process, with members representing relevant ministries and economic bodies (KSA-SEC 2005).

The privatisation strategy drawn up by the Privatisation Committee was accepted by the Supreme Economic Council in June 2002, and in November of that year the Council of Ministers approved the listing of public utilities and activities which were targeted for privatisation (SAGIA 2004f). The latter listing was extensive: water supply and drainage; water desalination; telecommunications; air transportation; railways; some roads (expressways); airport services; postal services; flour mills and silos; seaport services; industrial city services; government shares in some government corporations (including the Saudi Electric Company, banks, the Saudi Basic Industries Corporation [SABIC], the Saudi Arabian Mining Company, the Saudi Telecommunications Company, and local oil refineries); government shares in paid-up capitals of joint-venture companies in Arab and Islamic countries; hotels, sports clubs, and a wide range of municipal, educational, social, agricultural and health services. The scope of what was being proposed was impressive.

Close consideration appears to have been given to devising a framework for privatisation which would ensure that the economy benefited fully. In a document entitled 'Basic Issues to be Dealt with in the Privatisation Process', which formed part of the privatisation strategy, stress was laid on creating a proper regulatory framework for the privatised sectors, with the establishment of regulatory agencies; devising a systematic method for setting tariffs for services which were previously subsidised through government corporations; creating procedures for some public enterprises to be restructured prior to sale; bringing in strategic partners to cope with the largest privatisation projects; and fostering the correct business environment for privatisation by ensuring the proper functioning of capital markets and promoting human resource development among the Saudi population (SAGIA 2004a). Privatisation, then, was not being regarded primarily as an easy way for the government to meet its budget deficit, but as a process involving structural transformation.

6.4.2   The regulatory framework

Five significant measures reforming the regulatory conditions governing the economy were introduced over the 2000–6 period. First, and perhaps most crucial, was the Law on Foreign Direct Investment. Prior to April 2000, foreign investment was only permitted in the Kingdom if it fulfilled three conditions: undertakings had to be 'development projects'; investments had to generate technology transfer; and there had to be a Saudi partner with at least 25 per cent equity. Applications for licences tended to take a long time, except for those where the government was a partner. Foreign companies and individuals, apart from other GCC citizens, could not own land or engage in internal trading and distribution activities.

The new law was endorsed by the Council of Ministers in April 2000 and became effective in June of that year (SAGIA 2004e). A framework for future legislative and regulatory activities was established by the law, intended to enhance the country's investment climate and attract capital. Critical elements of the new law, and of the executive rules of the law which were enacted at the same time, were:

- Companies could now be 100 per cent foreign-owned (except in certain specified sectors), and foreign and Saudi companies were to be treated on an equal basis. Previously, the Foreign Capital Investment Committee had usually demanded 51 per cent Saudi ownership. Under the new law, foreign companies could apply for low-cost loans from the Saudi Industrial Development Fund (SIDF), on the same terms as Saudi companies. These could cover up to 50 per cent of a venture.
- Foreign companies were now allowed to own land for licensed activities and for housing employees. Previously, the Saudi partner had been required to hold the land.

Perhaps most significant of all, however, was the role given to SAGIA as a facilitator for foreign investment, speeding up investment decisions and reducing bureaucracy. SAGIA was mandated under the new law to make a decision on all investment applications within 30 days, and in the event of failing to meet that deadline was required to issue the licence forthwith. The basis on which decisions on issuing licences were made, moreover, were made very explicit, with investment being permitted in all areas except for those specified on a 'negative list'. The minimum investments for licences to be issued were also specified: SR25 million for agricultural projects, SR5 million for industrial projects, and SR2 million for service projects.

Guarantees against the full or partial confiscation of investments were made more specific than they had been before, as also were the arrangements for foreign investors to repatriate funds and transfer money so as to fulfil contractual obligations. For the first time, foreign companies were given authority to act as sponsors for non-Saudi staff.

As a corollary to the Foreign Direct Investment Law, the Council of Ministers enacted a Real Estate Law later in the same year (SAGIA 2004g). The law was sub-titled 'The System of Real Estate Ownership and Investment of Non-Saudis', giving the entitlement to non-Saudis to own real estate for their private residence.

Second, the Corporate Tax Law, enacted in July 2004 (SAGIA 2004d). This too related primarily to foreign investment. Attracting more foreign investment required changes to the taxation levied on such investment. Prior to 2000 the main rate of corporate tax for foreign investors stood at 45 per cent. In the light of the low rates of corporate tax in the smaller states of the Gulf, this acted as a strong disincentive for foreign investors. The comparison with tax regulations covering Saudi companies, moreover, emphasised the disadvantage to foreign investors. For Saudi companies there was no corporate tax but simply an obligation to pay the 2.5 per cent *zakat* contribution, which in practice was not rigorously or consistently enforced.

The introduction of tax reductions for foreign investors preceded the enactment of the new law. In 2000 the overall rate for foreign investors was reduced to 30 per cent. The new Corporate Tax Law in July 2004 spelt out in greater detail than before the precise details and procedures of the Saudi tax system. The rate of corporate tax fell further to 20 per cent (SAGIA 2004d). For investments in the hydrocarbons sectors, however, a higher rate was payable: 30 per cent in natural gas investment activities, and 85 per cent in oil and hydrocarbons production. In practice, foreign investors could still only enter the latter field in conjunction with ARAMCO.

Although the taxation changes improved the environment for investors, the level of taxation on foreign businesses was still substantially more than in other Gulf countries. In the United Arab Emirates and Bahrain, for example, no corporate tax was levied. The decision to reduce corporate tax, therefore, was unlikely to lead investors to shift investment from the smaller Gulf states to Saudi Arabia. There was some danger that it would cut the government's non-oil income without necessarily leading to a major boost to foreign investment. Nonetheless, the new law did clarify the regulations and procedures with regard to tax, and as such could be expected to increase confidence among potential investors.

Third, the Capital Markets Law, enacted in June 2003 (SAGIA 2004b). The objective of this law, regulating the capital markets, was to attract those with available capital to invest more of it in Saudi companies, thereby increasing the funds at the disposal of companies and strengthening their ability to invest. Some of the capital which would be attracted to a larger and better-regulated stock market would no doubt come from within the country. It was also hoped, however, that Saudis with holdings outside of the country would repatriate all or part of these holdings once the investment opportunities had become clear and sufficiently protected by regulation. There were estimates that some $1 trillion was held by Saudi citizens outside of the country. The scale of what might be gained, therefore, was immense. The reform of the capital markets was intended to encourage such a capital movement and to encourage Saudis with money to look to domestic rather than foreign investment.

Prior to the adoption by the Council of Ministers of the Capital Markets Law, Saudi Arabia did not have a stock exchange. It had been possible to trade shares through the national securities depository centre, but there was no regulatory framework facilitating such trading or protecting the interests of investors. The law formally established the Saudi Arabian Stock Exchange (SASE), whose activities were to be regulated by a Saudi Arabian Securities and Exchange Commission. The latter, now named the Capital Markets Authority, was duly set up in June 2004. It was made responsible for organising the capital market, protecting investors from unfair practices, achieving efficiency and transparency in securities transactions, and developing and monitoring all aspects of the trade in securities (SACMA 2005). Trading in the SASE was limited to GCC nationals, but non-GCC nationals could participate through investing in mutual funds offered by Saudi Arabian banks.

Fourth, the Copyright Law (SAGIA 2004c). Intellectual property rights were important: investors (especially foreign investors) needed to know that they were operating in a market where copyrights on their products were respected. In June 2003, the Council of Ministers approved a new Copyright Law, replacing the previous 1990 law. The 2003 law, which came into effect six months after publication in the official gazette, protected intellectual property rights in the fields of literature, arts and sciences, computer programs, audio recordings and visual displays.

The legal change was consistent with the requirements of the WTO's Agreement on Trade Related Aspects of Intellectual Property Rights (TRIPS).

There remained doubts, however, as to whether the Saudi government would enforce the law effectively enough to meet external requirements. In 1995 Saudi Arabia was placed on the US's 301 Priority Watch List, and at the time of writing the country remains on the list despite the new law. The List comprises the countries which, in the view of the US Trade Representative, 'do not provide an adequate level of Intellectual Property Rights protection or enforcement' and are pursuing 'the most onerous or egregious policies that have an adverse impact on US right holders' (US-TRO 2004).

A new Patent Law was passed by the Council of Ministers in July 2004 (KSA-CM 2004), covering integrated circuits, plant varieties and industrial designs. Formulated with a view to meeting the requirements of TRIPS, the law was expected to improve Saudi Arabia's position with regard to the 301 Priority Watch List.

Fifth, the Cooperative Insurance Companies Control Law, which was approved by the Council of Ministers in July 2003. This was aimed at regulating the insurance sector, creating a legal framework within which insurance companies could operate, and opening the sector up to competition (*MEED*, 6.12.04). Foreign investors were now, for the first time, able to enter this field.

6.4.3   Changing patterns of governmental expenditure

Table 6.6 shows that actual expenditure grew significantly over the period covered by this chapter. Much of this is accounted for by development expenditure and was in keeping with the development plans. In non-development fields, however, there appears to have been substantial additional expenditure. Some was made possible by increases in the annual budgets, but much was in excess of those. The extent to which actual expenditure was outstripping budgeted expenditure over a prolonged period was in fact greater than ever before. The excess appears to be accounted for by rises in recurrent and defence expenditure. The former stemmed in part from the decision to increase all public-sector salaries by 15 per cent in 2005. Within the development sectors, as shown by Tables 6.4 and 6.7, the distribution of budgeted spending between the different sectors was consistent with that which had been envisaged in the Seventh Plan.

Despite the rise in expenditure, however, the government's finances showed a surplus over this period, in all years except 2001 and 2002 (when revenues slipped back for a limited time). After so many years

Table 6.6 Budgeted and actual revenues and expenditures, 2000–6 (SR million)

| | Revenues | | Expenditures | | Surplus/deficit |
	Budgeted	Actual	Budgeted	Actual	Actual
2000	157,000	258,065	185,000	235,322	22,743
2001	215,000	228,159	215,000	255,140	−26,981
2002	157,000	213,000	202,000	233,500	−20,500
2003	170,000	293,000	209,000	257,000	36,000
2004	200,000	392,291	230,000	285,200	107,091
2005	280,000	564,335	280,000	346,474	217,861
2006	390,000	N/A	335,000	N/A	N/A

Source: Saudi Arabian Monetary Agency (2006) *Forty-Second Annual Report.* Riyadh: SAMA.

Table 6.7 Breakdown of governmental expenditures in the Seventh Plan period

		Economic resources development	Human resources development	Social and health development	Infrastructure development	Total
Seventh Plan	SR billion	54.4	276.9	92.6	61.4	485.3
	%	11.2	57.1	19.1	12.6	100.0

Source: Kingdom of Saudi Arabia, Ministry of Planning (2005) *Eighth Development Plan 2005–2009.* Riyadh: Ministry of Planning.

through most of the 1980s and 1990s when there had been a continuing deficit in these finances, this marked a substantial change. The government had reason to feel that it had regained a situation of financial strength.

6.5 The record of achievement in economic and social development

6.5.1 The growth and composition of Gross Domestic Product

At the time of writing, accurate GDP figures for 2006 were not yet available. The figures given here, therefore, go up to 2005.

GDP at current prices grew very quickly between 2000 and 2005, as can be seen from Table 6.8. This growth, however, stemmed largely from the rising price of oil. GDP at constant prices (see Table 6.9) expanded at a slower rate. Over the span over the Seventh Plan (through to the end of 2004) it increased by 3.7 per cent per annum. In 2005 it achieved a faster rate of growth, at 6.6 per cent. Among the different fields of activity,

Table 6.8 Growth in Gross Domestic Product, 2000–5 (current prices, SR million)

Year	Total GDP ^{a}
2000	697,007
2001	679,163
2002	699,680
2003	796,561
2004	929,946
2005	1,150,627
Total	4,952,984

^{a}Total except import duties.
Source: Kingdom of Saudi Arabia, Central Department of Statistics (2000–6) *Statistical Abstracts.* Riyadh: Ministry of Planning.

non-oil manufacturing was growing quickly (8.1 per cent) as also were transport, storage and communications (9.6 per cent) and financial services (9.4 per cent). This can be seen from Table 6.10.

6.5.2   The balance of payments and trade

The balance of payments moved back into surplus in 2000 and remained in surplus for the rest of the period except for 2002 (see Table 6.11). In the latter year, export earnings from oil were low due to the temporary fall in oil prices. After 2003 the size of the surplus rose sharply, standing at $68.9 billion in 2005–a level substantially higher than had been reached before.

The 'Other commodity exports' item in the current account rose some three-fold over this period, from $6.6 billion in 2000 to $19.0 billion in 2005. This was significant, indicating that non-oil exports were now making a real contribution to the well-being of the economy. Petrochemical exports constituted the major part of non-oil exports. The non-oil contribution was clearly dwarfed by oil exports while the price of oil was at a peak, but it could now remain as a bedrock of profitability and a source of foreign exchange should the price of oil falter. Also significant, albeit less positive, was the continuing high level of workers' remittances. Although the level of these had fallen slightly since the mid-1990s, they remained a major drain on foreign exchange. Judging by these figures, there was little indication that the government's Saudisation policy was working.

Commodity imports grew substantially over the period, reflecting the buoyancy in the economy and the population's greater spending power. Some of the latter, in 2005, came from the rise of government salaries. While there is evidence that some private capital was being repatriated

Table 6.9 GDP by kind of economic activity, 1998–2005 (producers' values, constant prices at 1999, SR million)

	1998	1999	2000	2001	2002	2003	2004	2005
Industries and other producers except producers of government services:								
Agriculture, forestry and fishing	33,676	34,443	35,789	35,992	36,454	36,751	37,874	39,518
Mining and quarrying	191,915	175,566	188,251	179,937	164,901	195,055	207,742	220,325
(a) Crude petroleum and natural gas	189,476	173,102	185,735	177,388	162,311	192,452	205,088	217,639
(b) Other	2,440	2,464	2,517	2,550	2,590	2,603	2,654	2,685
Manufacturing	60,191	62,800	65,794	68,700	71,082	76,142	81,314	87,088
(a) Petroleum refining	18,101	18,021	18,660	18,515	18,063	19,914	21,634	22,585
(b) Other	42,090	44,779	47,134	50,186	53,019	56,227	59,680	64,502
Electricity, gas and water	7,511	8,174	8,561	9,515	9,955	10,569	11,259	11,866
Construction	40,406	39,437	41,755	42,123	43,181	45,550	48,517	51,178
Wholesale and retail trade, restaurants and hotels	42,394	45,992	48,183	50,079	52,210	54,204	56,893	60,392
Transport, storage and communication	27,186	27,893	29,015	31,277	33,455	35,046	37,863	41,508
Finance, insurance, real estate and business services	70,020	73,824	76,544	79,113	82,560	84,793	88,490	94,469
(a) Ownership of dwellings	40,682	42,221	43,176	44,080	45,115	46,080	47,924	50,110
(b) Other	29,338	31,603	33,368	35,033	37,445	38,713	40,566	44,360
Community, social and personal services	20,620	21,377	22,478	23,481	24,792	25,552	26,754	28,194
Less imputed bank services charge	11,493	12,340	13,422	14,029	14,859	14,804	14,954	15,536
Sub-total	482,426	477,166	502,948	506,189	503,731	548,858	581,751	619,001
Producers of government services	115,728	116,789	120,289	123,075	126,040	129,326	132,148	141,533
Import duties	9,987	9,634	9,714	7,152	7,459	7,854	8,274	8,972
Gross Domestic Product (GDP)	608,141	603,589	632,951	636,417	637,230	686,037	722,173	769,506

Source: Kingdom of Saudi Arabia, Ministry of Planning (2005) *Achievements of the Development Plans.* Riyadh: Ministry of Planning.

Table 6.10 Percentage growth in sectors of the Gross Domestic Product, 2000–5

	2000	2001	2002	2003	2004	2005 (prelim. est.)
Agriculture, forestry and fishing	3.91	0.57	1.28	0.81	3.06	4.34
Mining and quarrying	7.23	−4.42	−8.36	18.29	6.50	6.06
(a) Crude petroleum & Natural Gas	7.30	−4.49	−8.50	18.57	6.57	6.12
(b) Other	2.15	1.31	1.57	0.50	1.96	1.17
Manufacturing	4.77	4.42	3.47	7.12	6.79	7.10
(a) Petroleum refining	3.55	−0.78	−2.44	10.25	8.64	4.40
(b) Other	5.26	6.48	5.65	6.05	6.14	8.08
Electricity, gas and water	4.73	11.14	4.62	6.17	6.53	5.39
Construction	5.88	0.88	2.51	5.49	6.51	5.48
Wholesale and retail trade, restaurants and hotels	4.76	3.93	4.26	3.82	4.96	6.15
Transport, storage and communication	4.02	7.80	6.96	4.76	8.04	9.63
Finance, insurance, real estate and business services	3.69	3.35	4.36	2.70	4.36	6.76
(a) Ownership of dwellings	2.26	2.09	2.35	2.14	4.00	4.56
(b) Other	5.59	4.99	6.88	3.39	4.79	9.35
Community, social and personal services	5.15	4.46	5.58	3.07	4.70	5.38
Less imputed bank services charge	8.78	4.51	5.92	−0.37	1.01	3.89
Sub-total	5.40	0.64	−0.49	8.96	5.99	6.40
Producers of government services	3.00	2.32	2.41	2.61	2.18	7.10
Total except import duties	4.93	0.97	0.08	7.69	5.27	6.53
Import duties	0.83	−26.37	4.29	5.30	5.35	8.44
Gross Domestic Product (GDP)	4.86	0.55	0.13	7.66	5.27	6.55

Source: Calculated from data in Saudi Arabian Monetary Agency (2000–4) *Annual Surveys.* Riyadh: SAMA.

from the US and elsewhere as a result of the events of 11 September 2001, this was offset by other private capital leaving the country. Over-all the balance on private capital movements became considerably more negative.

6.6 The contribution and composition of the private sector

The contribution of the private sector to GDP over this period grew steadily, rising at the end of it to a level which was substantially higher

Table 6.11 Balance of payments, 2000–5, (US$ billion)

	2000	2001	2002	2003	2004	2005
Current account						
Exports and incoming transfers						
Oil exports	70.7	60.1	63.6	82.0	110.4	162.0
Other commodity exports	6.6	8.2	8.7	11.0	15.3	19.0
Investment income	3.3	4.1	3.7	3.0	4.3	5.0
Service exports	5.0	5.2	5.4	6.0	6.2	6.9
Total	85.6	77.6	81.4	102.0	136.2	192.9
Imports and outgoing transfers						
Commodity imports	34.3	36.8	38.2	44.8	56.3	73.5
Payments for services			22.0	14.4	14.4	14.7
Workers' remittances	15.0	15.1	15.9	14.8	13.6	14.0
Total	71.3	68.0	69.5	74.0	84.3	102.2
Current account balance	14.3	9.6	11.9	28.0	51.9	90.7
Capital movements						
Oil sector and government capital transactions (net)	−1.9	0.0	−0.7	−0.6	−0.3	0.5
Private capital movements (net)	−1.0	−7.7	−12.8	−10.0	−17.9	−27.8
Commercial bank movements (net)	1.0	−0.8	−3.4	3.6	−1.6	5.5
Total	−1.9	−8.5	−16.9	7.0	−19.8	−21.8
Balance of payments surplus/deficit	12.4	0.9	−5.0	21.0	32.1	68.9

Source: Saudi Arabian Monetary Agency (1970–2006) *Annual Reports*. Riyadh: SAMA.

(in constant as well as current prices) than ever before. As a proportion of total GDP at constant prices, the private-sector share maintained, and slightly exceeded, the level it had achieved in 1999 (see Table 6.12). A higher share had been achieved in the mid-to-late 1980s, but that was attributable mainly to the low level of oil prices and production, and the effects which this had on government spending. In the 2000–5 period, the relatively substantial private-sector share occurred at a time when oil prices and production were high and government spending was increasing rapidly.

Significant growth, moreover, was taking place in fields which were crucial to the future development of the economy (see Table 6.13). Manufacturing recorded an average growth rate of 5.5 per cent. Transport, storage and communications grew at 6.9 per cent annually, and electricity, gas and water at 7.1 per cent. In the two latter fields the high rates of growth probably reflected in part the transfer to the private sector of some state-owned enterprises, especially in telecommunications and electricity provision.

Table 6.12 Private-sector share in the Gross Domestic Product, 1998–2005 (constant prices at 1999, SR million)

	Private sector	% of total	Oil sector	% of total	Government sector	% of total	GDP
1998	244,891	40.9	215,357	36.0	137,905	23.1	598,154
1999	255,200	43.0	198,988	33.5	139,767	23.5	593,955
2000	266,437	42.8	212,652	34.1	144,148	23.1	623,237
2001	276,254	43.9	204,365	32.5	148,646	23.6	629,265
2002	287,667	45.7	189,112	30.0	152,992	24.3	629,772
2003	298,970	44.1	221,545	32.7	157,668	23.2	678,183
2004	314,924	44.1	236,459	33.1	162,516	22.8	713,899
2005[a]	335,807	44.2	250,522	32.9	174,205	22.9	760,534

[a]Preliminary data.
Source: Kingdom of Saudi Arabia, Ministry of Planning (2000) *Achievements of the Development Plans*. Riyadh: Ministry of Planning.

Table 6.13 Percentage growth in private-sector fields of activity, 2000–4, by plan-period (compounded, at current prices)

	Plan VII average
Agriculture, forestry and fishing	1.43
Mining and quarrying	3.00
Manufacturing	5.45
Electricity, gas and water	7.12
Construction	3.85
Wholesale and retail trade, restaurants and hotels	4.24
Transport, storage and communication	6.89
Finance, insurance, real estate and business services	3.69
Community, social and personal services	4.45

Source: Kingdom of Saudi Arabia, Ministry of Planning (2000) *Achievements of the Development Plans*. Riyadh: Ministry of Planning.

Construction grew rather more substantially than in the previous period, at an average rate of 3.9 per cent, while agriculture expanded at about the same slow rate it had maintained since the early 1990s, 1.4 per cent.

Gross fixed capital formation in the private sector, which had grown substantially in the final four years of the previous period, continued on the same trend throughout the 2000–5 period (see Table 6.14). As a proportion of total GFCP it declined, due to the higher levels of public-sector expenditure made possible by increased revenues and the provisions of the Seventh and Eighth Plans, but it still made up at least two-thirds of the total.

Table 6.14 Gross fixed capital formation by sectors, 2000–5 (current prices, SR million)

Year	Govt. (non-oil)	% of total	Private sector (non-oil)	% of total	Oil sector	% of total	Total
2000	16,353	13.26	92,953	75.37	14,018	11.37	123,324
2001	17,508	13.88	94,347	74.82	14,240	11.29	126,095
2002	18,121	14.15	97,459	76.10	12,486	9.75	128,066
2003	23,291	15.73	103,676	70.00	21,131	14.27	148,098
2004	30,386	19.43	109,040	69.74	16,921	10.82	156,347
2005	40,970	23.50	115,037	65.99	18,310	10.50	174,317

Source: Saudi Arabian Monetary Agency (1986–2000) *Annual Surveys*. Riyadh: SAMA.

6.7   The changing pattern of employment

The size of the civilian labour force expanded substantially over this period. The total labour force expanded by about one million between 1999 and 2004 (see Table 6.15). Although the numbers of those in manufacturing industry, agriculture, and the oil and gas sector increased, the major growth occurred in the categories described as 'Other producing sectors' and 'Private services'. The former category appears to include activities in construction, electricity, etc., while the latter covers commerce, transport, finance, real estate and domestic service. The proportion of Saudis in the civilian workforce rose from 37.5 per cent of the total in 1999 to

Table 6.15 Civilian employment by economic activities, 1999 and 2004

	1999		2004	
	000's	%	000's	%
Producing sectors except oil and gas				
Agriculture	567.1	7.8	596.7	7.2
Manufacturing industries	638.5	8.8	650.6	7.85
Other producing sectors	1,236.5	17.1	1,680.3	20.3
Service sectors				
Private services	3,703.2	51.2	4,148.3	50.1
Government services	1,001.2	13.8	1,105.4	13.3
Oil and gas	83.8	1.2	100.5	1.2
Total	7,230.3	100.0	8,281.8	100.0

Sources: Khayat, Dina (2005) 'Female Employment in Saudi Arabia' unpublished PhD thesis, University of Exeter, pp. 39–42. All figures from Kingdom of Saudi Arabia, Ministry of Planning (1984–99) *Development Plans*. Riyadh: Ministry of Planning.

Table 6.16 Civilian employment by nationality, Saudi/non-Saudi, 1999 and 2004

	1999		2004	
	000's	*%*	*000's*	*%*
Saudi	2,712.0	37.5	3,536.3	42.7
Non-Saudi	4,518.3	62.5	4,745.5	57.3
Total	7,230.3	100.0	8,281.8	100.0

Sources: Khayat, Dina (2005) 'Female Employment in Saudi Arabia' unpublished PhD thesis, University of Exeter, pp. 39–42.

42.7 per cent in 2004, with some 824,300 more Saudis now in employment. The underlying trend, however, was not as favourable to the Saudisation objective as these figures suggest. Despite attempts to reduce the size of the non-Saudi workforce, the absolute number of non-Saudis in the workforce was still rising. In the course of these five years, the number had increased from 4,518,300 to 4,745,500 (see Table 6.16).

7 The record of reform

Progress, constraints and requirements

7.1 Introduction

The immediate objective of this chapter is to assess the extent to which the reform measures mentioned in the last chapter have been successful. Behind this, however, there is a broader concern. Chapter 5 showed that, at the end of the 1990s, there remained many ways in which the Saudi political economy did not cohere with the developmental state model. Most importantly, it did not have the legal and regulatory framework which such a state required, and the leading circles in the private sector had little confidence in their ability to work effectively with the government. Since 2000, as has been shown in Chapter 6, substantial legal and regulatory changes have occurred. Most of these have been of the kind which leading elements in the private sector had wanted. The issue that arises from this, and which is the broader issue covered in the chapter, is whether the Saudi state now falls into the developmental state pattern. Besides acting as an assessment of the impact of the reform process, therefore, the chapter is also a conclusion to the book: a statement of the stage which Saudi political economy has reached, and its prospects for the future.

The two dimensions – assessing the success of the reforms, and defining the characteristics of Saudi Arabia's contemporary political economy – are of course closely linked. The 'success' of the reforms must, ultimately, be judged by whether they help fashion the economic conditions necessary for Saudi Arabia's further development. For this, the reforms must be situated in relation to the social and economic dynamics underpinning the state. The theoretical basis employed in this book makes use of the developmental state model to uncover and highlight some of these dynamics. A number of issues, therefore, are linked together in the analysis: whether the reforms have improved the effectiveness of the Saudi economic system; whether the country's current procedures, institutions and infrastructure now form a sound base for economic growth; and whether the relationship between the state and the private sector, as currently developing, can create an ongoing dynamic whereby Saudi Arabia can emerge as a major industrial/financial power.

The specific questions to which answers will be sought, in this assessment of the success of the reforms and the characteristics of the country's contemporary political economy, are the following:

- Will the legal, financial and institutional structures which are now in place enable the private sector to act as a critical motor of Saudi Arabia's economic growth?
- Does the country's social and physical infrastructure constitute a sound basis for promoting economic expansion?
- Is the economy linked into the wider global setting in a manner which will enable it to develop effectively? (This will inevitably relate primarily to the framework created by membership of the World Trade Organisation.)
- Has the government's policy on privatisation proved capable of creating a more competitive and effective economic order?
- Does the stock market operate as an effective instrument for raising capital and channelling investments to productive purposes?
- Does the labour market provide the calibre and skills needed for successful economic development, at rates of pay which are competitive internationally?
- Are the state institutions, and the manner in which they are linked to the private sector, geared to framing coherent development policies and implementing them?

It is worth noting at this stage that the overall evaluation of Saudi Arabia's political economy cannot rest simply on the balance between negative and positive outcomes on each of the issues just mentioned. The social impact of the outcomes also needs to be considered. An economic strategy cannot be deemed successful if it creates social dynamics which are going to be destabilising and ultimately destructive of social and political harmony. Without such harmony the economic strategy itself may not be sustainable. The social dimensions of the current pattern of economic development in the Kingdom are, therefore, also given attention in this chapter. This is done after the potential for, and likely shape of, economic development have been assessed.

Some of the data used in this chapter come from published statistical and documentary sources. Use is also made, however, of a series of interviews which the author conducted with prominent businessmen in the spring and summer of 2006. Some of the same questions were asked of this group as had been asked of the group of businessmen interviewed in the 1990s by Malik. The interviews did not seek to cover a representative survey of business opinion, but rather focused on some ten individuals playing key roles in the private sector. Their perceptions were deemed important due to these roles, not because they necessarily represented a wider range of business opinion. Nonetheless, many of their views do also find expression in the meetings of the various Chambers of Commerce in the country, which are becoming increasingly significant and open fora for debate.

There is a central thread to the argument pursued through the sections which follow. It is that, while large parts of the Saudi economy are not structured in such a way to prosper in a competitive global economy, there are significant parts of the economy which have all the characteristics, dynamics and facilities needed for global success. The industries which are in this latter category are mainly in sectors where Saudi Arabia has the greatest comparative advantage. Their relationships with the Saudi state are supportive and productive rather than extractive in either direction. They have the potential to obtain for the Saudi economy a major stake in the global market for some critical products, especially petrochemicals. Saudi Arabia's political economy is likely in the future, therefore, to have this paradoxical aspect: a relatively small but highly effective part of the economy, playing an increasingly important global economic role, surrounded by a larger economic hinterland of Saudi companies and undertakings struggling to compete. With the opening up of the Saudi domestic market to foreign competition, the 'struggle to compete' will occur in domestic as well as global markets. At one level the economy will cohere with the model of the developmental state; at another it will have insufficient competitiveness for developmental success. Oil revenue creates the social and economic dynamics that make this kind of hybrid economy possible. A new social contract between the state and the population may be needed if the problems of the economic hinterland are to be addressed effectively. This would, in turn, make possible a more favourable social outcome for the population and reinforce the country's social stability.

7.2   Will the legal, financial and institutional structures which are now in place enable the private sector to act as a critical motor of Saudi Arabia's economic growth?

The legal, financial and institutional reforms, as documented in Chapter 6, are of fundamental significance to the shaping of Saudi Arabia's current economic development. This section will, therefore, concern itself not just with the suitability of the existing arrangements but also with some wider economic developments. While not all the latter stem simply from the reform process, they cannot usefully be disentangled from that process.

There has clearly been substantial new legislation affecting economic life in Saudi Arabia since 2000. Besides what was mentioned in Chapter 6, moreover, numerous other smaller pieces of legislation relating to the good running of the economy have been issued. Most of these have taken the form of clarifications of existing procedures rather than substantive changes. Most were adopted specifically to satisfy WTO requirements, and the background to their being issued can be found in the *Report of the Working Party on the Accession of the Kingdom of Saudi Arabia to the World Trade Organisation* (WTO 2005). The Working Party Report has a listing of the documentation which the Saudi government provided in its application for WTO membership. Among the smaller legal and regulatory changes referred to are the royal decrees enacting laws on Commercial Data (25.6.02) Competition Policy (22.6.04) and Trademarks (7.8.02); the Council of Ministers resolutions implementing the Vienna Convention on the Law of Treaties (1.9.02); introducing an Import Licensing Law to clarify the procedures required for import licences (16.6.02); laying down Regulations for the Protection of Confidential Information (4.4.05); and the technical directives issued by the Saudi Arabian Standards Organisation to specify the standards applied within the country (18.5.04 and 18–19.7.05). Altogether, Saudi Arabia enacted 42 new laws and created nine new regulatory bodies to bring it into alignment with WTO rules (WTO 2005: 1–8).

The significance of the new and/or clarified regulations is not limited to any substantive changes which they may have introduced. A major part of their significance lies precisely in the clarification of economic processes and procedures. They are available in English as well as Arabic, and all future regulations must (under WTO rules) be available in both languages. In the process of negotiating WTO entry (and in the negotiation of the 38 bilateral trade agreements which were needed to prepare for membership) the Saudi government had to produce 7,000 pages of documentation, in answer to 3,400 questions (SAMBA 2006: 6). It is now easier for businesses, especially foreign businesses, to know their rights and what procedures are necessary for them to conduct business. At least in terms of their overall structure, the key laws (such as the Foreign Investment Law) are comparable to those in other countries seeking investment. The tax system is generous to investors, and indeed probably too generous at the domestic level.

Government ministries have, at the same time, been issuing more detailed statistics and information than before, and government institutions have been more open in producing information on the economy.

The web page of the Ministry of Planning, for example, provides substantial statistical information on the economy, such as would be needed for businesses which are planning to invest, and most ministries have web pages which provide information on the laws and regulations which relate to their own fields of activity. As will be shown later, there are some areas, particularly those which relate to labour, in which the information provided is confusing and/or inaccurate. The statistics produced by the Saudi Arabian Monetary Agency are detailed and tend to be reliable.

The central institution created to promote private-sector investment within the new regulatory framework – the Saudi Arabian General Investment Authority (SAGIA) – has generally operated effectively. In its role as a one-stop shop for companies seeking to invest in the Kingdom (especially foreign companies), it has acted both as a facilitator for businesses wishing to invest and as the authority which decides on investment applications and their revocation. In both respects it has played a useful role, discharging its duties efficiently. The process of setting up a business and acquiring the necessary licences has been made easier. Besides fulfilling the duties just mentioned, SAGIA has also played a wider role in promoting the competitiveness of the Saudi economy, especially in the industrial field. Among the measures it has taken have been the establishment of investors' services centres at the main airports and the economic cities, preparing specialised economic reports on the different regions to inform investors, promoting public/private partnerships, and holding fora devoted to the means by which competitiveness can be enhanced (SAGIA 2007). In effect it has become a powerful lobby group working for economic reform in the Kingdom.

The rate at which licences for new investments have been approved since 2003 has increased substantially. How much of this is due to the effectiveness of SAGIA, and how much to the improved climate for investment, is impossible to say. Both factors have, no doubt, contributed to the increase. From the initiation of its activities in 2001 through to March 2004, SAGIA issued some 2,200 licences, for projects whose value totalled some SR56 billion. By the end of November 2005 a total of 3,112 licences had been issued for projects to a value of SR152 billion (*Arab News*, 6.6.06). The more recent licences were for larger projects than before. In 2006 the increase was even more substantial. In that year alone 1,389 licences were issued, carrying a total value of SR253 billion. In announcing its annual results for 2006, SAGIA predicted that the total for 2007 might be in the region of SR300 billion (SAGIA 2007). Most of the initial licences given by SAGIA were for foreign and joint investment, but over the years the proportion from Saudi investors has steadily risen, reaching 42.7 per cent in 2006 (*Arab News*, 6.6.06).

The granting of a licence is not necessarily followed by an actual investment, and usually there is a delay of two or three years before it is
known whether the investment will materialise. A SAGIA report on foreign investment in June 2005 projected that, based on previous experience,
some 80 per cent of all licences would be followed by an actual investment (SAGIA 2005: 20). Statistics on foreign and domestic investment
since 2003 do indeed show investment growing rapidly. Table 6.14 shows
gross fixed capital formation growing on average by about 12 per cent per
annum between 2003 and 2005. The increase during 2006 seems to have
been significantly higher, although the official figures for this were not
available at the time of writing.

One reflection of the impact of the regulatory changes comes in the
rising position which Saudi Arabia is given in the league tables which
rank countries according to the ease with which business is conducted.
The rise has been particularly marked in the years since 2003. The Doing
Business Report for 2006 ranks Saudi Arabia as 38th in the world in ease
of doing business, out of a total of 175 countries covered. The report
was prepared under the auspices of the World Bank and the International
Finance Corporation. In 2004 the Kingdom ranked 64th. The 2006 report
placed Saudi Arabia as the best country for doing business in the Arab
world, and ahead of some developed countries. It was just ahead of Spain
and Portugal and a little behind France (Doing Business 2006).

Yet this ranking is misleading. It is based on a composite figure made
from a variety of different elements. An analysis of performance in the
different areas which contribute to the composite suggests that the Saudi
economy remains uncompetitive in some key areas. The economy scored
well on such components as paying taxes (where the low or in some
cases non-existent taxes are well known), registering property, employing
workers (a surprising outcome, given that Saudi businessmen complain
about the difficulty of firing Saudi employees) and trading across fron-
tiers. In some other highly important areas, however, the Saudi economy
was ranked very low: 156th for starting a business, 99th for protecting
investors, 97th for enforcing contracts and 87th for closing a business
(Doing Business 2006). While in all of these areas the Saudi economy was
little worse, and often better, than most other Arab economies, it came out
substantially worse than some key competitors within the region (in particular the United Arab Emirates and Bahrain) and outside. The performance
bore no comparison with the norm in OECD countries. The details which
the Doing Business Report provides about procedures in some of these
areas, moreover, add to the bleakness of the picture. Starting a business in
Saudi Arabia was estimated as involving 13 procedures, taking 39 days,
and costing 58.6 per cent of the per capita income. The improvement in

ease of doing business since 2004, moreover, might not be sustained. In the 2005 Doing Business Report, Saudi Arabia had come in at 35th, so in 2006 it slipped back three places (Doing Business 2005). The Global Competitiveness Report of the World Economic Forum did not list Saudi Arabia in 2005 and 2006, perhaps because the information needed for that listing was not available.

Interviews with businessmen registered agreement with the picture just outlined: business conditions were seen as having improved while remaining inappropriate to the efficient and effective operation of the economy in some significant respects. There were still, it was stated, large areas where bureaucratic red tape remained heavy and in practice restrictive. Most businesses employed 'fixers' whose role is specifically to liaise with government departments in order to secure permissions and authorisations, which should really be only procedural. Some of these latter practices were seen as involving petty corruption, which often entailed facilitation through beneficial personal relationships: presenting gifts to officials to speed up the performance of tasks, which they should be doing anyway. An interviewee from one medium-sized company reported that his company had a fund of SR3 million to finance this side of its operations. There were suggestions that major projects could involve more significant pay-offs to senior officials. Interviewees were convinced that the setting up of companies in Saudi Arabia took longer than elsewhere, with a suggestion that it could be done in two days in Dubai as against up to two months in Saudi Arabia.

Reports from the IMF and some other international financial institutions continue to point to the continued inadequacy of the financial instruments at the disposal of the Saudi government, with no income tax on Saudi citizens, no corporate tax on Saudi companies beyond the obligation to pay *zakat* (a religious tax coming to 2.5 per cent of profits, whose proceeds are intended to be used for charitable purposes), and no value-added tax. The contention of the IMF is that the government needs such instruments so as to be able to shape economic and social processes in the country more effectively (IMF 2006). They could be used to encourage certain types of economic activity while discouraging others, focus economic development on regions which need investment most, and redistribute wealth so as to ensure greater social equality.

Overall, the regulatory changes made in recent years appear to have been of most benefit to those Saudi companies which are seeking to expand through alliances with foreign investors. While the changes may benefit all parts of business, the dynamic which drove them was the need to satisfy the needs of foreign investors. They needed the reassurance, guarantees and transparency they could obtain elsewhere. The Saudi companies for whom international alliances and foreign participation are of most relevance are in the petrochemicals, banking, power and water sectors. In petrochemicals, the scale and character of production requires such alliances, together with foreign investment in their domestic projects, if they are to pursue global production and marketing strategies. In banking, a foreign input into the local operation is required for the bank to achieve its global role. It was mentioned in interviews that foreign participation also helps a company to avoid unwarranted interference or obstruction by authorities within the Kingdom. Government personnel would, it was said, be more circumspect in dealing with companies with foreign connections, knowing that the foreign partner might have less compunction than a local businessman in seeking legal redress. Large companies, developing areas of the economy which are regarded as critical for Saudi Arabia's long-term future, allied to major international corporations, have every means to cut through the bureaucratic hindrances which remain within the system. Smaller companies will have less interest in international alignments, and less practical ability to pursue them. They will also be more vulnerable to bureaucratic obstruction or predatory behaviour.

7.3 Does the social and physical infrastructure constitute a sound basis for promoting economic expansion?

The substantial funding which was put into the development of the social and physical infrastructure in the 1970s and early 1980s created a structure of communications and services which was suited to the needs of that time. The existing state of physical and social infrastructure does, however, have deficiencies when seen from the perspective of contemporary needs. The latter must, moreover, be placed within the context of comparability in the global environment.

With the physical infrastructure, part of the problem lies with the lower levels of physical infrastructure expenditure in the late 1980s and 1990s, and the lack of effective maintenance or modernisation of some of the facilities. Businessmen interviewed referred to inadequacies in airport services (with Jiddah airport singled out for particular criticism), shortages of industrial land, problems in telecommunications, difficulties in obtaining sufficient supplies of water and power (with the facilities in Jiddah again attracting particular criticism), and the absence of suitable rail networks to transport heavy goods around the country (interviews 2006). A report by the National Commercial Bank in 2004 suggested that a total of $267 billion of investment would be needed to cover basic infrastructural improvements over a 20-year period. Subsequent reports have suggested that the need would be significantly more than this (NCB 2004).

Such existing shortages and inadequacies as there are, however, are not likely to inhibit the expansion of business. On the one hand, the past few years have seen some improvements in infrastructure. On the other, the government already has plans in place for massive developments in infrastructure. Much of this involves private investment operating within a framework devised and overseen by the government – as with the power and water developments which are now underway. The government's current plans are to raise $624 billion in foreign direct investment over the period through to 2020, and a significant part of this would be for investment in infrastructural schemes: $170 billion for water and electricity, and $100 billion for ports, highways and railways (*Arab News*, 16.1.06). In the course of 2005–6, moreover, the government announced the establishment of four new economic cities at Rabigh (the King Abdallah Financial District), Ha'il, al-Madinah and Jizan, together with that of the King Abdallah Business City in Riyadh. It was expected that a further economic city would be established in Tabuk, and perhaps one more in the eastern part of the country. While the practicability and feasibility of some of these latter developments remain unclear, the likelihood is that the areas in the country where businesses can obtain modern and effective facilities will grow.

Human resource expenditure, as shown earlier, has increased substantially over the past 15 years. Paradoxically, however, this element of the infrastructure may prove most problematic for the business sector (at least parts of it). The problem lies in the framework within which education is delivered. This has not changed significantly, despite frequent governmental references to syllabus reform. A strong intention for reform has been present in government circles, but the practical effects have focused more on presentational changes to school textbooks (removing passages which Western observers have seen as antagonistic to regional and global harmony) rather than gearing the system to the needs of a fast-changing global environment. For the requirements of the business sector, the crucial inadequacies identified in recent interviews remain similar to what they were in Malik's 1998 survey. Except in certain specific areas, the education system was seen as failing to produce sufficient graduates with the calibre and skills which the private sector required, and with the creativity and commitment necessary for global competition.

A 2005 analysis of the output of the educational system, and its relevance for the employment needs of business, outlined some of the problems. Despite an emphasis on graduating more students with technical, scientific and engineering specialisations, 44 per cent of students graduating in 2003 emerged with arts-based qualifications, and about 20 per cent with *sharia'a*-related qualifications. Whereas there were skills gaps and resultant job opportunities in scientific and technical fields, there was an excess of graduates who could take on administrative and clerical positions. Labour productivity in the non-oil sector was low, although rising fast in the leading industrial sectors of the economy. 64 per cent of Saudis in employment were either in general administration or education, with no more than 3 per cent in manufacturing. Female labour constituted only 5 per cent of the labour force, and 69 per cent of female employees were either in education or in health (Taher 2005).

In practice, the weaknesses in Saudi Arabia's human resources infrastructure are unlikely to hold back the development of the leading business sectors. Many of the key personnel running the organisations and corporations in the petrochemical, oil, energy-intensive industrial and financial sectors were educated outside of the country, as also were some of the scientific and technological personnel who operate the factories. The best of Saudi education, moreover, is of high quality. The King Fahd University for Petroleum and Mineral Resources (where the instruction is in English, and the specialisations studied are predominantly in the scientific and technological fields) produces engineering graduates who are as good as those graduating anywhere else in the world. A further reality is that the petrochemical and energy-intensive industries where Saudi Arabia has an international competitive advantage do not require a large employment base. They require a small number of highly skilled and qualified personnel. Mostly, such personnel are available within the country, but to the extent that they are not they can be brought in from outside. The resources are available for the best people on the international market to be recruited, and the close governmental/private sector links within the industries concerned mean that any tendency to hold up permissions for this kind of labour can be resolved.

Some of the needs for graduates with higher levels of scientific and technical skills will, no doubt, be filled through the new scholarship programmes instituted in 2005 and 2006, to send large numbers of Saudis abroad for training. Some of these are being sent to Western countries, mainly the US, but significant numbers are now being sent to the Far East, South-East Asia and South Asia. The countries concerned are Singapore, Malaysia, India, China and South Korea. The educational provision in these Asian countries is considered best suited to training Saudi students in practically-oriented technical and scientific fields–the fields which have assured the success of the countries concerned, whose record Saudi Arabia now needs to emulate.

The optimistic view given above, however, refers only to the needs of the leading business sectors. For the remainder of the economy, which will have to rely primarily on the output of the Saudi educational system, the prospects are not so good and the need for substantial educational reform is more acute. The social implications of leaving the educational system unreformed, and its graduates relegated to jobs which do not require high levels of proficiency, would be severe. The need to improve the quality and character of the graduates of Saudi universities remains, for reasons which are both economic and social.

7.4   Is the economy linked into the wider global setting in a manner which will enable it to develop effectively?

Saudi membership of the WTO is clearly central to any assessment of Saudi Arabia's position in the global economy. The period which has elapsed since the country became a member in December 2005 is too brief for conclusions to be drawn from actual membership experience, but the implications of the accession agreement are fairly evident. Moreover, 12 years passed between Saudi Arabia's initial application for membership and its ultimate accession, and over this period many of the crucial changes which membership entails were made. Change, in other words, preceded membership in some fields rather than followed it. A report by SAMBA put the extent of the changes made in the run-up to membership as follows: 'In the process of preparing for membership, Saudi Arabia enacted 42 new trade-related laws, created nine new regulatory bodies, and signed 38 bilateral agreements' (SAMBA 2006: 3). The Kingdom's external tariffs had come down considerably since negotiations began, from a level where they stood at 12 per cent for three-quarters of Saudi imports in 1993, to 5 per cent for more than three-quarters of Saudi imports in 2003. The level of import tariffs would, the SAMBA report pointed out, be reduced further following WTO accession (in stages), but the most substantial changes had already taken place.

An analysis of the implications of WTO membership will therefore form the focus of this consideration of how conditions in the global economy will impinge on Saudi Arabia's economy in the future. While the focus here is on the impact of WTO membership on Saudi Arabia, it should be remembered that Saudi membership was itself of some importance to the WTO. As the world's 13th largest merchandise exporter and 23rd largest importer in the year prior to accession, Saudi Arabia is a major global trading power which needs to be inside the system. On 11 December 2005 it became the 149th member of the WTO.

A significant part of the extended negotiations over Saudi membership of the WTO took the form of negotiations between Saudi Arabia and its main trading partners. Bilateral agreements with these countries had to be reached before membership could proceed. The two main trading partners were the US and the EU, both of whom had important interests at stake in the negotiations. The achievement of the agreements, therefore, required a deal to be struck. The central objective of the Saudi government in the negotiations was for the US and EU (followed by other countries) to lift duties on Saudi petrochemical products as a condition for Saudi Arabia opening its own markets. On the US/EU/WTO side, the Saudi government had to open its markets, placing upper limits on tariffs, removing protective barriers to trade, allowing more foreign participation in service sectors (such as banking), liberalising regulations on foreign investment, and improving the business climate in such areas as the protection of intellectual property rights. The bilateral agreements which were reached, and ultimately the agreement for WTO membership, were based on this balance of interests, with Saudi Arabia gaining considerably more favourable terms for the entry of its petrochemicals into global markets than the industrial powers had initially wanted to concede.

The measures to open up the economy, which the Saudi government agreed upon, were significant. They involved major changes to the way in which the economy operated. The government committed itself to reduce tariffs (including those in some key areas which had previously been protected), and to open up its service sectors to foreign participation. The opening up to foreign investment had already taken place. Customs duties were to be reduced over a five-year period on 870 industrial and agricultural commodities, representing 12 per cent of the commodities listed on the Saudi tariff schedule. While this percentage may seem to constitute a small part of the total, they in fact comprised most of the commodities which had retained high tariff barriers–around the 20 per cent level, rather than the 5 per cent which applied to most imports. Among the industries affected are those producing confectionery, plastics, paper, metal, steel pipes and lubricating oils. In some other areas duties were to be reduced to zero, as in telecommunications equipment, computers and computer accessories. Some key agricultural products (such as dates, wheat, poultry, eggs, vegetables and some fruits) would continue to benefit from higher tariffs, on the grounds that the Saudi government had invested heavily in the development of these products. At the same time the Saudi government committed itself to reducing its domestic support for agriculture (which had, in any case, been falling) by 13.3 per cent over a ten-year period (SAMBA 2006: 5–14).

Saudi Arabia also made significant commitments with regard to its service sector. Twelve main fields of service activity were targeted in this respect, together with 155 sub-fields and four administrative or delivery structures. In practice this comprised most of the major fields of service activity. They now became open for cross-border delivery and for receiving foreign investment. The measures did not involve the removal of all restrictions, but they did envisage that the key sectors would be considerably more open than before, most crucially in banking, insurance, wholesale and retail trade, and franchising. The requirements that foreign companies should act through Saudi-owned agencies were phased out by the agreement, so that foreign companies could now act as agents themselves as well as establish joint-venture partnerships with Saudi companies. Given that much of the private sector in Saudi Arabia has been built up around agencies for foreign companies, this is a significant change. Nonetheless it would seem probable that many foreign companies would continue to use the established agencies, as many of the latter had developed important distribution networks and servicing and repair facilities which could not easily be replicated (WTO 2005).

The Saudi government also agreed to implement all WTO rules on accession, rather than passing through a transitional phase where the WTO rules would not be applied. The latter provision meant that it had to apply regulations on intellectual property rights, foreign investment, transparency in trade issues, legal recourse for trade partners, and elimination of technical barriers to trade, all from 11 December 2005 (SAMBA 2006: 3). In practice, as has been shown in Chapter 6, most of the relevant legislation to comply with these rules had been enacted between 2001 and 2004.

During the years of negotiation, some prominent Saudis had feared that accession would force the Kingdom to change long-held social and political policies and practices in the country. Among these were permitting the import of pork products and alcohol, opening up trade with Israel, abandoning the emphasis on Saudisation, and charging less than the international price for the oil and gas used as energy or feedstock in the country's petrochemical industries. None of this, however, was required by the accession agreement.

In return for these changes, Saudi Arabia made a substantial gain. WTO membership gave its key industrial products greatly enhanced access to international markets – with full access assured once the transition to the conditions of membership is completed in 2009. The government was not required to give a commitment to change the pricing of feedstock or energy for domestic industry. Given the importance of petrochemical exports to the country's development strategy, and the manner in which its exports had previously been blocked from entry into many key markets, this was a major change. Previously the advanced industrial powers had strongly resisted such a move, on the grounds that their own petrochemical industries would be undercut. Saudi Arabia was seen as enjoying too great a competitive advantage, for as long as it was supplying its industry with feedstock and energy at much lower prices than those which held on the international market. The major Saudi beneficiary of WTO accession in this regard was, of course, the petrochemicals industry, and in particular SABIC, which dominates petrochemical production within the Kingdom.

The nature of the advantage which the Saudi petrochemical industry now has internationally, at least in comparison with the same industries in developed countries, can be seen by comparing the price of natural gas (the main feedstock for petrochemicals) in the US and in Saudi Arabia. In the US, the price is $14 per million BTUs, whereas in Saudi Arabia it stands as $0.75. The Saudi side was also fortunate that the Chemical Tariff Harmonisation Agreement (1995) had come into force, substantially reducing global tariffs on chemical imports – including all 64 of the chemicals which SABIC and its affiliates exported. The country's ability to develop new projects in this field, therefore, has been greatly strengthened (SAMBA 2006: 17). The petrochemicals industry can continue to benefit from low-cost feedstock and low-cost energy supply, at the same time as benefiting from the removal of the high tariffs which previously inhibited exports.

No change would occur with regard to the country's crude oil exports. Crude oil would not benefit from any greater market access than before. This, however, was of little significance. Tariffs on oil imports around the world are generally zero or very low, so there was not much which Saudi Arabia could have gained on this score. Domestic taxes on oil and oil products are the major factor raising the price of oil in Western countries, but these are not covered by WTO regulations.

In other industries, the prospects for private-sector companies are not so bright. Many of them have enjoyed protection from their inception, without raising themselves to a level where they can compete with foreign competition domestically, and on the global market they may well decline and fail. Much may depend on their ability to forge alliances and partnerships with foreign companies which will reinforce their competitive ability. Those who can do this may succeed, while the remainder may find themselves squeezed out of the market place.

There are some other aspects of WTO membership which should also be put in the balance. Membership has increased transparency and predictability in the Saudi commercial environment, as was pointed out in Section 7.2. It has also provided a context within which Saudi Arabia could, if it so chooses, pool its strength with that of other developing and industrialising countries in the WTO (led at present by Brazil, India and China). It could then become part of the bloc seeking to shift the advantage of international trading practices away from the interests of the developed industrialised world.

7.5 Has the government's policy on privatisation proved capable of creating a more competitive and effective economic order?

Privatisation of state-owned enterprises has generally been deemed important for two different reasons in the literature of the international financial institutions. First, it is seen as increasing productivity through reducing the role of the 'bureaucratic' public sector. Second, it encourages the growth of private-sector-led investment growth, a significant proportion of which will be from foreign sources. The latter, it is contended, will increase efficiency and introduce new technology. Both of these arguments have been used in justifying an extensive privatisation policy in Saudi Arabia, both in the context of WTO membership and outside of it. As has been mentioned in earlier chapters, it has been proclaimed as a policy in all recent Saudi development plans. The pace at which it has advanced, however, has been slow.

The main measures of privatisation were initiated in the later part of 2002, after the guidelines had been laid down. The most important such measure so far has been the initial public offering for 30 per cent of the Saudi Telecommunications Company (STC), which was held between 17 December 2002 and 6 January 2003. The company is the country's sole fixed line provider, and up to 2005 was the only one with a licence to run a mobile network. This was the first major government sell-off since the part privatisation of SABIC in the early 1980s. There was strong demand for the sale: according to the Finance Ministry, the government generated a net US$4 billion from the sale of 90 million shares. Around one-third of the shares were sold to two state-run pension funds, the Retirement Pension Directorate (RPD) and the General Organisation for Social Insurance (GOSI), which together hold some 65 per cent of total government debt. The remainder of the shares were sold to Saudi citizens (Niblock 2006: 136). With the public offering of STC shares, STC rapidly became the largest publicly traded company in Saudi Arabia (Zahid 2004). As the government retained majority control of the company, however, it seems unlikely that the trading of the company's shares will lead to a radical change in its operation.

Two other initial public offerings were announced in 2004, both involving companies playing substantial roles in the economy. In May 2004 the Supreme Economic Council approved the long-awaited sale of the government's stake in the National Company for Co-operative Insurance (NCCI). The initial public offering duly took place in December 2004 and January 2005, with 7 million NCCI shares being put on the market at SR205 each. This was equivalent to about 70 per cent of the company's total capital. The offering was over-subscribed by 11.5 times (Zawya 2005). The Supreme Economic Council also approved in May 2004 the privatisation of the Saudi Arabian Mining Company (MAADEN). Wide-ranging restructuring of the latter company has already begun in order to sell it off in different parts. According to the company, the precious metals business will be the first to be sold off. It was announced late in 2005 that an initial public offering for shares in 50 per cent of the company would take place at the end of 2006, but at the time of writing (July 2007) this had not yet taken place.

Many other privatisation projects which have been envisaged and widely discussed over the years still remained at the planning stage when this book was being written. An initial public offering for the 50 per cent of shares in the National Commercial Bank held by the government was expected. This had been initially mentioned as a possibility in 2004 (Dun and Bradstreet 2004: 25), but has still not been implemented. The much-heralded sale of some of the government's 70 per cent equity participation in SABIC has still not taken place, although in the course of 2005 SABIC announced an initial public offering of 35 per cent of its holding in one of its subsidiaries, the Yanbu National Petrochemicals Company (Yansab). The sale of more of the government shares in SABIC would, of course, be particularly significant. The company accounts for about 10 per cent of world petrochemical production, and with the new projects which it has in hand that percentage will continue to increase (US Embassy 2004). The Saline Water Conversion Company has been planning a move towards privatisation, and consultants have been appointed to advise on this move. It was intended that the privatisation would take place in 2008. The sale of Saudi Arabian Airlines (SAUDIA) continues to be debated, and the belief that this was likely to go ahead in the near future was strengthened when a new director for the airline was appointed in June 2006. The new director was Khalid al-Milhum, who had successfully carried through the privatisation of the Saudi Telecommunications Company. Such plans as have been made public so far, however, relate to the sale of some of the services associated with the airline rather than the airline itself.

The privatisation of services in a number of fields has been advancing. The privatisation of the management and operation of local and international airports has been announced; some of the ports services have been privatised; the postal services are now being operated by private operators;

and plans for the privatisation of urban transport systems and of some medical care facilities are being discussed.

The slow progress of privatisation is to some extent justified by the need to establish appropriate regulatory frameworks first, in order to ensure that the process does not involve the stripping of state assets, the establishment of privately owned monopolies and the exploitation of consumers. But the elaboration of the regulatory frameworks has itself not been given urgent attention. A further problem is that the government has sometimes indicated that jobs should not be cut following privatisation (Malik 1999: 258). This removes one of the perceived major benefits of the privatisation process – to eliminate unproductive jobs and to improve efficiency.

Whether the slow rate of privatisation matters to Saudi Arabia's emergence as a developmental state, however, can be questioned. The Saudi companies and institutions which are most critical for Saudi Arabia in gaining a stake in the global markets are already effectively managed and directed. Many of them are majority-owned by the state, with SABIC at the forefront. There is no particular reason to believe that SABIC would be better able to achieve its global objectives if the government sold its 70 per cent share. MAADEN is also a well-run state-owned company which is expected to play an important role in developing the global reach of the economy.

The parts of the economy which suffer from the slow pace of privatisation are those which are not at the cutting-edge areas of Saudi Arabia's industrial development strategy. Smaller companies, not working in the fields of comparative advantage which the Saudi government is seeking to develop, are the ones which could benefit most from the privatisation of state-owned enterprises. Their benefit could come through taking over some of these operations themselves, but it might also come from the better services which a more competitive system could deliver. At present, they certainly suffer the inefficiency and bureaucracy which characterises some services currently run by the state or by municipalities. The slow rate of privatisation, then, affects them most.

Progress on privatisation should not be confused with a wider process of opening up new opportunities for the private sector, such as giving licences to private entrepreneurs to enter fields of investment which had previously been closed to them. The latter process has in fact advanced substantially. One aspect of this has been the developments in the power and water sectors referred to earlier. It has happened in other fields also. In August 2004 the Council of Ministers licensed a foreign company (the UAE-based Etisalat) to establish and operate the second mobile phone network in the country. In June 2003 the Supreme Economic Council opened up the Saudi aviation sector to private enterprise, making it possible for Saudi-owned private companies to operate domestic airline services.

Two new airline companies have now been licensed. In October 2003 the Saudi Arabian Monetary Agency (SAMA) announced that it would allow Deutsche Bank AG to begin independent operations in the Kingdom, and in the course of 2004 similar announcements were made with regard to the American bank JP Morgan Chase and the French BNP Paribas. This was the first time such banks had been allowed in since the 1970s, when the banking industry was nationalised (Dun and Bradstreet 2004: 50). A number of other banking licences have subsequently been given. Private health clinics, hospitals and educational facilities are also developing. These developments may be more important than the privatisation of some of the larger and more successful state-owned enterprises.

7.6 Does the stock market operate as an effective instrument for raising capital and channelling investments to productive sectors?

The creation of a well-regulated financial market is an important element in the reform process. The intention in creating the Saudi Arabian Stock Exchange (*al-Tadawul*), as mentioned in Chapter 6, was to make it easier to float companies, provide better opportunities for Saudi citizens to invest their money domestically, and to increase the capital available to companies for their expansion and development.

There has, as a result, indeed been an explosion of share-ownership in Saudi Arabia. This had begun even before the new Capital Markets Law was enacted in June 2003. It was initially driven by the new liquidity in the market stemming from the rise of oil revenues and government expenditure. It was perhaps also affected by the reluctance of some Saudis to risk their money in investments abroad after the deterioration of US–Saudi relations in the wake of 9/11. At the beginning of July 2003 the Tadawul All-Share Index (TASI) stood at about 3,000. By the end of August 2004 it had passed the 9,000 mark, in November 2005 it reached 15,000, and at the end of February 2006 it peaked at about 21,000 (SAMBA 2005, 2006, 2007). The market capitalisation of the Saudi stock market had risen from $158 billion in 2003, through $307 billion in 2004, to a total value of $745 billion in January 2006 – a sum which was approximately equal to that of all of the other Arab stock markets combined. The second largest was that of the United Arab Emirates, which was valued at $210 billion. The concentration of market capitalisation in a small number of companies was considerable: 57 per cent of total capitalisation was accounted for by the largest five companies.

The price/earnings index for Saudi shares in 2005 stood at 44 per cent. This was very high, given that the price/earnings index for shares on the

London Stock Exchange in that year was 18 per cent (and elsewhere the earnings were generally less). More than half of the adult Saudi population became involved in share-dealing. Many took out large loans to finance their purchase of shares, or else sold houses or cars to raise the money. Figures on consumer debt give some indication of what was happening. In 2002 consumer debt came to less than SR60 billion; in 2005 it stood at more than SR240 billion (SAMA 2003, 2006). In 2002 most of the debt had been related to real estate, credit cards and cars, whereas in 2005 three-quarters of the debt was ranked under the broad title 'Other'. It seemed that the stock market was achieving its purpose: raising substantial sums of money for the development of the companies concerned, and creating wealth among shareholders.

The period which followed the peak of February 2006, however, showed that the sharp rise in the TASI and of market capitalisation lacked a secure foundation. A dramatic and continuing fall in the index ensued. By the beginning of April the index had fallen back to 15,000. Although it then staged a rally, this was short-lived. By the middle of that year it stood at around 10,000. In the later part of 2006 the decline continued, falling below the 7,000 mark in November 2006. The market capitalisation fell by about $500 billion. The price/earnings ration stood at about 15 per cent in January 2007 (SAMBA 2007: 12, 22). Early in 2007 the TASI was mostly fluctuating around the 8,000 mark.

While the unrealistic expectations of investors no doubt contributed to the false bubble which had been created in 2004 and 2005, substantial responsibility also lay with the character, imperfections and inadequate regulatory arrangements of the market itself. Those with substantial funds to invest were able to draw profit from forcing up the price of a particular stock. Sometimes, it seems, small groups of wealthy investors bought and sold the shares of a particular company among themselves, creating an ever-rising spiral and giving the impression to others that substantial profits could be made from purchase of the share concerned. Smaller investors would see the trend and, assuming that the spiral would continue, purchased the share concerned. The assumption was often made that a sharply rising price might be brought about by insider information (someone within the company divulging the scale of prof-its which the company was realising). In some cases there was indeed such insider dealing, which itself distorted the market, but in other cases the rumoured profits had no basis in fact. Smaller investors bor-rowed substantial sums of money to finance share purchases in these conditions. Some of the banks, rather than advising against unrealis-tic speculation, encouraged individuals to take on higher levels of debt (interviews 2006).

This was not a sound basis on which to build the confidence of Saudi investors in putting their money into the market, or to arrange the investment of excess funds for sound developmental purposes. A small number of very wealthy individuals profited greatly from the stock market bubble: having set the rising spiral in motion, they knew the right time to sell their shares. Those benefiting came from a variety of backgrounds. Some were members of the royal family, others were from large business families. Although some smaller investors were fortunate in selling their shares at the right time, the majority did not. Large numbers of bankruptcies resulted. The blame for what had happened, however, should not rest simply on the shoulders of individuals who had used or misused the system. A range of institutions is needed if a capital market is to constitute an effective financial instrument, channelling funds from those who wish to invest and putting it in the hands of those who are developing economic projects. The ability of the SASE to act in this manner was limited by the absence of investment banks, independent brokerage firms, asset management firms, etc., and by the inadequacy of venture capital (Zahid 2004).

At the end of 2004 there were still only 71 companies listed on the Saudi stock exchange, and in some sectors only one company was represented. By the beginning of 2007 the number had risen to 87, but the market remained narrowly based. Approximately one-third (32.5 per cent) of stock market capitalisation consisted of government-owned stock, with the general public holding 52 per cent, foreign investors holding 8.7 per cent and founders/institutions holding 6.8 per cent. Most of the market capitalisation was concentrated in the banking (47.6 per cent) and industrial (25.2 per cent) sectors. Most of the industrial capitalisation was contributed by SABIC (NCB Market Review and Outlook 26.11.06).

Despite the severe problems which had occurred in the stock market during 2006, there were some aspects where it was continuing to play the role for which it was required. Most importantly, an increasing number of companies were coming on to the stock exchange through arranging initial public offerings of shares (IPOs). In the course of 2005 there were four IPOs, with National Cooperative Commercial Insurance, Bank al-Bilad, SADAFCO and al-Marei entering the stock market. The two latter companies were food-producing undertakings. In 2006 there were nine more IPOs: Yansab Petrochemicals, the Al Drees Petroleum and Transport Company, the Saudi Research and Marketing Group (owners of newspapers), the Paper Manufacturing Company, the Emaar Economic City Company (which was developing the King 'Abdallah Economic City), Red Sea Housing, the Saudi International Petrochemicals Company, Al Babtain Power and Telecommunications, and the Fawaz Abdulaziz Alhokair Company (clothing and fashion distributors) (SAMBA 2007: 13).

The companies whose share prices maintained their value best were those in petrochemicals and communications.

7.7   Does the labour market provide the calibre and skills needed for successful economic development, at rates of pay which are competitive internationally?

The pressures on Saudi employers to recruit the most effective and best-value labour will inevitably increase in the future. The character of the economic relationships inherent in membership of the World Trade Organisation leads strongly in this direction. As the Saudi domestic market becomes more open to foreign competition (some of it based in surrounding countries, shipping goods across the border), and Saudi companies seek a larger share of the global market for their products, the cost-effectiveness of their labour force will be a critical issue in determining their success. The Saudi government's laudable aim of promoting Saudisation will be a hindrance to these activities unless Saudi manpower is indeed competitive. It needs to be competitive both with labour which could be brought from elsewhere (migrant labour), and with labour in countries which produce rival products. Otherwise, production will move elsewhere.

Before proceeding further with the analysis, an explanation needs to be given of the statistical basis for estimating the composition of the Saudi labour force. So far in this book, the employment figures which have been given are those which appear in the country's development plans. These are prepared under the auspices of the Ministry of Planning. As they are the only ones which provide a continuum from the beginning of the planning process, they are valuable in showing trends and changes of direction. They stand at variance, however, to figures on employment which in recent years have been produced by the Ministry of Labour. The latter appear to be more accurate, based on the actual numbers of those who are registered as employed, and are used in the statistical information produced by the Saudi Arabian Monetary Agency. They cover exclusively civilian manpower, which is the claim made by the Ministry of Planning for its figures also.

Whereas the Ministry of Planning statistics (see Tables 6.15 and 6.16) show an overall total of 8,281,000 in the labour force in 2004, the Ministry of Labour puts the figure for the same year at 6,754,904. It seems likely that the Ministry of Planning takes a broader view of what is meant by 'civilian employment' and also includes some who are not formally registered as employed. The Ministry of Labour figures, as a result, show a much smaller Saudi labour force for 2004: 1,385,587, as opposed to 3,536,300.

The absolute size of the non-Saudi workforce, moreover, is considerably larger in the Ministry of Labour statistics: 5,369,317, as against 4,745,500. The Ministry of Labour figures may include some migrants who are working but do not carry legal authorisation for employment. The implications of this for the proportion of the workforce constituted by Saudi labour are stark: the percentage of Saudis in the workforce falls from 42.7 per cent to 20.5 per cent (SAMA 2006).

The absence of an independent means of unravelling the realities behind the divergent statistics on employment makes it impossible to arrive at an accurate figure for the composition of the Saudi labour force. Three observations, however, are worth making at this stage. First, the weakness of the statistical information on employment is itself a problem. Without a clear and generally accepted knowledge of how large the labour force is, and how it is composed, it is difficult to frame coherent plans for the country's economic future. Second, the more negative aspects of the employment scene, as documented in previous chapters, could in reality be yet worse than was suggested. The likelihood is that they are. The Ministry of Labour figures show the rate of increase in the non-Saudi labour force substantially exceeding that of the Saudi labour force in 2003 and 2004 (SAMA 2006). Third, many of the claims made in government literature about the substantial proportion of Saudis working in the private as opposed to the public sector are based on weak foundations. On the basis of Ministry of Planning figures, it is sometimes claimed that up to 80 per cent of Saudis work in the private sector. The authors' own estimates are that, of the whole Saudi labour force (including in this case those working in security and the armed forces, as well as civilian employment), some 60 per cent are drawing salaries from governmental institutions. Of the remaining 40 per cent, moreover, some are employed by companies which are majority-owned by the government, and where government employment practices continue to affect the terms and nature of employment.

The impact which government salaries have on the salaries earned by Saudis, therefore, remains crucial – and exerts a strong impact on the terms and conditions on which Saudis are prepared to work for the private sector. The leading industrial, finance and IT-related companies in the private sector pay more for the best expertise than the government does, and some parts of the Saudi educational system are producing graduates of outstanding calibre (interviews 2006). Reference has already been made, for example to engineers graduating from the King Fahd University for Petroleum and Mineral Resources. The private sector is eager to employ them and rewards them generously. The same does not apply, however, at lower levels of skill and expertise. For most Saudis emerging from the educational system, whether from schools or universities, the salaries and conditions are better in the public sector. If they are unable to find jobs in the latter, they may take employment in the private sector. They would tend, however, to see it as an inferior option, and perhaps as a stopgap until a public-sector position becomes available. Advertisements for public-sector jobs are sometimes accompanied by street unrest as applicants jostle to submit their applications. This occurred, for example, in April 2006 when 10,000 Saudi men sought to submit applications for 500 jobs advertised by the passports department. Police had to be called in to control the demonstration which ensued. Some applicants believed that their applications were being disregarded, while others were unable to reach the office where applications were being accepted (*Arab News*, 21.4.06).

Different estimates are made of the level of unemployment in Saudi Arabia. In 2002, the government for the first time released employment and labour force data. Based on figures gathered at the end of 1999, overall unemployment (male and female) was put at 8.1 per cent, with Saudi male unemployment at 6.8 per cent and female unemployment at 15.8 per cent (SAMBA 2002: 1). In July 2004 new figures were released. Using data gathered in 2002, the total number of unemployed was given as 300,000, representing 9.6 per cent of the available labour force. Saudi male unemployment stood at 7.6 per cent, and female unemployment at 21.7 per cent (KSA-CDS 2005). A 2007 figure prepared by the chief economist of the Riyadh Bank, using data from official sources, shows male unemployment at 9 per cent and female unemployment at 22 per cent (Khan 2007: 243). The economist goes on to suggest, however, that the real number may be higher. The problem which this poses is intensified by the age-groups most affected by unemployment. It is highest among those in their twenties – males and, even more so, females. The social effects which follow from this cannot be ignored.

The figures on unemployment, moreover, do not convey the full extent of the employment problem facing the country. The unemployment rate constitutes a proportion of the 'available labour force'. The latter, however, only comprises a relatively small part of the Saudi population. According to the figures of the Saudi Central Department of Statistics, only 19 per cent of the Saudi population (35.3 per cent of the working-age population) forms part of the labour force (Niblock 2006: 116). This ranks among the lowest labour force participation rates of any country in the world, against an average 33 per cent in the rest of the Middle East, and 45 per cent in Europe. The phenomenon is in part accounted for by the low level of female employment. The 2002 figures show that only 6.6 per cent of Saudi females above the age of 15 were employed (KSA-CDS 2005). The same figures, however, also indicate that significant numbers of men did not form part of the available labour force due to being unable to work, whether on grounds of disablement or for other unspecified reasons. Some 308,389 men were in this category, constituting about 6.7 per cent of all Saudi men over 15 (KSA-CDS 2005).

Underlying these various employment problems is the issue of productivity. Labour productivity is low: many of those in employment would be more gainfully employed elsewhere, but it is not in their interest to change their employment. To do so would leave them with a lower salary and more difficult working conditions. Nor is it in the interest of private-sector employers to seek to attract them. It is cheaper for them to obtain labour from outside the country, if they can obtain the necessary permission, and the dynamics of WTO membership provide a further rationale for such a strategy.

The realities of the dilemmas inherent in the employment problem are, of course, well known to the Saudi government. The emphasis on Saudisation in all recent development plans, the practical measures which have been implemented over the past five years by the Minister of Labour to impel business to employ Saudis, the introduction of industrial training courses, and the allocation of half of total expenditure in the Seventh and Eighth Plans to education and training, are all evidence of this awareness and of the attempt to act on it. Considerable determination has been shown in attempting to implement the practical measures to restrict employment of non-Saudis. The reality which arises with the imposition of Saudisation, however, is that the skilled, motivated and effective Saudi labour which the private sector needs is not available, or at least not sufficient. Without a more thorough reordering of the educational system, the problem is likely to remain. There is, moreover, one further problem: the differential in cost between employing Saudis and non-Saudis. At present, for those in the median levels of employment, Saudi employees are paid two to three times the salaries of non-Saudi employees with the same educational qualifications. The absence for facilities for women in many workplaces also has cost implications: the separate facilities may put on an added initial cost, but salaries for females are on average one-half of the salaries earned by men with the same educational qualifications (Niblock 2006: 116). Pressures from the government for business to Saudiise are likely to become greater with the growth of population and unemployment, but the international economic pressures on business to operate competitively will also increase.

An area where the problem over Saudi employment is not problematic is that of the oil sector, the petrochemicals industry and financial services. In these sectors, the numbers employed are relatively small and there is an adequate supply of well-qualified Saudis to take the jobs which arise.

Much of the labour may remain migrant, but skilled positions are increasingly filled by Saudis. There is no indication that these parts of the economy will be held back by moves towards Saudisation, especially if these are well planned with enough time given to reach the government's targets. For the rest of the economy it will be considerably more difficult to combine Saudisation with the increased competitiveness which the global market will require.

7.8   Are the state institutions, and the manner in which they are linked to the private sector, geared to framing coherent development plans and implementing them?

This issue covered here is central to determining whether the Saudi state coheres with the developmental state model. The analysis is built on the data which has been presented earlier in this chapter and in previous chapters. It has been shown that in many ways the Saudi state is operating effectively in guiding the development of the country's economy. In many respects, moreover, the relationship between the state and the private sector has been structured so as to help Saudi Arabia gain a major stake in the global industrial market – a stake based on production and not on simple rentier extraction and export. It is also evident, however, that this pattern does not hold sway in all areas. In some aspects of Saudi economic life, the state is not acting effectively in developmental terms and the relationship between the state and the private sector does not promote productive development. The latter areas are often characterised by predatory behaviour, and policies driven by short-term or individual interests, rather than developmental coherence.

In order to assess the extent and nature of developmental characteristics in the Saudi state, it is important first to take stock of the aspects which reflect this model of political economy. First, the central core of planning in Saudi Arabia is well organised, coherent in its approach and objectives, geared towards the exploitation of the comparative economic advantages which the country possesses, and appropriately directed to Saudi Arabia gaining a major stake in global industrial markets. It concerns itself both with efficient exploitation of the resources which have created the country's existing wealth, and developing new areas of economic activity that will sustain the economy if and when the exporting of crude or refined oil and natural gas ceases to be viable or profitable. The most significant testimony to this planned coherence is the development plans, which have over the years become increasingly well structured and well conceived. The more micro-level plans produced for developments in the key areas – petrochemicals, oil and finance in particular – are similarly well conceived.

Second, the central government institutions, the state-owned enterprises and the state-led companies with responsibility for promoting the country's central economic strategies are effective and well organised. The reference to 'central economic strategies' relates specifically to policies geared towards gaining for Saudi Arabia an important stake in global industrial and financial markets. The bodies concerned operate in a manner which is largely free from the influence of personal interests or political obstruction. Crucial among them are the relevant departments in the key government ministries (mainly in the Ministry of Finance and the Ministry of Planning and National Economy), the Saudi Arabian Monetary Agency (SAMA), the Saudi Arabian General Investment Authority, ARAMCO, the Saudi Arabian Basic Industries Corporation (SABIC), the Royal Commission for Jubail and Yanbu, and the mining corporation MAADEN. To some extent these bodies can be seen as islands of excellence. The surrounding environment may be characterised by rather different practices and procedures, but that does not impinge significantly on how these islands of excellence function.

In certain respects the islands of excellence are cut off from the rest of the country and function according to different rules. The clearest example of this is the industrial cities of Jubail and Yanbu, where the administrative, social and physical management of the area is outside the structures used to administer the rest of the country. They are managed by the Royal Commission for Jubail and Yanbu, which is dedicated to providing an environment which renders business activity (especially in the field of petrochemicals) straightforward, efficient and unbureaucratic The new economic cities, it seems, are intended to exist in similar bubbles of efficiency, also cut off from the bureaucratic hindrances affecting other parts of the country's administration. Whether these latter developments will be similarly successful, however, is yet to be seen.

The relative autonomy of the islands of excellence reflects a governmental awareness of their importance. They are crucial to the country's existing economic well-being and its future prospects. To put the coherence of their operations in doubt would have widespread and damaging effects. One indication of the importance which the state leadership attaches to them is the high calibre of those appointed to lead and manage them. These individuals enjoy, moreover, easy access to the highest levels of government. Problems which they encounter can be settled quickly and effectively through personal channels rather than passing through cumbrous bureaucratic processes. Despite constituting islands shielded from the wider environment, they nonetheless enjoy close links among themselves. Both in terms of the personal relations between the leading elements within them, and some of the institutional links, they cooperate towards their common objectives.

Third, the state has now fashioned the access to global markets which a developmental state requires. The framework of Saudi Arabia's accession to the World Trade Organisation ensures that access, on terms which are favourable to the critical sectors at the crux of the developmental strategy.

Fourth, the leading elements in those parts of the private sector needed for the development strategy can be regarded as enjoying a degree of embedded autonomy in the Saudi state. The nature of this embedded autonomy is no doubt rather different from that which exists in the developmental states of the Far East and South-East Asia. In the Saudi case, the embedded autonomy rests less on institutional structures than on personal channels of communication. The webs of committees and business–government liaison groups which characterise the Asian form of embedded autonomy are either not present in Saudi Arabia, or else are not as significant as other channels of communication.

The reference to 'personal channels of communication' in Saudi Arabia may suggest that the practice is predatory rather than developmental, but such an understanding would be mistaken. The measure of autonomy enjoyed by business interests in the key developmental fields is based in part on the character of their resource base. Their wealth is not dependent on the state and indeed much of it is held outside of the state (part of the estimated $1 trillion worth of assets which the Saudi private sector owns abroad). Some of them, indeed, have accumulated much of their capital from their activities outside of the country. Moreover, the Saudi state needs their involvement if it is to achieve its developmental objectives, for they can supply a significant amount of the investment, cooperative alignments with international corporations, and expertise which are required. They do not need, therefore, to act in a predatory manner. The major gains which they seek are attainable through the development policies of the state.

In some ways these business elements are so closely embedded in the structures of the state that the dividing line between them and the managers of state companies and corporations is blurred. Many of the latter are now led by individuals who have come in from the private sector. In some ways, this can be seen as a takeover of state institutions by the leading elements of the private sector, accepted by the state so that the country's developmental objectives can be met. It is distinct from a situation where individual businessmen draw private benefit from state institutions and distort the developmental process. While the pattern may be different from Asian embedded autonomy, the contention here is that it serves the same purpose. Embedded autonomy need not always take the same form.

It may, furthermore, be questioned whether the Asian pattern is quite so devoid of personal channels of communication as the literature suggests. The role of *guan-shi* (personal contacts from which individuals benefit – the equivalent of the Arabic *wastah*), for example, clearly plays an important part in the economy of Taiwan.

The strength of the leading business elements is given further backing by two other aspects of Saudi Arabia's political economy and society. The first is the extensive and well-resourced character of the Saudi private sector in general, and the degree to which it has become increasingly organised and articulate. The size and strength of the sector is reflected in the statistics on private-sector growth presented in the earlier chapters. The Chambers of Commerce have become stronger than before, and the transformation of their governing boards into majority-elected bodies has increased their sense of communal solidarity and independence. The businessmen who are leading the development of strategic sectors, therefore, can put themselves forward to government personnel as championing the rights and interests of a wider private sector (whether accurately or not). This is a sector of Saudi society, moreover, whose support the government needs for reasons of political interest. Second, most of the leading business elements come from families which are socially influential, often outside of the country as well as within. They have the social confidence to speak their views freely and openly.

It must be stressed now that the picture which has been painted above does not cover the overall relationship between the state and the private sector in Saudi Arabia. It relates specifically to one part of the private sector: that which is present in the parts of the economy which are at the forefront of the government's development strategy. Outside of this small, but highly important, sphere, the relationship between the private sector and the state does not fit well with the developmental state model. Chapter 5 and the earlier part of this chapter have both shown that the wider relationship is, in many ways, flawed. Much of the wider private sector is, no doubt, profitable, and there are many well-run businesses, but the sector's relationship with the state does not have the dynamic through which a productive, well-balanced and coherent pattern of development can emerge. The relationship needs to be reshaped if that objective is to be achieved.

Saudi Arabia, therefore, is emerging as a hybrid developmental state. It has created the mechanisms and the economic linkages to achieve one of the key objectives of a developmental state. It is well placed to gain a significant stake in the global industrial economy through the activities of its petrochemical and financial sectors. But whereas the developmental states of Asia achieve a rounded process of development through such a strategy, with the wider economy operating on the same competitive basis as the leading core, this is as yet not happening in Saudi Arabia. The availability of oil revenue has in Saudi Arabia's case made it possible for inefficient and predatory behaviour to co-exist with a highly effective and developmentally directed core.

7.9   The social dimension and the Saudi developmental state: conclusion

The social implications of an economic strategy which is capable of achieving success in some key sectors, but struggles with uncompetitive and restrictive practices in others, are likely to be far-reaching. The issue of employment is central here. For social stability the Saudi economy needs to be capable of producing the jobs which the growing population needs, and the dynamics of the global economy (with Saudi Arabia's accession to the WTO) will require employment to be competitive in skills, ability and price. Within the existing framework of policy, there is considerable doubt as to whether current patterns of development in Saudi Arabia will indeed create sufficient and appropriate employment prospects for the growing population of Saudi Arabia. The sectors which will lead the way in creating a stake for Saudi Arabia in the global industrial market are ones which do not employ large numbers.

One indication of the employment needs of the future is the rate of increase of the population. The Saudi population through the decades of the 1980s and 1990s was growing at a rate of 3.9 per cent per annum – one of the highest population growth rates in the world (World Bank 2004: 40). Although the rate of increase has now fallen to about 3 per cent, and is expected to fall to 2.6 per cent by the end of the decade, the increase will still be substantial. The US Census Bureau estimates that Saudi Arabia's population will double between 2003 and 2050, rising from 24 million to 50 million (US-CB 2004). These figures include non-Saudis resident in the country, but the prediction in these figures is that both the absolute numbers and the proportion of non-Saudis in the population will fall. As would be expected, the major expansion in the Saudi population is among the young, with some 70 per cent of the population now below 30. The available Saudi labour force, therefore, is growing at an even higher rate than the population. The Seventh Development Plan estimated that the available labour force will grow at about 4.7 per cent per annum in the period through to 2020 (255,000 new workers annually). Over the 2000–2 period, employment in the public and private sectors combined was expanding by less than 90,000 jobs annually, absorbing about one-half of the job-seekers coming on to the labour market at that time (SAMBA 2002: 3).

The estimates in the Seventh Development Plan, moreover, may well be an underestimate, given that women are likely to become more demanding in seeking employment. The economy, therefore, will need to be functioning at a significantly higher level if it is to satisfy the employment needs of the population.

Yet it would be wrong to suggest that these problems are insoluble. Saudi labour can become as competitive as that elsewhere, and if that happens the employment problem can gain resolution. To achieve this, however, requires a more radical and transformative approach than is on offer at present. Clearly the quality of Saudi labour needs to be improved through training and education, but what is required is more than simple training. A different intellectual climate within the schools and universities is needed, and different approaches to teaching. More emphasis has to be placed on creativity, and on the individual finding his or her own way ahead. There are many within the country who are trying to bring this about. The cushioning of labour in the state system, whether in terms of salary or employment conditions, will need to be brought to an end, thereby enabling the private sector to attract Saudi labour at appropriate rates of pay. Women will need to be given more opportunities to enter employment and remain in it. The salaries and conditions of migrant labour need to be improved, not just for humanitarian reasons but to prevent it from undercutting Saudi labour.

The policies just proposed are often advanced by those who advocate a reduction in the role of the state. They propose that welfare be removed so as to allow the private sector to set the parameters of economic and social life. That, however, is not the contention here. To some extent it is the opposite. The state needs to be providing more and better welfare for the population if the necessary transition is to be achieved. The removal of the cushioning of labour in government institutions, for example, has to be accompanied by a strengthening of the safety-nets which protect the population's standard of living. People need to be assured that if they lose their employment, or suffer a deterioration in its conditions, they will not fall into poverty. They need to have access to assured unemployment benefit, retraining in different and more productive employment, educational support for their children, and other basic requirements. The Saudi population needs to be able to draw benefit from the wealth of their country, but to do so through excellent health and education provision, transport facilities, access to leisure activities and other facilities and services, rather than through the guarantee of but unproductive jobs. In this way a new basis can be laid for employment in the country, with Saudis gaining their incomes by productive employment. As has been shown earlier, many are already employed on this basis, and there is no reason why such a practice should not encompass the whole population.

What is needed for such a strategy is a new social contract, where the employed population abandons some of the security it currently enjoys through protected conditions, but gains in return a framework of support enabling Saudis to compete effectively with labour elsewhere. Without such a policy, the social gap between the economically gainful parts of the population and the remainder will grow, intensified by the inequalities engendered by occasional predatory behaviour. Such a situation would be damaging to the social stability of the country, undermining the effectiveness even of those economic sectors which are destined for global pre-eminence.

Glossary

Asabiyah capitalism   Crony capitalism based on family connections.

Guan-shi   Personal connection, used to win favours (Chinese version of the Arabic *wastah*).

Halalah   Unit of currency in Saudi Arabia, with 100 *halalah* equal to 1 riyal.

Riyal   Principal unit of currency in Saudi Arabia (pegged at $1 = SR3.75 since 1982).

Shari'a   Islamic law.

Wastah   Personal connection, used to win favours.

Zakat   Taxation-type levy founded on Islamic precepts.

Notes

Chapter 1

1 The definition of the state provided by the World Bank (1997: 20), which follows the line of many others and is as useful as any, is 'the set of institutions that possess the means of legitimate coercion, exercised over a defined territory and its population, referred to as society. The State monopolises rulemaking within a territory through the medium of an organised government'.

2 Some of these may go beyond what is found in many neoclassical accounts.

3 The World Bank (1997: 41) noted that markets could not develop far without effective laws.

4 Williams (1991: 181, 183) also argues that research and development, which is central to economic and cultural development should be encouraged by government, as markets are likely to fund only a very small amount.

5 This was also noted by *Cammack et al.* (1988: 59, 66–7).

Chapter 3

1 All percentage figures of growth over a plan-period cover the five years from the first year of the plan to the last full year before the beginning of the next one. In the case mentioned here, for example, the years covered are 1970, 1971, 1972, 1973 and 1974.

Chapter 5

1 Some of the material on which this chapter is based has been published before in a chapter by Monica Malik in Wilson, R., with Al-Salamah, A., Malik, M., and Al-Rajhi, A., *Economic Development in Saudi Arabia*. London: Routledge, 2004. The analysis here, however, focuses specifically on the aspects which are relevant to this book, and has been organised around that.

Bibliography

Books, reports and theses

Aarts, Paul and Nonneman, Gerd (2005) *Saudi Arabia in the Balance: Political Economy, Society, Foreign Relations*. London: Hurst.

Abdeen, Adnan M. and Shook, Dale N. (1984) *The Saudi Financial System*. New York: John Wiley.

Abdel-Rahman, Osama (1987) *The Dilemma of Development in the Arabian Peninsula*. London: Croom Helm.

Al-Ajmi, Khaled M. (2003) 'Quality and Employability in Higher Education: The Case of Saudi Arabia', PhD dissertation, Middlesex University.

Al-Awaji, Ibrahim M. (1971) 'Bureaucracy and Society in Saudi Arabia', PhD dissertation, University of Virginia.

Albers, Henry Herman (1989) *Saudi Arabia: Technocrats in a Traditional Society*. New York: Peter Lang.

Al-Dekhayel, Abdulkarim (1990) 'The State and Political Legitimation in an Oil-Rentier Economy: Kuwait as a Case Study', unpublished PhD thesis, University of Exeter.

Al-Dukheil, Abdulaziz Muhammad (1995) *The Banking System and its Performance in Saudi Arabia*. London: Saqi Books.

Al-Farsy, Fouad (1989) *Saudi Arabia: A Case Study in Development*. London: Stacey International.

—— (1990) *Modernity and Tradition: The Saudi Equation*. London: Kegan Paul International.

Al-Harthi, Mohammed A. (2000) 'The Political Economy of Labor in Saudi Arabia: The Causes of Labor Shortage', PhD dissertation, State University of New York.

Al-Humaid, Mohammed I. A. (2003) 'The Factors Affecting the Process of Saudization in the Private Sector in the Kingdom of Saudi Arabia: A Case Study of Riyadh City', PhD dissertation, University of Exeter.

Al-Mabrouk, Saud A. (1991) '"Dutch Disease" in a "Small" Open Economy: The Case of Oil in Saudi Arabia', PhD dissertation, Colorado State University.

Al-Rawaf, Othman (1980) 'The Concept of Five Crises in Political Development: Relevance to the Kingdom of Saudi Arabia', PhD dissertation, Duke University.

Al-Sarhan, M. N. H. (1995) 'Privatisation in the Context of the Saudi Arabian Economy – An Examination of the Attitudes of the Saudi Private Investors Towards Privatisation in Saudi Arabia', unpublished PhD thesis, University of Loughborough.

Auty, Richard M. (1990) *Resource Based Industrialization: Sowing the Oil in Eight Developing Countries.* Oxford: Clarendon Press.

Azzam, Henry (1988) *The Gulf Economies in Transition.* London: Macmillan.

—— (1993) *Saudi Arabia: Economic Trends, Business Environment and Investment Opportunities.* London: Euromoney.

—— (1997) *The Emerging Arab Capital Markets: Investment Opportunities in Relatively Underplayed Markets.* London: Kegan Paul International.

Bakr, Mohammed A. (2001) *A Model in Privatization: Successful Change Management in the Ports of Saudi Arabia.* London: London Centre of Arab Studies.

Bannock, G., Baxter, B. and Davis, E. (1992) *Dictionary of Economics.* London: Penguin

Barsalou, Judith M. (1985) 'Foreign Labor in Sa'udi Arabia: The Creation of a Plural Society', PhD dissertation, Columbia University.

Bashir, Faisal Safooq (1977) *A Structural Econometric Model of the Saudi Arabian Economy, 1960–70.* London: Wiley-Interscience.

Beling, Willard A. (1980) *King Faisal and the Modernisation of Saudi Arabia.* Boulder, CO: Westview Press.

Birks, Stace J. and Sinclair, Clive A. (1980a) *Arab Manpower: The Crisis of Development.* London: Croom Helm.

British Offset Office (1995) *Al Yamamah Offset.* London: British Offset Office.

Business International (1981) *Saudi Arabia – Issues for Growth. An Inside View of an Economic Power in the Making.* London: Business International.

—— (1985) *Saudi Arabia – A Reappraisal.* Geneva: Business International SA.

—— (1989) *Economic Recovery in Saudi Arabia – The Role of the Private Sector.* London: Business International.

Cammack, P., Pool, D. and Tordoff, W. (1988) *Third World Politics.* London: Macmillan.

Carter, John R. L. (1984) *Merchant Families of Saudi Arabia.* London: Scorpion.

Champion, Daryl (2003) *The Paradoxical Kingdom.* New York: Columbia University Press.

Chaudhry, Kiren A. (1997) *The Price of Wealth.* Ithaca, NY: Cornell University Press.

Cole, Donald P. (1975) *Nomads of the Nomads: The Al-Murrah of the Empty Quarter.* Chicago: Aldine.

Cordesman, Anthony (2003a) *Saudi Arabia Enters the Twenty-First Century: The Military and International Security Dimensions.* London: Praeger.

—— (2003b) *Saudi Arabia Enters the Twenty-First Century: The Political, Foreign Policy, Economic, and Energy Dimensions.* London: Praeger.

Cragg, C. (1996) The New Maharajahs: the Commercial Princes of India, Pakistan and Bangladesh. London: Random House.

Cunningham, Robert B. and Sarayrah, Yasin K. (1993) *Wasta: The Hidden Force in Middle Eastern Society*. London: Praeger.

Cypher, James M. and Dietz, James L. (1997) *The Process of Economic Development*. London: Routledge.

Dahlan, Ahmed H. (1990) *Politics, Administration and Development in Saudi Arabia*. Brentwood: Amana.

De Gaury, Gerald (1966) *Faisal: King of Saudi Arabia*. London: Barker.

Dequin, Horst (1967) *The Challenge of Saudi Arabia: The Regional Setting and Economic Development as a Result of the Conquest of the Arabian Peninsula by King 'Abdul 'Aziz Al Sa'ud*. Hamburg: D. R. Gotze.

Dun and Bradstreet (2004) *Country Report: Saudi Arabia*. London: Dun and Bradstreet.

Economist Intelligence Unit (EIU) (1997) *1996–7 Saudi Arabia Country Profile*. London: EIU.

—— (1998) *Investing, Licensing and Trading in Saudi Arabia*. London: EIU.

—— (1999) *Financing Operations in Saudi Arabia*. London: EIU.

—— (2004) *Country Report: Saudi Arabia*. London: EIU.

El-Ghonemy, Mohamed Riad (1998) *Affluence and Poverty in the Middle East*. London: Routledge.

El-Mallakh, Ragaei (1982) *Saudi Arabia, Rush to Development*. Baltimore: Johns Hopkins University Press.

—— and El-Mallakh, Dorothea (eds) (1981) *Saudi Arabia*. Toronto: Lexington Books.

Ernst and Young (1992) *Doing Business in Saudi Arabia*. New York: Ernst and Young International Business Series.

Evans, Peter (1995) *Embedded Autonomy: States and Industrial Transformation*. Princeton, NJ: Princeton University Press.

Field, Michael (1985) *The Merchants: The Big Business Families of Saudi Arabia and the Gulf States*. Woodstock, NY: Overlook Press.

First, Ruth (1980) 'Libya: Class and State in an Oil Rentier Economy', in P. Nore and T. Turner, eds, *Oil and Class Struggle*. London: Zed Press.

Gelb, Alan et al. (1988) *Oil Windfalls: Blessing or Curse?* New York: Oxford University Press.

Hajrah, Hassan Hamza (1982) *Public Land Distribution in Saudi Arabia*. London: Longman.

Hertog, Steffen (2006) 'Segmented Clientalism: The Politics of Economic Reform in Saudi Arabia', PhD thesis, University of Oxford.

Ibrahim, Saad Eddin and Cole, Donald P. (1978) *Saudi Arabian Bedouin: An Assessment of Their Needs*. Cairo: American University Press.

International Monetary Fund (IMF) (1995) *International Financial Statistical Yearbook*. Washington, DC: IMF.

—— (1998a) *Saudi Arabia – Recent Economic Developments and Selected Issues*. Unpublished.

—— (1998b) *Saudi Arabia – Staff Report for the 1998 Article IV Consultation.* Unpublished.

—— (1999) *World Economic Outlook.* Washington, DC: IMF.

—— (2001) *Saudi Arabia – Staff Report for the 2001 Article IV Consultation.* Unpublished.

—— (2006) *IMF Executive Board Concludes 2005 Article IV Consultation with Saudi Arabia.* Washington, DC: IMF.

Islami, A. Reza S. and Kavoussi, Rostam M. (1984) *The Political Economy of Saudi Arabia.* Seattle: University of Washington Press.

Jeddah Chamber of Commerce and Industry (1995) *The Impact of GATT on the Business Sector of the Kingdom of Saudi Arabia.* Jeddah: Jeddah Chamber of Commerce and Industry.

Johany, Ali D. (1980) *The Myth of the OPEC Cartel: The Role of Saudi Arabia.* New York: John Wiley.

——, Berne, Michele and Mixon Jr, Wilson, J. (1986) *The Saudi Arabian Economy.* London: Croom Helm.

Kanovsky, Eliyahu (1994) *The Economy of Saudi Arabia: Troubled Present, Grim Future.* Washington, DC: Washington Institute for Near East Policy.

Kerr, Malcolm H. and Yassin, El-Sayed (1982) *Rich and Poor States in the Middle East.* Boulder, CO: Westview Press.

Khan, Zahid (2007) *Riyad Bank Weekly Economic Briefing* 7.4.07

Killick, T. (1995) *IMF Programmes in Developing Countries: Design and Impact.* London: Overseas Development Institute.

Kingdom of Saudi Arabia, Central Department of Statistics (KSA-CDS) (1968) *Statistical Yearbook.* Riyadh: Ministry of Finance and National Economy.

—— (1971) *Statistical Yearbook.* Riyadh: Ministry of Finance and National Economy.

Kingdom of Saudi Arabia, Central Planning Organisation (KSA-CPO) (1970) *First Development Plan, 1970–75.* Riyadh: Central Planning Organisation.

Kingdom of Saudi Arabia, Ministry of Planning (KSA-MOP) (1975) *Second Development Plan, 1975–80.* Riyadh: Ministry of Planning.

—— (1980) *Third Development Plan, 1980–85.* Riyadh: Ministry of Planning.

—— (1985a) *Fourth Development Plan, 1985–1990.* Riyadh: Ministry of Planning.

—— (1985b) *Achievements of the Development Plans 1970–1985.* Riyadh: Ministry of Planning.

—— (1989) *Achievements of the Development Plans 1970–1989.* Riyadh: Ministry of Planning.

—— (1990) *Fifth Development Plan, 1990–1995.* Riyadh: Ministry of Planning.

—— (1995) *Sixth Development Plan, 1995–2000.* Riyadh: Ministry of Planning.

—— (2000) *Seventh Development Plan, 2000–2004.* Riyadh: Ministry of Planning.

—— (2005) *Eighth Development Plan, 2005–2009.* Riyadh: Ministry of Planning.

—— (2006) *Achievements of the Development Plans 1970–2005.* Riyadh: Ministry of Planning.

Kingdom of Saudi Arabia, Social Security Department (KSA-SSD) (n.d.) *The Achievements of Social Security, 1962–77*. Riyadh: Ministry of Labour and Social Affairs.

Knauerhase, Ramon (1975) *The Saudi Arabian Economy*. New York: Praeger.

Krueger, Anne O. (1993) *Political Economy of Policy Reform in Developing Countries*. Cambridge, MA: MIT Press.

Lackner, Helen (1978) *House Built on Sand: A Political Economy of Saudi Arabia*. London: Ithaca Press.

Lal, Deepak (1997) *The Poverty of 'Development Economics'*. London: Institute of Economic Affairs.

Lipsky, George A. (1959) *Saudi Arabia: Its People, Its Society, Its Culture*. New Haven: HRAF Press.

London Business School (1989) *Staying the Course: Survival Characteristics of the Family Owned Business*. London: London Business School.

Long, David E. (1997) *The Kingdom of Saudi Arabia*. Gainesville: University Press of Florida.

Looney, Robert E (1982) *Saudi Arabia Development Potential, Applications of an Islamic Growth Model*. Lexington, MA: Lexington Books.

—— (1990b) *Economic Development in Saudi Arabia: Consequences of the Oil Price Decline*. London: JAI Press.

Malik, Monica (1999) 'Private Sector and the State in Saudi Arabia', PhD dissertation, University of Durham.

Masood, Rashid (1989) *Economic Diversification and Development in Saudi Arabia*. New Delhi: Sangam Books.

McLoughlin, Leslie (1993) *Ibn Saud: Founder of a Kingdom*. London: Macmillan.

Meier, Gerald M. (1995) *Leading Issues in Economic Development*. Oxford: Oxford University Press.

Metz, Helen (1993) *Saudi Arabia: A Country Study*. Washington: Library of Congress.

Ministry of Industry and Electricity (1996) *Industrial Statistical Bulletin*. Riyadh: Ministry of Industry and Electricity, Kingdom of Saudi Arabia.

Moliver, Donald, M. and Abbondante, Paul J. (1980) *The Economy of Saudi Arabia*. New York: Praeger.

Montagu, Caroline (1994) *The Private Sector of Saudi Arabia – A Personal View on its Role in the Kingdom's Economy*. London: Committee for Middle East Trade (COMET).

Mutawakil, G. (n.d.) *Business and Law in Saudi Arabia*. Riyadh: Falcon Press.

Nader, M. and Alameldin, M. (1994) *A Legal Practical Guide for the Businessman in Saudi Arabia*. Jeddah: Nader Law Offices.

Nahedh, Munira (1989) 'The Sedentarisation of a Bedouin Community in Saudi Arabia', PhD dissertation, University of Leeds.

National Center for Financial and Economic Information (1991) *Report on the Development of the Service Sector in the Kingdom of Saudi Arabia – An Update*. Riyadh: Ministry of Finance and National Economy, Kingdom of Saudi Arabia.

Niblock, Tim. (1980) *Dilemmas of Non-oil Economic Development in the Middle East*. London: Arab Research Centre.

—— (ed.) (1980b) *Social and Economic Development in the Arab Gulf*. London: Croom Helm.

—— (ed.) (1981) *State, Society and Economy in Saudi Arabia*. London: Croom Helm.

—— (ed.) (1982) *Iraq: The Contemporary State*. London: Croom Helm.

—— (2000) *'Pariah States' and Sanctions in the Middle East: Iraq, Libya and Sudan*. London: Lynne Rienner.

—— (2006) *Saudi Arabia: Power, Legitimacy and Survival*. London: Routledge.

Nyrop, Richard F. (1985) *Area Handbook for Saudi Arabia*, 4th edn. Washington: Government Printing Office.

Okruhlik, Mary G. (1992) 'Debating Profits and Political Power: Private Business and Government in Saudi Arabia', unpublished PhD thesis, University of Texas, Austin.

Plant, Raymond (1991) *Modern Political Thought*. Oxford: Blackwell.

Poulanzas, Nicos (1974) *Political Power and Social Classes*. London: New Left Books.

Presley, John R. (1984) *A Guide to the Saudi Arabian Economy*. London: Macmillan Press.

—— and Westaway, A. J. (1989) *A Guide to the Saudi Arabian Economy*. London: Macmillan Press.

Richards, Alan and Waterbury, John (1996) *A Political Economy of the Middle East: State, Class and Economic Development*. Boulder, CO: Westview Press.

Romahi, Mohamed A. (2005) *The Saudi Arabian Economy: Policies, Achievements and Challenges*. New York: Springer.

Sabri, Sharaf (2001) *The House of Saud in Commerce*. New Delhi: I. S. Publications.

Saudi-American Bank (SAMBA) (2002) *Saudi Arabia's Employment Profile* Riyadh: SAMBA.

—— (2005) *The Saudi Economy at Mid Year 2005*. Riyadh: SAMBA.

—— (2006) *Saudi Arabia and the WTO*. Riyadh: SAMBA.

—— (2007) *The Saudi Economy: 2006 Performance, 2007 Forecast*. Riyadh: SAMBA.

Saudi Arabia Business Information and Economic Research Centre (SABIERC) (1997) *The SABIERC Economic Report on Saudi Arabia*. London: SABIERC.

Saudi Arabian General Investment Authority (SAGIA) (2005) *Foreign Direct Investment Survey Report*. Riyadh: SAGIA.

Saudi Arabian Monetary Agency (SAMA) (1977) *Fifteenth Annual Report*. Riyadh: Research and Statistics Department, Kingdom of Saudi Arabia.

—— (1979) *Seventeenth Annual Report*. Riyadh: Research and Statistics Department, Kingdom of Saudi Arabia.

—— (1986) *Twenty-Fourth Annual Report*. Riyadh: Research and Statistics Department, Kingdom of Saudi Arabia.

—— (1995) *Thirty-First Annual Report.* Riyadh: Research and Statistics Department, Kingdom of Saudi Arabia.

—— (1997) *Thirty-Third Annual Report.* Riyadh: Research and Statistics Department, Kingdom of Saudi Arabia.

—— (1998) *Thirty-Fourth Annual Report.* Riyadh: Research and Statistics Department, Kingdom of Saudi Arabia.

—— (2003) *Thirty-Nineth Annual Report.* Riyadh: Research and Statistics Department, Kingdom of Saudi Arabia.

—— (2006) *Forty-Second Annual Report.* Riyadh: Research and Statistics Department, Kingdom of Saudi Arabia.

Saudi Consulting House (1995) *Investing in Saudi Arabian Industry.* Riyadh: Saudi Consulting House, Kingdom of Saudi Arabia.

Saudi Development and Training Company (1996) *The Saudi Labour Market – The Experience and Understanding of Saudi Development and Training Company.* Dammam: Saudi Development and Training Company Ltd.

Saudi Export Development Center (1993) *Saudi Export Directory.* Riyadh: Abdeli Krome.

Saudi Industrial Development Fund (1997) *The Saudi Industrial Development Fund Annual Report.* Riyadh: Ministry of Finance and National Economy, Kingdom of Saudi Arabia.

Shaw, John A. and Long, David E. (1982) *Saudi Arabian Modernisation: The Impact of Change on Stability.* New York: Praeger.

Sirageldin, M. (1984) *Saudis in Transition: The Challenges of a Changing Labour Market.* Oxford: Oxford University Press.

Soufi, Wahib A. and Mayer, Richard T. (1991) *Saudi Arabian Industrial Investment: An Analysis of Government–Business Relationships.* Westport, CT: Quorum Books.

Tbeileh, Faisal H. (1991) *The Political Economy of Legitimacy in Rentier States: A Comparative Study of Saudi Arabia and Libya.* PhD Dissertation, University of California.

Todaro, Michael P. (1997) *Economic Development.* Addison-Wesley, MA, London: Longman.

Transparency International. (2004) *Background Paper to the 2004 Corruption Perceptions Index: Framework Document.* Berlin: Transparency International.

Turner, Louis, and Bedore, James M. (1979) *Middle East Industrialisation: A Study of Saudi and Iranian Downstream Investments.* London: Royal Institute for International Affairs.

Twitchell, Karl S. (1953) *Saudi Arabia, with an Account of the Development of its Natural Resources.* Princeton, N.J.: Princeton University Press.

Understanding Global Issues. (1999) *Asia's Financial Crisis – Causes, Effects and Aftershocks.* Issue 98/11. Cheltenham: Understanding Global Issues.

United Nations Conference on Trade and Development (UNCTAD). (2004) *World Investment Report.* Geneva: UNCTAD.

US-Saudi Business Council. (2005) *The Oil and Gas Sector in the Kingdom of Saudi Arabia.* Washington: USBC.

Wade, Robert (1990a) *Governing the Market.* Princeton, NJ: Princeton University Press.

Waznah, Abdel-Hakim (1996) 'Privatisation of Public Enterprises in Saudi Arabia: General Framework and Case Study', unpublished PhD thesis, University of Exeter.

Willams, R. (1991) 'The Inevitabilty of Symbiosis: States, Markets and R&D' in M. Moran and M. wright, eds., *The Markets and the state: Studies in Interdependence.* New York, St Martin's Press.

Wilson, Peter W. and Graham, Douglas F. (1994) *Saudi Arabia: The Coming Storm.* New York: M. E. Sharpe.

Wilson, Rodney (1998) *Banking and Finance in the Middle East 1999.* London: Financial Times Business.

——, with Al-Salamah, Abdallah, Malik, Monica and Al-Rajhi, Ahmed. (2004) *Economic Development in Saudi Arabia.* London: RoutledgeCurzon.

Woodward, Peter (1988) *Oil and Labour in the Middle East: Saudi Arabia and the Oil Boom.* New York: Praeger.

World Bank (1989) *Developing the Private Sector, a Challenge for the World Bank Group.* Washington, DC: World Bank Group.

—— (1997) *World Bank Annual Report.* Washington, DC: World Bank.

—— (1999) *1998/9 World Bank Development Report.* Washington, DC: World Bank.

—— (2004) *World Bank Indicators.* Washington, DC: World Bank.

World Trade Organisation (2005) *Report on the Working Party on the Accession of the Kingdom of Saudi Arabia to the World Trade Organisation.* WT/ACC/SAU/61. Geneva: WTO.

Yabuki, Susumu (translated by Harmer, Stephen M.) (1995) *China's New Political Economy: Giant Awakens.* Boulder, CO: Westview Press.

Yamani, Mai (2000) *Changed Identities: The Challenge of the New Generation in Saudi Arabia.* London: Royal Institute of International Affairs.

—— (2004) *Cradle of Islam: The Hijaz and the Quest for an Arabian Identity.* London: I. B. Tauris.

Young, Arthur N. (1983) *Saudi Arabia: The Making of a Financial Giant.* New York: NewYork University Press.

Articles, chapters in books and conference papers

Abdel-Fadil, M. (1987) 'The Macro-Behaviour of Oil-Rentier States in the Arab Region', in Hazem Beblawi and Giacomo Luciani (eds), *The Rentier State.* London: Croom Helm.

Al-Hajjar, Bandar and Presley, John (1993) 'Managerial Inefficiency in Small Manufacturing Businesses in Saudi Arabia: A Constraint upon Economic Development', *Industry and Development,* 32, pp. 39–54.

—— (1996) 'Small Business in Saudi Arabia', in J. W. Wright (ed.), *Business and Economic Development in Saudi Arabia.* London: Macmillan.

Al-Hejailan, Salah (June 1998) 'Legal Developments in Saudi Arabia', unpublished paper presented at SOAS, London.

Al-Mutrif, I. A. (1999) 'Saudiisation in Private Sector: New Challenges in Human Resource Development', *Saudi Commerce and Economic Review*, March, 59, pp. 16–21.

Al-Saleh, N. O. (November 1996) 'Kingdom's Top 100 Companies Face Global Challenges', *Arab News Top 100 Saudi Companies Supplement*, pp. i–xvi.

Amsden, Alice (1979) 'Taiwan's Economic History: A Case of Etatisme and a Challenge to Dependency Theory', *Modern China*, 5(3), pp. 341–380.

Anderson, R. E. and Mertinez, A. (1998) 'Supporting Private Sector Development in the Middle East and North Africa', in Nemat Shafik (ed.), *Prospects for Middle Eastern and North African Economies*. London: Macmillan.

Auty, Richard M. (1988) 'The Economic Stimulus from Resource-Based Industry in Developing Countries: Saudi Arabia and Bahrain', *Economic Geography*, 64(3), pp. 126–45.

Ayubi, Nazih N. (1992) 'Political Correlates of Privatisation Programs in the Middle East', *Arab Studies Quarterly*, 14(2 & 3), pp. 39–56.

Beblawi, Hazem (1987) 'The Rentier State in the Arab World', in Hazem Beblawi and Giacomo Luciani (eds), *The Rentier State*. London: Croom Helm.

Birks, Stace J. and Sinclair, Clive A. (1980b) 'The Oriental Connection,' in Tim Niblock (ed.), *Social and Economic Development in the Arab Gulf*. London: Croom Helm, pp. 135–160.

Birks, Stace J. and Sinclair, Clive A. (1981) 'Manpower in Saudi Arabia, 1980–85', in Ragaei and Dorothea El-Mallakh (eds), *Saudi Arabia*. Toronto: Lexington Books.

Cammack, Paul (1991) 'States and Markets in Latin America', in Michael Moran and Maurice Wright (eds), *The Market and the State: Studies in Interdependence*. New York: St Martin's Press.

Chaudhry, Kiren A. (1992) 'Economic Liberalisation in Oil-Exporting Countries: Iraq and Saudi Arabia', in Iliya Harik and Denis Sullivan (eds), *Privatisation and Liberalisation in the Middle East*. Bloomington: Indiana University Press.

Cheng, Tun-jen (1990) 'Political Regimes and Development Strategies: South Korea and Taiwan', in Gary Gereffi and Donald Wyman (eds), *Manufacturing Miracles*. Princeton, NJ: Princeton University Press.

Diwan, Ishac, Yang, Chang-po and Wang, Zhi (1998) 'The Arab Economies, the Uruguay Round Predicament, and the European Union Wildcard', in Nemat Shafik (ed.), *Prospects for Middle Eastern and North African Economies*. London: Macmillan.

Evans, Peter (1991) 'The Classical Economist, Laissez-Faire and the State', in Michael Moran and Maurice Wright (eds), *The Market and the State: Studies in Interdependence*. New York: St Martin's Press.

—— (1992) 'The State as Problem and Solution: Predation, Embedded Autonomy, and Structural Change', in Stephen Haggard and Robert Kaufman (eds), *The Politics of Adjustment*. Princeton, NJ: Princeton University Press.

Garawi, A. and Schmidt, M. E. (1996) 'The Saudi Arabian Managerial Environment: A Review Essay and Lecture' in J. W. Wright (ed.), *Business and Economic Development in Saudi Arabia*. London: Macmillan.

Giugale, Marcelo and Mobarak, Hamed (1996) 'Introduction: The Rationale for Private Sector Development in Egypt', in Marcelo Giugale and Hamed Mobarak (eds), *Private Sector Development in Egypt*. Cairo: American University Press.

Harik, Iliya (1992) 'Privatisation: The Issues, the Prospects, and the Fears', in Iliya, Harik and Denis Sullivan (eds), *Privatisation and Liberalisation in the Middle East*. Bloomington: Indiana University Press.

Hertog, Steffen (2005) 'Segmented Clientalism: The Political Economy of Saudi Economic Reform Efforts', in Paul Aarts and Gerd Nonneman (eds), *Saudi Arabia in the Balance*. London: Hurst.

Hoekman, Bernard (1998) 'The World Trade Organization, the European Union, and the Arab World: Trade Policies Priorities and the Pitfalls' in Nemat Shafik (ed.), *Prospects for Middle Eastern and North African Economies*. London: Macmillan.

Holmes, P. (1987) 'France: State-Sponsored Development in the First NIC', *IDS Bulletin*, 18(3), pp. 13–17.

Jenkins, Rhys (1991) 'Learning from the Gang: Are There Lessons for Latin America from East Asia?', *Bulletin of Latin American Research*, 10(1), pp. 37–54.

—— (1992) '(Re-)interpreting Brazil and South Korea', in Tom Hewitt, Hazel Johnson and David Wield (eds), *Industrialization and Development*. Oxford: Oxford University Press.

Jomo, Kwame S. (1998) 'Introduction: Financial Governance, Liberalisation and Crisis in East Asia', in Kwame S. Jomo (ed.), *Tigers in Trouble: Financial Governance, Liberalisation and Crisis in East Asia*. London: Zed Books.

Karl, Terry Lynn (1999) 'The Perils of the Petro-State: Reflections on the Paradox of Plenty', *Journal of International Studies*, 53(1), pp. 32–48.

Koch-Weser, C. (1996) 'Private Sector Development: Realizing the New Paradigm for Growth in the Middle East', in Marcelo Giugale and Hamed Mobarak (eds), *Private Sector Development in Egypt*. Cairo: American University Press.

Krueger, Anne O. (1974) 'The Political Economy of Rent-Seeking Society', *American Economic Review*, LXIV, June, pp. 291–303. Reprinted in Deepak Lal (ed.) (1992) *Development Economics, 3*. Aldershot: Edward Elgar.

Krugman, Paul (1998) 'Saving Asia: It's Time to Get Radical', *Fortune*, September, pp. 27–32.

Lall, Sanjaya (1994) 'Industrial Policy: The Role of Government in Promoting Industrial and Technological Development', *UNCTAD Review*, pp. 65–90.

Lee, K.-H. (1998) 'Does the South Korean Crisis Challenge the East Asian Model', *SOAS Economic Digest*, 2(1), pp. 24–30.

Linderoth, Hans (1992) 'Target Revenue Theory and Saudi Arabian Oil Policy', *Energy Policy*, 20, pp. 1078–1088.

Livingstone, Ian (1993) 'Promotion of Small- and Medium-Scale Industry with Imported Labour: Policy and Prospects in the States of the Persian Gulf', *Industry and Development*, 32, pp. 71–120.

Looney, Robert E. (1989) 'Saudi Arabia's Development Strategy: Comparative Advantage vs. Sustainable Growth', *Orient*, 30(1), pp. 75–96.

—— (1990) 'Oil Revenue and the Dutch Disease in Saudi Arabia: Differential Impacts on Sectoral Growth', *Canadian Journal of Development Studies*, XI(1), pp. 119–133.

—— (1991) 'The Viability of Saudi Arabian Industrial Diversification Efforts: The Consequences of Declining Government Expenditures', *Rivista Internazionale di Scienze Economiche e Commerciali*, XXXVIII, pp. 17–44.

—— (1996) 'Saudi Arabia's Economic Challenge', *JIME Review*, Autumn, pp. 37–47.

Luciani, Giacomo (1987) 'Allocation vs. Production States: A Theoretical Framework' in Hazem Beblawi and Giacomo Luciani (eds), *The Rentier State*. London: Routledge.

Luciant, Giacomo (2005) 'From Private Sector to National Bourgeaisie Saudi Arabian Business', in Aarts, Paul and Nonneman, Gerd (eds) *Saudi Arabia in the Balance: Political Economy, Society Foreign Affairs*, London: Hurst.

Mahdavy, Hossein (1970) 'The Patterns and Problems of Economic Development in Rentier States: The Case of Iran', in Michael A. Cook (ed.), *Studies in the Economic History of the Middle East*. Oxford: Oxford University Press.

Merriam, John G. and Fluellen, Anthony J. (1992) 'Arab World Privatisation: Key to Development?', *Arab Studies Quarterly*, 14(2 & 3), pp. 57–67.

Metwally, M. M. and Abdel Rahman, A. M. M. (1996) 'The Structure and Performance of Saudi Business Enterprises', in J. W. Wright (ed.), *Business and Economic Development in Saudi Arabia*. London: Macmillan.

NCB Economist (1992) *The Agricultural Sector*. The NCB Economist, 2(9).

—— (1993) *Small Industries in Saudi Arabia*. The NCB Economist, 3(6).

—— (1994) *A Larger Role for the Saudi Private Sector*. The NCB Economist, 4(3).

—— (1996) *The Saudi Electrical Sector*. The NCB Economist, 6(3).

—— (1997) *Economic Outlook: 1997*. The NCB Economist, 7(1).

—— (1998a) *WTO and Globalization of the Middle East Enterprise*. The NCB Economist, 8(2).

—— (1998b) *The GCC Insurance Industry: Challenges and Opportunities*. The NCB Economist, 8(4).

—— (1999a) *The Saudi Arabian Economic Outlook for 1999*. The NCB Economist, 9(1).

—— (1999b) *Structure of Gulf Banking and the Effects of Globalization and Financial Liberalization*. The NCB Economist, 9(2).

—— (1999c) *Foreign Direct Investment in Saudi Arabia: Stimulating Structural Changes and Global Integration*. The NCB Economist, 9(3).

—— (2005) *Quarterly Economic Update*. The NCB Economist, 15, 4 issues.

Niblock, Tim (1982) 'Social Structure and the Development of the Saudi Arabian Political System', in Tim Niblock (ed.), *State, Society and Economy in Saudi Arabia*. London: Croom Helm.

—— (1993) 'International and Domestic Factors in the Economic Liberalization Process in Arab Countries', in Tim Niblock and Emma Murphy (eds), *Economic and Political Liberalization in the Middle East*. London: British Academic Press.

Obeid, M. and Shafie, A. B. (1999) 'Outlook for Petrochemicals', *Saudi Commerce and Economic Review*, March, 59, pp. 28–33.

Parkinson, F. (1984) 'Latin America, Her NICs and the New International Economic Order', *Journal of Latin American Studies*, 16, pp. 127–141.

Rehfuss, D. (1996) 'Oil and the Development of the Saudi Economy', *Middle East Insight*, February (253), pp. 50–65.

Richards, Alan (1993) 'Economic Imperatives and Political Systems', *Middle East Journal*, 47(2), pp. 217–227.

Rodrik, Dani (1990) 'How Should Structural Adjustment Programs Be Designed?', *World Development*, 18(7), pp. 933–947.

Rueschemeyer, Dietrich and Evans, Peter (1985) 'The State and Economic Transformation: Towards an Analysis of the Conditions Underlying Effective Intervention', in Peter Evans, Dietrich Rueschemeyer and Theda Skocpol (eds), *Bringing the State Back In*. New York: Cambridge University Press.

Said, Mona, Chang, Ha-Joon and Sakr, Khalid (1991) 'Industrial Policy and the Role of the State in Egypt: The Relevance of the East Asian Experience', in Heba Handoussa (ed.), *Economic Transition in the Middle East – Global Challenges and Adjustment Strategies*. Cairo: American University Press.

Salameh, Ghassan (1980a) 'Political Power and the Saudi State', *MERIP Reports*, No. 91, Spring, pp. 20–25.

—— (1981) 'Saudi Arabia: Development and Dependence,' *Jerusalem Quarterly*, No. 20, Summer, pp. 109–122.

—— (1987) 'Islam and Politics in Saudi Arabia', *Arab Studies Quarterly*, Summer, pp. 306–326.

Saudi-American Bank (SAMBA) (2005) *The Saudi economy at Mid-year 2005*. Riyadh: SAMBA.

Saudi Arabian Monetary Agency (2003) *Thirty-Nineth Annual Report*. Riyadh: Research and Statistics Department, Kingdom of Saudi Arabia.

—— (2006) *Forty-Second Annual Report*. Riyadh: Research and Statistics department, Kingdom of Saudi Arabia.

Schotta, C. (1996) 'Saudi Arabia in a Global Economy – Challenges and Opportunities', *Middle East Insight*, February (253), pp. 39–43.

Shihata, I. (1996) 'Legal and Regulatory Framework for Private Sector Development in Egypt', in Marcelo Giugale and Hamed Mobarak (eds), *Private Sector Development in Egypt*. Cairo: American University Press.

Singer, Hans (1988) 'On the Blessings of "Outward Orientation": A Necessary Correction', *Journal of Development Studies*, January, pp. 232–236.

Skocpol, Theda (1982) 'Rentier State and Shi'a Islam in the Iranian Revolution', *Theory and Society*, 11(3), pp. 46–82.

—— (1985) 'Bringing the State Back In: Strategies of Analysis in Current Research', in Peter Evans, Dietrich Rueschemeyer and Theda Skocpol (eds), *Bringing the State Back In*. Cambridge: Cambridge University Press.

Stevens, Paul (1981) 'Saudi Arabia's Oil Production', in Tim Niblock (ed.), *State, Society and Economy in Saudi Arabia*. London: Croom Helm, pp. 214–234.

—— (1986) 'The Impact of Oil on the Role of the State in Economic Development: A Case Study of the Arab World', *Arab Affairs*, Summer, pp. 87–101.

Stiglitz, Joseph (1998) 'Asia's Reckoning: What Caused Asia's Crash? – Bad Private-Sector Decisions', *The Wall Street Journal*, 4 February, A22.

Taecker, Kevin (1996) 'Private Sector Growth, Fiscal Dicipline, and Planning – A Long-Term View of the Saudi Economy', *Middle East Insight*, February (253), pp. 44–49.

—— (1999) 'Budget: Govt. Economic Role Shrinking, But Private Sector to Grow', *Saudi Commerce and Economic Review*, March, 59, pp. 13–15.

Taher, Nahed (2005) 'Role of Saudi Women in Building a Knowledge-Based Economy', paper presented to a conference convened under UN auspices in Riyadh, 17–19 December.

Turck, Nancy (1998) 'Dispute Resolution in Saudi Arabia', *International Lawyer*, Summer (22), pp. 415–444.

Wade, Robert (1990b) 'State Intervention in Outward-Looking Development: Neoclassical Theory and Taiwanese Practice', in Gordon White (ed.), *Developmental States in East Asia*. London: Macmillan.

—— (1990) 'Industrial Policy in East Asia: Does it Lead or Follow the Market?', in Gary Gereffi and Donald Wyman (eds), *Manufacturing Miracles*. Princeton, NJ: Princeton University Press.

Walters, Alan (1989) 'Liberalization and Privatization: An Overview' in S. El-Nagger (ed.), *Privatization and Structural Adjustment in the Arab Countries*. Washington, DC: IMF.

Waterbury, John (1991) 'Twilight of the State Bourgeoisie', *International Journal of Middle East Studies*, 23, pp. 1–17.

Waterbury, John (1994) 'Democracy without democrats? The Potential for Liberalisation in the Middle East', in G. Salame (ed.), *Democracy without Democrat: the Renewal of Politics in the Muslim World*. London: (I.B. Tauris); pp. 23–47.

Wright, J. W. and Albatel, Abdullah H. (1996) 'Private Sector Finance: Problems Faced by Fourth and Fifth Year Development Plans', in J. W. Wright (ed.), *Business and Economic Development in Saudi Arabia*. London: Macmillan.

Zahid, Khan (2004) 'Investment Challenges Facing Oil-Rich MENA Countries: The Case of Saudi Arabia', paper presented to the OECD Conference on Mobilising Investment for Development in the Middle East and North Africa Region, held in Istanbul, 11–12 February.

Zarrouk, Jamel E. (1998) 'The Uruguay Round Agreements and Their Implications for the Middle East Countries', *Forum*, 1(4), pp. 6–7.

Internet sources

AMEINFO (2003) 'Prince Sultan bin Salman bin Abdulaziz Highlights Tourism Opportunities', accessed at www.ameinfo.com/28402.html, January 2005.

Doing Business (2005) 'Doing Business: Economic Rankings', accessed at www.doingbusiness.org, April 2006.

——(2006) 'Doing Business: Economic Rankings', accessed at www. doingbusiness.org, April 2007.

Kingdom of Saudi Arabia, Central Department of Statistics (KSA-CDS) (2005) 'Social Statistics Labour Force Survey', accessed at www.planning.gov.sa/ statistic/sindexe.htm, February 2005.

Kingdom of Saudi Arabia, Council of Ministers (KSA-CM) (1997) 'Privatisation Objectives and Policies', Decision No. 60, August 1997, accessed at www.sec.gov.sa/english/list.asp?s_contentid=22&s_title+&ContentType= & Cat, February 2005.

——(2004) 'The Patent Law 2004', Decision No. 56, July 1997, accessed at www.the-saudi.net/business-center/patent-law.htm, February 2005.

Kingdom of Saudi Arabia, Supreme Economic Council (KSA-SEC) (2005) 'Privatisation Objectives and Policies', accessed at www.sec.gov.sa/english/ list.asp?s_contentid=22&s_title+&ContentType=&Cat, January 2005.

Migration Policy Institute (2005) 'Saudi Arabia's Plan for Changing its Workforce', accessed at www.migrationinformation.org, January 2005.

National Commercial Bank (NCB) (2004) 'Saudi Arabia: Business and Economic Developments', accessed at www.saudieconomicsurvey.com/ html/reports.html, January 2005.

Saudi Arabia Information Resource (SA-IR) (2005) 'Supreme Economic Council', accessed at www.saudinf.com/main/e111.htm, March 2005.

Saudi Arabian Capital Markets Authority (SACMA) (2005) 'About the Capital Markets Authority', accessed at www.cma.org.sa, January 2005.

Saudi Arabian General Investment Authority (SAGIA) (2004a) 'Basic Issues to be Dealt with in the Privatisation Process', accessed at www.sagia.gov.sa/ innerpage.asp, December 2004.

——(2004b) 'Capital Markets Law 2003', accessed at www.sagia.gov.sa, December 2004.

——(2004c) 'Copyright Law 2003', accessed at www.sagia.gov.sa, December 2004.

——(2004d) 'Corporate Tax Law 2004', accessed at www.sagia.gov.sa, December 2004.

——(2004e) 'Foreign Direct Investment Law 2000', accessed at www.sagia. gov.sa, December 2004.

——(2004f) 'Privatisation Announcements', accessed at www.sagia.gov.sa/ innerpage.asp December 2004.

——(2004g) 'Real Estate Law 2000', accessed at www.sagia.gov.sa, December 2004.

—— (2005a) 'Gas Projects', accessed at http://www.sagia.gov.sa/innerpage.asp? ContentID=7&Lang=en&NewsID=238, January 2005.

—— (2005b) 'Negative List', accessed at www.sagia.gov.sa/innerpage.asp, February 2005.

—— (2007) 'Saudi Arabian General Investment Authority Results in 2006', accessed at www.sagia.gov, April 2007.

Transparency International (TI) (2002) 'Bribery Payers' Index', accessed at www.transparency.org/cpi/2002/bpi2002.en.html, December 2004.

United Nations Conference on Trade and Development (UNCTAD) (2004a) 'Country Fact Sheet: Saudi Arabia', accessed at www.unctad.org/fdstatistics, December 2004.

United States Census Bureau (US-CB) (2004) 'IDB Summary Demographic Data for Saudi Arabia', accessed at www.census.gov/cgi-bin/ipc/idbsum?cty=SA, December 2004.

United States Embassy, Riyadh (US-E) (2004) 'Saudi Arabia: Economic Trends 2004', accessed at www.usembassy.state.gov/riyadh, December 2004.

United States Energy Information Administration (US-EIA) (2004a) 'Energy Topics: Historical Data', accessed at www.eia.doe.gov, November 2004.

—— (2004b) 'Saudi Arabian Gas Projects', accessed at www.eia.doe.gov/emeu/cabs/saudi.html, December 2004.

United States Trade Representative Office (US-TRO) (2004) '2004 Special 301 Report: Watch List', accessed at www.ustr.gov/Documents_Library/Reports_Publications/2004.html, December 2004.

World Bank (1995) *Private Sector Development in Low Income Countries*. Washington DC: World Bank.

World Bank (2005) 'Doing Business in Saudi Arabia', Washington, DC: World Bank, accessed at www.rru.worldbank.org/doingbusiness, January 2005.

World Health Organisation (WHO) (2005) 'Child and Adult Mortality Statistics', accessed at www.who/int/countries, January 2005.

World Trade Organisation (WTO) (2005b) 'Accessions: Saudi Arabia', accessed at www.wto.org/english/thewto_e/acc_e/al_arabie_saoudite_e.htm, January 2005.

Zawya (2005) 'Saudi Arabian Equities', accessed at www.zawya.com/Equities, January 2005.

Newspaper and magazine references used

Arab News, Jiddah
Financial Times (*FT*), London
Middle East Economic Digest (*MEED*), London
Reuters, London
NCB Economist (2006) *Quarterly Economic Update*. The NCB Economist, 16,4 issues.
Saudi British Bank (1999) *Saudi Economic Bulletin 1.12.99*

Index

Saudi Consolidated Electricity
    Company 113
Saudi Credit Bank 67
Saudi Development and Training
    Company 165
Saudi Electricity Company 112
Saudi Industrial Development Fund
    187, 204
Saudi Industrial Investment
    Fund (SIDF) 170
Saudi Investment Bank 26
Saudi Ports Authority 24, 67
Saudi Public Transport Company
    (SAPTCO) 26
Saudi Telecommunications Company
    (STC) 26, 112, 187, 214, 215
Saudi telephone and telegraph system 112
'Saudisation' 139, 140, 141, 159,
    164, 170
Savola 160
services sector 74, 122
Shaker family 135
Sharbatly family 135
share-ownership 217
shari'a 166, 209, 231
Shobokshi family 135
Sinclair, Clive A. 51, 234, 241
Skocpol, Theda 15–16, 19
social development: 1962–70 44; 1970–85
    72; 1985–2000 106, 116; 2000–6 184
social dynamics: of private sector 88, 131;
    of state policies 10–14
social groupings, rentier states 17
social implications of economic
    strategies 228
social infrastructure, as basis for
    economic expansion 207
social provision 47; 1962–70 47; 1970–85
    82; 1985–2000 123
social role of public sector 146
Social Security Department (KSA-SSD)
    47, 237
Somalia 5
Soufi, Wahib A. 68, 148
South Korea 13
Standard Oil Company of California
    36, 68
state centrality/capacity 20
state involvement, depth of 5–10
state policies, social dynamics of 10–14
state socialist model 54
state, economy–related functions 7
state-aided capitalism 6–7, 157
state-centric regimes 34

state-controlled enterprises 26
state-owned banks 9; subsidies/loans 68
state-owned enterprises 26; creation
    of 8–9
state-sponsored capitalism 5, 9, 34, 97
Stiglitz, Joseph 9
stock market 26, 31, 146, 162, 168, 169,
    190, 201
subsidies 66, 102–3, 134, 140, 143
Sudairi family 135
Supply-side developments 178
Supreme Council for Petroleum and
    Minerals (SCPM) 186
Supreme Council of Tourism (SCT) 186
Supreme Economic Council (KSA-SEC)
    186, 187, 215, 216

Tadawul All–Share Index (TASI) 217
Taecker, Kevin 181, 245
Taher, Nahed 209
Taiwan 8, 13
Tamimi family 135
tariff protection 3, 157
taxation 17, 20, 21, 151, 182, 189, 231
technology acquisition: promotion of 9;
    vision for 165
Tehran agreement (1970) 52
telecommunications 26, 82, 112,
    170, 214
Ten-Point Programme (1962) 39
Texaco 68
theoretical approaches 4–21
tourism 186, 187, 246
trade: 1962–70 47; 1970–85 79;
    2000–6 193
trade sector 112–13
Turck, Nancy 166

underemployment 115
unemployment 98, 141, 142, 159, 174,
    177, 184, 222
Unilever 133, 159
United Arab Emirates 189, 205, 217
United Saudi Bank (USB) 160
universities 82, 92, 124, 165, 210,
    221, 229
US Census Bureau (US-CB) 228
US Embassy 215
US Trade Representative 191
US–Saudi Business Council 2
US: 301 Priority Watch List 191; concern
    with Saudi domestic conditions 217;
    petrochemical duties 202, 207; as
    trading partner 211

SAUDI ARABIA

Power, Legitimacy and Survival

Tim Niblock, University of Exeter, UK

Saudi Arabia provides a clear, concise yet analytical account of the development of the Saudi state. It details the country's historical and religious background, its oil rentier economy and its international role, showing how they interact to create the dynamics of the contemporary Saudi state.

The development of the state is traced through three stages: the formative period prior to 1962; the centralisation of the state, and the initiation of intensive economic development, between 1962 and 1979; the re-shaping of the state over the years since 1979. Emphasis is placed on the recent period, with chapters devoted to:

- the economic and foreign policy problems which now confront the state.
- linkages between Saudi Arabia and Islamic radicalism, with the relationship/conflicts involving al-Qa'ida traced through from events in Afghanistan in the 1980s
- the impact of 9/11 and the 2003 Gulf War
- identification of major problems facing the contemporary state and their solutions.

Saudi Arabia provides a unique and comprehensive understanding of this state during a crucial time. This book is essential reading for those with interests in Saudi Arabia and its role in Middle Eastern politics and on the international stage.

The Contemporary Middle East
March 2006: 234x156: 224pp
Hb: 978-0-415-27419-7:
£75.00 / $135.00
Pb: 978-0-415-30310-1:
£19.99 / $35.95

Tim Niblock is Professor in the Institute of Arab and Islamic Studies at the University of Exeter, UK.

Contents

Routledge
Taylor & Francis Group